The FREEDOM FIGHT

The New Drug and the Truths That Set Us Free

"The growing problem of porn addiction has taken ground in millions of lives, and it's time to fight it with the only power that overcomes—the power of Christ. Ted Shimer has taken this problem by storm and gives readers the hope and restoration they need to fight this battle and win."

—**CRAIG GROESCHEL,** Pastor of Life.Church
New York Times Best-Selling Author

"There is no more immediate problem in western civilization than the presence of pornography. Young men and women are having their entire adult lives robbed from them. The church will be forced to deal with this issue one way or another. Ted Shimer's book gives a biblical perspective, analysis, and path to follow. Any person in ministry had best read this book."

—**PASTOR TOMMY NELSON,** Denton Bible Church
Board Member, Dallas Theological Seminary

"As someone who has studied pornography for the last twenty-five years, I can confidently say Shimer does a masterful job of weaving together accurate statistics, science, and personal stories that bring the material to life. The array of topics he covers so well in one book is very impressive. I highly recommend his landmark book."

—**DR. JOHN FOUBERT,** Author of *How Pornography Harms*

"*The Freedom Fight* combines God's Word with expansive research and personal stories to paint a clear picture of true freedom. This book will be a powerful tool for any leader who is shepherding men and women through the process of recovery."

—**JONATHAN JP POKLUDA**
Best-selling author of *Welcome to Adulting*
Lead Pastor of Harris Creek in Waco, TX

"Working with men for over forty years, I have witnessed firsthand the explosive plague of pornography sweeping over our country. That being the case, we desperately need the insights of my friend, Ted Shimer, and the help his book *The Freedom Fight* provides. It powerfully awakens us to how extensive the bondage of pornography is. But even more importantly, it offers us a real path to freedom. Ted Shimer has answers. Life-giving answers. I highly recommend his book."

—**DR. ROBERT LEWIS**, Pastor, Author
Founder of Men's Fraternity

"The Freedom Fight is a critical weapon in the arsenal for purity and holiness. Shimer delivers a clear diagnosis of root issues and attacks the problems from every dimension: spiritually, psychologically, physiologically, and practically. I believe the Lord will use this work to give hope to many helping them break the chains of addiction."

—**BRIAN LEWIS**, Senior Leader, Campus Outreach

"*The Freedom Fight* is the most needed discipleship resource in the Church today. Ted Shimer has been a master disciple-maker for over thirty years. He combines this experience with deep theological roots and the best clinical training of the day. This book will equip you to disciple others out of a porn habit that has gripped their lives. The results have been disciples who are not only free but also more Word-filled, authentic, and passionate about the King and His Kingdom."

—**DR. STEVE SHADRACH,** Founder of Student Mobilization
and Center for Missions Mobilization

"Ted Shimer has given us a long-overdue, practical, accessible, biblically and theologically-sound, research-informed resource that provides very real hope and help and practical solutions that can lead to the *'freedom'* that God wants us to experience and enjoy. No pie-in-the-sky platitudes. It is the fruit of thousands-of-hours of interviews, reviewing the latest medical and brain-based research, and real-life hands-on application with men and women around the world. *The Freedom Fight* will inform, educate, and even transform those who apply its truths. This is one resource that you'll refer to many times in the years ahead … and want to share with others."

—**GARY J. OLIVER, THM, PHD**
Licensed Clinical Psychologist, Clinical Director
The Center for Healthy Relationships
John Brown University

"I have counseled men and women in the church who are battling with sexual brokenness for over thirty years and have written fifteen books on the subject. So when I say I am profoundly excited about Ted Shimer's book, it is for very practical reasons. This book is unique because it cuts through all the psychobabble of the day and presents in concise bullet points the core of the issues. You are going to be provoked, stimulated, and brought to a new depth of comprehension regarding the problem of and solution for sexual brokenness."

—**DR. TED ROBERTS,** Founder of Pure Desire Ministries
Pastoral Sex Addiction Professional-Supervisor
Co-Creator of Conquer Series

"To all who feel stuck … help has arrived! This is the book we have been waiting for!"

—**DR. TODD AHREND**, Founder, The Traveling Team

"Porn enters my room and sits on my sofa every single day as a therapist in one capacity or another. Ted Shimer does an excellent job of explaining the what, why, and how behind porn addiction in a way everyone can understand. Ted also does a beautiful job of revealing where true freedom resides … in Christ. The principles in this book provide a therapeutically sound and scripturally inspired path for successful recovery ... for freedom."

—**SUSAN GOSS, MED, MS**
Licensed Marriage & Family Therapist
Licensed Professional Counselor
Founder of Tangible Truth Ministries

"We are in the middle of an epidemic. It is not Covid-19, nor is it opioid addiction, but this crisis is equally destructive. Porn and sex addiction has invaded our nation, and many are in desperate need of help and freedom. This book is a great tool for helping people restore healthy sexuality. Ted Shimer's work is thoroughly researched and field-tested. I am grateful for this contribution to the Kingdom of God."

—**DR. SAM HANNON**, Fellowship Bible Church of Northwest Arkansas

"This book is really excellent! It's well-written and filled with valuable information and insights. Ted doesn't just describe the seriousness of the problem, backed up with solid data and research, but he also gives clear direction and hope for recovery."

—**KEN HARRISON,** CEO, Promise Keepers

"For the past twenty years, I have mentored college women. The number of Christian women struggling with porn or other unwanted sexual behaviors has exploded in the last several years. *The Freedom Fight* is a desperately needed resource to understand the 'whys' behind what's going on and a real guide for the path to freedom. If you're working with women of any age, this is a resource you need."

—**TONYA ZUNIGHA,** Director of Women's Ministry,
Faith Bible Church, Edmond, Oklahoma

"*The Freedom Fight* does an excellent job of combining Scriptural wisdom with practical application that's having a lasting impact in people's lives. It has been the perfect complement for our men to continue their journey toward lasting sexual freedom and wholeness. Thanks, Ted, for this excellent resource!"

—**BRYCE BOUCHARD**, The Navigators
Founder of Noblemen Ministries

"Having discipled students for 50 years, I know the value of passing on the 'whys' and 'how-tos' in any area of a disciple's transformation. Ted's book does both so well! He goes after the roots of porn addiction and then gives intentional disciple-makers the practical steps we need to help set people free. *The Freedom Fight* gives the sound scholarship, biblical understanding and practical help that I will use with the students I disciple."

—**ROGER HERSHEY**, Cru speaker and mobilize
Author of *The Finishers*

"Ted's book offers the strongest impact of any book that I've read because of his strategy of fighting back through second order change with biblical and neuroscience truths. This level of change is long-lasting because it goes to what's underpinning the problem, not just the abstinence from the behavior! *The Freedom Fight* is a must read for everybody!"

—**DR. ADRIAN HICKMON**
Founder of Capstone Addiction Treatment Center, LPC
Certified Sex Addiction Therapist-Supervisor

"The spiritual warfare being unleashed on the people of God by way of pornography must be understood and addressed. Shimer unpacks not just the destructive nature of porn but also Gospel-centered solutions that lead to freedom. I'm grateful there is a discipleship resource to equip both men and women to overcome a pornography addiction. Whether you struggle with pornography personally or you want to be equipped to help others, this book gives a clear path to freedom."

—**MO ISOM AIKEN**, New York Times Bestselling Author of *Sex, Jesus, and the Conversations the Church Forgot*

"*The truth will set you free*. In the 2,000 years since Jesus said that (John 8:32), each new generation needs to be taught and reminded of that truth. No one has done it better than my friend Ted Shimer. After a quarter-century working on the front lines of colleges and universities of America doing triage on pornography-infected young adults, Ted shares the battle-plan that has set thousands of the next generation free from sin's enslaving chains. I can't more strongly commend *The Freedom Fight* and its gifted author than I do."

—**DR. JOHN BARNETT**, Pastor, Author, Missionary, YouTuber

The FREEDOM FIGHT

The New Drug and the Truths That Set Us Free

TED SHIMER

HIGH BRIDGE BOOKS
HOUSTON

The Freedom Fight
by Ted Shimer

Printed in the United States of America
ISBN: 978-1-946615-55-8

High Bridge Books titles may be purchased in bulk for educational, business, fundraising, or sales promotional use. For information, please contact High Bridge Books via www.HighBridgeBooks.com/contact.

Published in Houston, Texas by High Bridge Books

To Amber, my beautiful bride and best friend.
You are an amazing wife, mother, and soulmate.
Thank you for all your love and support as we
serve the Lord together. Let's go another thirty!

Contents

Foreword

I have been sounding the alarm about pornography in the Church for a decade. I have been compelled to warn and educate believers about the pervasiveness and destructiveness of porn. As a result, many people have been pressuring me for years to write a book on pornography. When I read the manuscript of *The Freedom Fight,* I said, "Oh my gosh, this is better than anything I could have written."

That is saying a lot because I have authored or coauthored over 150 best-selling books that have sold over thirty million copies in total. I never thought I would say that about a topic, especially pornography. That is how blown away I was by what Ted has written. I decided at that moment instead of writing a book on pornography, I was going to take my energy, effort, and influence and promote this book as if it was my own. The Church needs to know and understand the message of this book.

This book is an answer to prayer for what I believe is the greatest threat to the Church today. We are in an epic spiritual battle, and our enemy is using pornography to destroy churches, pastors, marriages, and young people like never before. It is capturing the minds of the next generation, and few are sounding the alarm. Even fewer are offering real solutions. Ted Shimer does both in this book.

Ted's theological studies, his thirty-plus years of disciple-making, and his world-class clinical training for sex addiction uniquely qualify him to speak to the Church with authority. Ted does an excellent job of helping the reader understand the brutal facts of porn use and why it matters. It's one thing to sound the alarm so forcefully and accurately, but it's another to offer real solutions. The principles that Ted lays out to overcome porn addiction have a significant track record of bringing freedom. The solutions are biblical, gospel-centered, clinically proven, and effective.

This book is a must-read for every Christian leader in the home and church. We need more Christians who understand this issue and who are equipped to address it effectively. *The Freedom Fight* will equip you to take action, whether you need help in your own struggle with porn or you just need to be equipped to help others.

Some may question whether this is really needed for every Christian. Someone may wonder, how could this book be relevant for the Baby Boomer grandparents who never had issues with pornography. This book shows them the frontlines of the spiritual battle raging in the Church today so they can effectively pray for their leaders. It will help them know and understand what is going on in the world of their kids and grandkids. It will equip them to help others break free from the plague of our day. It will put them in a position to be a mentor to the next generation and offer real gospel-centered solutions that few have but so many need.

Whether pornography is a part of your past or not, you can get equipped to help the younger generation walk in genuine freedom and become a more fully devoted follower of Christ. The Body of Christ needs more believers who want to seize this opportunity to deposit the truth of God more deeply into the lives of those they disciple. If we think we are making disciples that will last but are not addressing this issue, we are fooling ourselves.

This book is a discipleship resource that the Church desperately needs. This is an opportunity for the Church and its leaders to show the relevance of God's Word and provide biblical and effective solutions. The first half of the book shows why porn is so devastating. The second half of the book unpacks the six roots of a pornography addiction that must be addressed to find freedom. Growth and development in key areas of a person's life are required for lasting freedom to be established.

If we think the impact of pornography is bad now, the research tells us a tsunami of destruction is coming. The future of the Christian home and church does not look bright. If there is no decisive action in the Church to address this issue, we are going to reap destruction to a greater level than we already are. My prayer is that pastors around the world will use this book in small groups in their church and among their youth to encourage their people to get equipped in this area. There is a hole in the discipleship of the Church that God can use this book to address.

Could it be that God will use the process of breaking His people free from porn to build more committed followers of Christ? Could it be that discipling people out of porn addiction is something God will use to bring revival to the Church? What if this is an opportunity to show the world the relevancy and power of the gospel and the Word of God to bring freedom to such a modern issue? This is an opportunity for the Church to shine the beauty and the power of the gospel for the glory of Christ.

—**Josh McDowell,** Author/Communicator

Introduction

In 2007, our ministry identified pornography as the number one obstacle to our mission of building spiritual leaders for Christ. Our purpose was in jeopardy because many of our aspiring leaders were addicted to porn. We knew we had to find a solution to this problem, or we would have to lower our standards for leadership. What we thought was a desperate situation was about to get dramatically worse—the iPhone came out later that year.

All our staff men started going through a porn addiction recovery program so we could be equipped to mentor students who were struggling. I started reading everything I could find on the topic. I walked with different staff who struggled with porn through a variety of addiction recovery programs. I later got clinically trained in porn addiction recovery. Through this process, it became clear that a holistic approach was essential for lasting freedom. There are physical, emotional, spiritual, and relational factors that must be addressed for freedom to last.

The Freedom Fight's gospel-centered approach is biblically-based, scientifically informed, and holistic. Unfortunately, some in the Christian community only address a porn addiction from a spiritual angle, but prolonged porn use changes a person's brain. The same God who created the soul created the brain, and both need attention in a porn addiction. God can immediately deliver someone, but He normally doesn't. He instead uses the process of healing to grow and develop the person to be more like Christ. Before His truth sets us free, it changes us. And because it changes us, the freedom lasts.

The stories in this book are real. I have changed names and, in some cases, the details to protect a person's identity. If I use a person's first and last name, that means they have already publicly shared their story.

In chapters 1-7, I explore the destructive nature of pornography. We look at how pornography use wages war on many fronts with devastating results. In the second two-thirds of the book (chapters 8-17), I focus on the roots of a porn addiction and get very practical about how to overcome them. The first third of the book lays important groundwork for the solutions that follow. Understanding the first section will help you more effectively apply the second section. So, whether you are reading this book for yourself or so you can be equipped to help others, both sections of the book are critical to winning the freedom fight.

This book is designed for both individuals and small groups. There are discussion questions for each chapter in the appendix.

Section One

The Brutal Realities of Porn's Impact

1

The Tsunami Is Coming

Mark grew up on a farm in rural Iowa. He learned to work hard raising crops and cattle. He loved his dog, Axel, who never left his side, whether he was doing his chores or wandering the farm. Mark was a good student and a standout athlete in football and track at the local high school. But behind what seemed like an ideal midwestern childhood was something darker, a plague that infects boys and girls like Mark on a daily basis. Mark was a porn addict.

He was nine when he first saw pictures of nude women on the internet. At twelve, he watched his first pornographic video. Throughout high school, pornography became a part of his weekly—if not daily—routine. The draw was more than just watching other people have sex. The hardcore imagery became a refuge and place of security in the midst of his parents' divorce. It was a place he could go to check out from the pain of his life. And though Mark knew watching porn was wrong, after years of use, he couldn't stop. He loved porn.

Mark went to college on a track scholarship and took his porn habit with him. But even while mired in addiction, Mark started to explore his faith and got plugged into a campus ministry. He decided to follow Christ, and his life changed as he started growing spiritually. As he did, he felt convicted about his porn habit and tried to stop watching it. He couldn't. He prayed for God to take it away. God never did. He continued following Jesus, though, and began sharing his faith and leading Bible studies. With increased leadership came an increased sense of shame and hypocrisy. He confessed his struggle to his mentor, the campus minister, but nothing seemed to work. Mark continued to limp along.

After graduation, Mark hoped to join the staff of the college ministry that had been so instrumental in his new faith. The problem? The ministry required twelve months of sobriety from pornography. Mark was motivated. He got a flip phone and upped his accountability. He found "freedom" long enough to get hired, but his sobriety did not last. Why? If you asked him now, he'd tell you this: he'd only focused on behavior modification and hadn't addressed the roots of his addiction. After a short stint of sobriety, Mark's addiction came back stronger than ever.

I began to walk with Mark through a variety of programs as we searched for freedom. He'd met a girl, was in love, and wanted to marry her. He loved his job. Both of those things were in jeopardy if he didn't break free from porn, and he knew it. So he took radical steps. He increased accountability again and sold his computer to make sure he had no internet access. His efforts still were not enough. When the urge hit, he'd sneak his roommate's phone or laptop and watch porn. Addicted people do risky things.

Week after week, we talked about Mark's addiction. I was puzzled. How could a man who is motivated and loves God continue in pornography use? How could an addiction sink its claws so deeply into someone?

Together, Mark and I became obsessed with uncovering a solution. We tried counselors, sex addiction therapists, and multiple online recovery programs. We found a one-month inpatient program, and Mark enrolled. When your best bet is to send someone to California for help, you know things are desperate. Nothing seemed to work.

Mark hated what he was doing but could not stop. And that's when the doubt set in. He prayed for God to set him free, yet he still struggled. This led him to wonder, "If I'm not experiencing the freedom the Bible promises, is my faith real? What's wrong with me?" He knew he'd experienced Christ's work in his life, which was evidenced by so much life change. Still, this unbreakable habit would not relent. In his utter shame and hopelessness, Mark even had passing thoughts of suicide.

Finally, Mark found a program that was eleven months long. At a cost of $5,500, it was a sacrifice for a young aspiring minister. But at the end of it, he found freedom. As we debriefed Mark's efforts to find freedom, we realized he had spent two-and-a-half years, attended several programs, and spent over $20,000. Although we were encouraged by Mark's progress, a sense of discouragement set in. This was not a viable pathway to freedom for the masses.

Everyone who struggles with porn struggles to varying degrees. Not every case is as extreme as Mark's. Still, the level of addiction seen in young adults is deepening each year. This reality strengthened my desire to find a Christ-centered, affordable, and effective solution. I explored and evaluated over twenty different porn addiction resources. I also went through the training to become a sex addiction professional-supervisor.[1] Ultimately, I went on to create The Freedom Fight, an online porn addiction recovery program that is both free and built on proven principles that are biblical, holistic, and effective.

Before someone can fully understand the solutions to a pornography addiction, they must appreciate how addiction happens and the brutal impact it has on the individual, their brain, and society. Only then can people fully appreciate the root factors that drive a porn addiction. And for each of these root factors, there are biblical, scientifically informed, and powerful solutions that lead to genuine freedom.

Observing the evolution of this issue over the last thirty years has made it clear: a tsunami of porn addiction is coming. This tsunami will wreck people's lives, their marriages, and their churches.

The Tsunami Is Coming

On December 26, 2004, an earthquake of a magnitude 9.1 struck off the coast of Indonesia. The immediate impact wasn't felt because it struck deep under the surface of the ocean. Just before 8 a.m., the ocean floor thrusted upward more than sixty feet because of the collision of the earth's plates along a 600-mile fault line. All the water displaced by this violent quake had to go somewhere. It pushed rapidly through the ocean, moving toward the shore at more than 500 miles per hour.

The sheer volume of water was barely noticeable until it reached the shoreline, where it grew into a huge wall, a wave reported to be over 100 feet high in some areas. There was little warning of the coming devastation. The people in coastal towns were caught completely off guard. The resulting tsunami was the deadliest in history, killing over 227,000 people in fourteen countries.[2]

Much like this tsunami, the destructive nature and enormous scale of pornography addiction are hidden from the masses. Much like a tsunami, the wave may not be seen until it is too late. And much like the tsunami that crushed so many communities in southeast Asia, the wave of porn addiction is gaining size and speed at an alarming rate. Today, we only partially see the impact of porn in culture, but there is a wave of devastation coming when today's youth who have been raised on porn grow up. If the Church does not wake up to the coming tsunami, the devastation will be catastrophic.

While I was writing this book, what was already a tsunami of epic proportions grew even worse. In January 2020, COVID-19 came to the American shores. As a result, state and local governments closed borders and businesses. They recommended people socially distance themselves from each other, shelter in place, and work from home. During the first three weeks of that lockdown, pornography consumption rose by 12%.[3] And this happened on top of the explosive growth the porn industry sees every year. This opportunity led the largest porn provider in the world to offer its premium package free for thirty days. Thirty days is long enough to hook new users for life. This savvy move increased their users by 24% worldwide, a statistic that represents millions of people.[4]

The destructive consequences of increasing porn addiction are coming. The next generation will experience them firsthand. The consequences will be worse than ever because each subsequent generation is getting more addicted than their predecessors.

The Law of Reaping and Sowing

Pornography has been around for decades, but historically, accessibility was the limiting factor to widespread use. Before the internet went mainstream in 1993, pornography was mostly available through magazines, videos, adult bookstores, or a friend's dad's stash. And purchasing pornography came with its own social obstacles, you had to walk into smut stores or endure shame and embarrassment at your local bookstore to get it. These inconveniences and obstacles kept exposure to pornography in check, at least until the dawn of the digital age.

With the internet, pornography became anonymous, affordable, and accessible from the comfort and in the secrecy of home. This ease of access led people around the country to pressure the government to pass legislation protecting young minds from pornographic material on the internet. However, the Supreme Court ruled that pornography is protected as free speech.[5] This ruling and others like it gave the green light to the porn industry. The number of online porn sites exploded overnight, and over the next decade, millions of people became addicted to porn.

As if the birth of the internet wasn't enough, two other technological shifts made porn more potent. The first shift was the invention of high-speed internet. Before 2006, photographs comprised the majority of pornography on the internet. High-speed internet, however, made it possible to click through an endless buffet of pornographic videos. The possibility of watching hardcore videos for hours at a time became a reality for millions of people. In fact, one man shared how the upgraded internet affected his porn addiction, saying, "High-speed porn changed everything. I began masturbating more than once a day. I found myself looking at porn prior to sex with my wife because she just couldn't do it for me anymore."[6]

A year after the birth of broadband, the iPhone made it possible to stream pornography to a handheld device. No matter what age or stage of life someone was in, anyone with a smartphone had their own personalized porn theater in their pocket or purse. This technology made it easier for adolescents to watch hardcore porn than it was for them to get a drink of water. Now, a teenager didn't even have to get out of bed to watch porn.

Bryan is a twenty-four-year-old porn addict who was raised in a Christian home. His story is not unusual.

> I started looking at porn when my parents bought me an iPhone. I was fourteen. I knew porn was there before, but I never had the opportunity to watch it regularly. My fascination grew, and by the time I was fifteen, I watched porn for at least an hour each day. I told my parents I was going to listen to music or play video games, and then I would disappear into porn. My parents never knew I even had a struggle with pornography until last year when my wife divorced me because of my porn addiction.

People wrongly assume that this unprecedented consumption of pornography is no big deal, but the Bible warns, "Do not be deceived: God is not mocked, for whatever one sows, that will he also reap. For the one who sows to his own flesh will from the flesh reap corruption" (Galatians 6:7-8). We tell ourselves it's not a big deal, but God's Word is true. If we continue to sow the seeds of pornography, we'll reap corruption, and ultimately, death.

The death and destruction that come with pornography aren't usually instant though. Often, pornography brings a slow death. What does it look like? I'll explain more throughout this book, but for now, consider the following deaths pornography leaves in its wake.

- *A slow death of a heart for God:* Those who view pornography more often reported lower levels of closeness to God and higher levels of religious doubts.[7]
- *A slow death of marriages:* Porn is mentioned as a significant reason in 56% of all divorces.[8]
- *A slow death of healthy sexuality:* People who watch porn are less satisfied with their sex lives than those who don't.[9]
- *A slow death of a heart to serve God:* Porn usage significantly decreases the likelihood that a person will serve or have a position of leadership in their church.[10]

Those paying attention in the secular world are observing the law of reaping and sowing when it comes to pornography. Consider four examples: an actor, an athlete, an author, and a musician.

Russell Brand is an award-winning actor and comedian. His life is marked by substance abuse and relational dysfunction, including his two-year marriage to Katy Perry. Of his pornography use, Brand said:

> I think my own past with pornography is the hub of my inner conflict and doubt. I know pornography is wrong… there's a general feeling, isn't there, in your core if you look at pornography that this isn't what's the best thing for me to do. If I had total dominion over myself, I would never look at pornography again. I would kick it out of my life… it's affecting my ability to relate to women, to relate to myself, to my own sexuality, to my own spirituality.[11]

Terry Crews, a former NFL linebacker and current actor, suffered the repercussions of porn addiction. Because of his addiction, he and his wife separated. During that separation, he came to realize he had to make a choice: love his wife or love porn. He chose his wife. Crews said:

> Pornography, it really, really messed up my life in a lot of ways. Pornography changes the way you think about people. People become objects. People become body parts. They become things to use rather than people to be loved.[12]

Atheist author Gary Wilson wrote, "Until recently, erectile dysfunction was rarely seen in men under forty. Now it is seen in teenagers as young as fifteen." Why? Wilson attributed the phenomenon to the use of porn. He went on to explain:

> By the time they find a real partner, perhaps as much as a decade later, some guys discover they have trained intensely for the wrong sport. These young men had simply conditioned their sexual response to screens, isolating, constant novelty, shock/surprise, fetish porn, and watching other people have sex… you become numb to real partners.[13]

Musician John Mayer has a net worth of $40 million and presumably could choose whatever sexual partner he wanted. He admitted in an interview that he prefers fantasy and masturbation to sex with a woman.[14] Mayer says porn has changed him. He says he will sometimes see 300 naked women before he ever gets out of bed to start his day. He said:

> I'm 100% straight as an arrow. But, look, because of all the porn I've watched, I'm now enamored with what I call 'the third kind.' It's not male, it's not female. It's a new creation.[15]

Whether they know it or not, these four men agree with the Scriptures. When a man sows to the flesh, he reaps corruption. But this is not just a man's issue. As we will see, pornography is advancing among women too. The law of Scripture is universal, applying to men and women alike.

Melodie Shekia was a twenty-two-year-old follower of Christ who attended a Christian college and served on the praise team at her church, where she was seen as a role model for the younger girls. In the secrecy of her room, though, Melodie was addicted to porn. She said, "I could barely sleep at night because of the guilt. I stopped praying, not because I wanted to stop, but because I thought God was angry with me. I was hiding from God."

She desperately begged God for deliverance, but there was something about porn that hooked her and wouldn't let her go.[16] Porn had a persistent power, one that called her back to itself. The urge to watch it seemed overwhelming. She had sown to her fleshly desires, and as a result, she was reaping a harvest.

"Don't be misled ... You will always harvest what you plant. Those who live only to satisfy their own sinful nature will harvest decay and death from that sinful nature" (Galatians 6:7-8 NLT). That decay and death is evident to Christian leaders today. As author Josh McDowell said, "Right at this moment, there's never been anything in history that is destroying more churches, more pastors, more marriages, more young people, than pornography."

The effects of pornography in society are so pervasive that they impact users and non-users. Men and women, young and old—no one is immune. This book is for anyone who wants to know the pathway to freedom for themselves or so they can be equipped to help others. Join me as we explore both the destructive impact of porn and how to overcome an addiction to it.

2

How Much? So What?

Andy Cimbala, a college minister, wrote about his own porn story. Though he'd seen pornographic photos in his younger years, the first time he watched a pornographic video, something was different. He explained:

> I was over at my friend's house, and he had porn in the VCR. As we were playing video games one moment, then somebody pressed play, and instead of a digital machine gun, I saw something far more exciting. From that point on, I was hooked. I had never felt so alive, such a rush! I wanted more of this. It was wrong, but I couldn't stop thinking about it. I loved porn.[1]

Andy goes on to share how his porn access remained limited until he was living alone in college. When he got to college and had unlimited access and privacy, he watched more porn than ever. His addiction deepened, and it took years to undo the damage.

Another example of the power of pornography is the story of Hannah, who became addicted to porn during her freshman year of high school. One day she saw something on social media that made her curious. Two taps later, she was looking at graphic sexual images. Her addiction took root in the privacy of her room as she scrolled through porn sites on her phone. Over the next three years, Hannah struggled with her addiction. Though the pornography gave her a high that distracted her from the pain of the moment, she was also distressed by what she was doing. Although she felt pornography ruining her, she still found herself returning to watch it over and over.[2]

Hannah and Andy's stories illustrate a common reality. Typically, people have exposure to pornography early, but addiction does not develop until they have consistent private access to it. And many teenagers have such private access. Ninety percent of teenage porn use occurs on their smartphones in the privacy of their own homes.[3]

The smartphone has enabled people to be more addicted to pornography than ever before. And this addiction is affecting our younger generations disproportionately. As we'll see in this chapter, the younger generation consumes more pornography than any previous generation, primarily because of the proliferation of the smartphone. The farther we move into the cell phone age, the more young people find themselves falling into the pit of addiction.

Consider the statistics: Before 2011, less than half of teenagers had access to smartphones. Today, 95% of teenagers in the US either own or have access to a smartphone.[4] This dramatic increase in cell phone usage has led to an increase in accessibility to hardcore porn. And from my own experience, each year, an increasing number of freshmen show up to college with deeper addictions to pornography.

Each year, the addictions grow in both breadth and depth. Why? Because there has never been this level of pornography access for young, moldable minds, minds ripe for pornography addiction. And yes, porn is one of the most addictive of all substances. In fact, some people have come to call pornography "the new drug." As we will see later, some drugs create a higher dopamine high than porn, but there are no drugs as accessible as the new drug. How hard would it be to break a cocaine habit if you always had it in your pocket?

Bad Habit vs. Addiction

Some people claim pornography isn't as much of an addiction as it is a bad habit. What is the difference between a bad habit and an addiction? The website Fight the New Drug explains:

> A habit is a pattern of behavior that begins with a cue or a trigger and ends with a memorable reward, often referred to as a "habit loop"—trigger, behavior, reward (think Pavlov and classical conditioning). On the flip side, an addiction begins with a behavior and evolves into a dramatic dependency that interferes with the normal functionality of one's life and the operation of one's brain.[5]

When a person desperately wants to stop a behavior they see as harmful, and they repeatedly try to stop it but can't, it may be an addiction. When the unstoppable behavior changes the brain in such a way to lock them into the behavior then the use of the term "addiction" seems appropriate. In Chapter 4, we'll see how porn hijacks the normal functioning of the brain. Whether you consider it a bad habit or an addiction, the world is beginning to recognize pornography as a significant problem.

The World Health Organization has recently recognized compulsive sexual behavior as a disorder.[6] What's more, sixteen US states have declared pornography to be a public health crisis.[7] Even secular establishments recognize the dangers of this phenomenon. Because of this, I would argue that it doesn't really matter whether someone calls it a bad habit or an addiction. Porn users are stuck in compulsive behavior and need help finding freedom from that behavior. Though the dangers of porn are becoming obvious, the appetite to consume it is growing. The staggering statistics bear it out.

Pornhub, the largest pornography website in the world, released its traffic statistics for 2019.[8] The website boasted:

- 42 billion visits
- 115 million daily visits
- 170 years of new content created

The site showed that the United States is by far the largest consumer of pornographic content (approximately 20% or more of all visits). That's enough visits for every man, woman, and child in the US to visit the site twenty-five times a year–and those statistics only represent one of tens of thousands of pornographic websites. And digging a little deeper, you'll find even more startling statistics about American porn use. Every *day* in the United States, there are an estimated:

- 2.5 billion emails sent that contain pornographic material
- 68 million searches related to pornography
- 116,000 searches for child pornography[9]

Based on multiple nationwide studies of pornography consumption, two out of three adult men watch porn monthly, about half view it weekly, and one out of four are daily users.[10] Within these statistics, there is a pattern: the younger a man is, the more likely he is to watch porn. In fact, a Barna Group survey found the following:

- The percentage of men in each age group who view porn at least *once a month*:
    - o 18–30-year-olds, 79%
    - o 31–49-year-olds, 67%
    - o 50–68-year-olds, 49%[11]

- The percentage of men in each age group who view porn at least *several times a week:*
  - 18-30-year-olds 63%
  - 31-49-year-olds 38%
  - 50-68-year-olds, 25%[12]

With each passing year, these percentages increase. Why? Because as younger generations age, they take their porn habit with them.

In 2019, Pornhub reported that 32% of the visitors to their site were women.[13] Here is the percentage of women in each age group who view porn at least *once a month:*

- 34% of 18–30-year-olds
- 13% of 31–49-year-olds
- 10% of 50–68-year-olds[14]

The same trend emerges whether the demographic consists of men or women. The younger the age group is, the larger the percentage of porn users is within it.

Today's youth are not just watching normal porn because technology allows them to see more deviant behavior in five minutes than their grandparents saw in a lifetime. Consider the content consumed by today's youth:

- 83% of boys and 57% of girls have seen group sex.

- 69% of boys and 55% of girls have seen same-sex intercourse.

- 39% of boys and 23% of girls have seen sexual bondage.

- 32% of boys and 18% of girls have seen bestiality.

- 18% of boys and 10% of girls have seen portrayals of rape or sexual violence.
- 15% of boys and 9% of girls have seen child pornography.[15]

The Christian Porn Problem

It might come as no surprise that there is virtually no difference in monthly porn use among non-Christian men (65%) versus Christian men (64%).[16] In fact, it might even be worse than the published statistics indicate. The Freedom Fight recently conducted a survey of over 750 Christian college men from over thirty different campuses across the country. Each of the men we surveyed was involved in a campus ministry, and each considered their faith to be a vital element in their lives. Many of them were leaders in their ministries. What we found was alarming—89% of the growing Christian men we surveyed watch porn, at least occasionally. More than six in ten view it at least weekly. More than half of these practicing Christian men say they are *addicted* to pornography.[17]

The Freedom Fight's recent survey of over 550 Christian women from over thirty university campuses across the US showed that 51% are watching porn at least occasionally. These aren't just any college women either. These women are practicing Christians, involved in campus ministry, and many of them are in leadership positions. Though their faith is important to them, pornography remains a part of their lives.[18]

Jessica Harris wrote in her book how easily ensnared she was by porn as a young Christian. She said:

> I first encountered pornography when I was thirteen. I hadn't gone looking for it. It found me. Within weeks, I was hooked. The next four years dragged me deeper into the toxic filth of immorali-

> ty. It wasn't an occasional thing; it was an everyday thing. It was an every-spare-moment thing. It was a stay-up-all-night-so-I-can-do-this thing. No matter what I tried, I could not stop.[19]

Jessica's story demonstrates the power of porn, even over people of faith. It is pervasive, compelling, and to many, is an unbreakable bond.

These are future Christian husbands, wives, fathers, mothers, and church leaders having their hearts and minds captured by porn. If nothing changes, the next generation of Christian homes and churches will be devastated at a rate never seen before.

So What?

Does all this porn consumption really matter? Does the fact that this generation of youth is consuming more hardcore material than any preceding generation make a difference? Consider the science.

In 2013, a research professor at the University of Montreal wanted to compare the behavior of men who viewed sexually explicit material with those who had never viewed it. Unfortunately, he had to cancel the whole project. Why? He could not find one man in his twenties who had not looked at porn.[20] This reality makes the following study even more significant.

In the 1980s, Dr. Dolf Zillman and Dr. Jennings Bryant conducted an experiment enlisting eighty male and eighty female college-age participants. The goal was to study the influence pornography has on shaping views. The study's subjects were divided into three subgroups: The Massive Exposure Group, The Intermediate Exposure Group, and The No Exposure Group.

Each group was shown five hours of media over a six-week period. The Massive Exposure Group only watched porn. The

Intermediate Exposure Group watched porn 50% of the time and watched normal media for the remainder. The No Exposure Group watched no porn at all.

According to Dr. Zillman's and Dr. Bryant's findings, there was a significant difference in responses to the following questions based on how much porn subjects watched. Consider, for instance, the differences in the responses of The Massive Exposure Group and the No Exposure Group to the following questions:

Is pornography offensive?

- The Massive Exposure Group – 26% yes
- The No Exposure Group – 75% yes

Should pornography be restricted from minors?

- The Massive Exposure Group – 36% yes
- The No Exposure Group – 83% yes

Do you support the women's rights movement? (males only)

- The Massive Exposure Group – 25% yes
- The No Exposure Group – 71% yes

Do you support the women's rights movement? (females only)

- The Massive Exposure Group – 52% yes
- The No Exposure Group – 82% yes

Average suggested prison sentence for a rapist?

- The Massive Exposure Group – six years
- The No Exposure Group – twelve years

For each of the above questions, The Intermediate Exposure Group's answers fell between the other two groups. This trend suggests a direct correlation between the amount of porn a person watches and how much it shapes one's perspective, particularly their perspective about the value of women in society.

The study also showed that raising pornography consumption directly increased the value subjects attached to casual sex and the hookup culture. Those who watched more porn placed a decreased value on the institution of marriage, the desire for children, and the need for faithfulness in a relationship. Those who watched more porn believed sexually deviant behavior is more common than it actually is.

The study also suggested that when something is normalized in a person's mind, they are more likely to practice it.[21] Modern surveys, like the one compiled by the Barna Group, have proven what this study suggested about the way porn changes people's perspectives. Specifically, in a 2016 survey, the Barna Group found that of those living in today's porn-saturated culture, only 55% of adults ages twenty-five or older believe viewing pornography is wrong.[22]

The Changing Definition of Porn

Because of the normalization of pornography, the definition of porn itself is changing. Only 57% of thirteen- to twenty-four-year-olds consider a fully nude and sexually arousing image to be pornography.[23] This means that 43% of today's youth would not consider the old Playboy centerfold porn.

These findings show what the 1980s porn exposure study predicted. The groups who watch more porn are more pro-porn. They do not see it as harmful, and to them, the definition of porn includes only more extreme versions of explicit material. These shifting definitions shape people's views, perspectives, and sexual tastes. In fact, research concluded that sexual tastes can be acquired through pornography consumption.[24] The Report on Digital Sexuality surveyed 11,000 porn users and concluded that the more porn someone watches, the more likely they are to be bisexual. The study shows there is a steady increase in the percentage of men who consider themselves bisexual for each level of frequency of porn use. The data shows:

- Of those watching porn once a week, 13% considered themselves bisexual.
- Of those watching porn a few times a week, 20% claim bisexuality.
- Of those watching porn several times a day, 27% consider themselves bisexual.

The director of the study concluded, "The more porn you watch, the more you may think, 'Hey, that's actually somewhat of a turn-on. Maybe I'm not as totally straight, or gay, as I thought.'"[25] Pornography encourages behavior by producing permission-giving beliefs that say, "What I am doing is normal, doesn't hurt anyone, and everyone is doing it."[26] And this, I suspect, is why many porn users—including Christians—find themselves experimenting with sexual behavior that goes against their morals, values, and even their sexual preferences. The messages people put in their minds shape them in ways they aren't always aware of.

The power of thoughts is significant, which is why God warns His people to be diligent about *every* thought that enters through the doorway of their minds. In 2 Corinthians 10:5, Paul writes that believers should "take every thought captive to obey Christ." The word "captive" comes from the Greek word meaning "a prisoner of war taken by spear." It is this kind of military diligence followers of Christ should exercise over every thought. The thoughts people think matter. Through what people feed their minds, they are either being conformed to the world or are being transformed to be like Christ.

There is no doubt, pornography is polluting people's minds. It is a weapon of the enemy, a disinformation campaign. It changes people's thoughts about sex. It feeds them lies about what is normal, fulfilling, and right. As we'll see, it brings people shame, which keeps them from experiencing God's love for them. But pornography doesn't just have psychological and spiritual repercussions. It wreaks very real havoc in society too.

3

Something Is Off

Carlos rarely dated in high school, which surprised many people. He was good-looking, athletic, and a fun-loving guy. Still, he didn't date because subconsciously he was comparing the girls he knew to the girls he watched in porn, and no one measured up. He could have the best girls through porn, and it was a lot less work. Through porn and masturbation, Carlos felt mostly satisfied. He still had occasional hookups to supplement the porn, and it gave him the most sexual pleasure for the least amount of work.

During his senior year, though, something happened that rocked Carlos. During one of his hookups, he was unable to get an erection. He tried to forget about it, but it happened again. He was embarrassed, ashamed, and surprised that he could have erectile dysfunction at such a young age. Turning to a little online research, he discovered he had all the symptoms of porn-induced erectile dysfunction (PIED). His porn consumption inhibited his ability to be aroused by an actual woman.

Carlos is not alone. PIED affects a growing number of teenagers and twenty-somethings every year. But PIED is not the only effect of our pornified culture. Sexlessness, teenage erectile dysfunction, the decline of marriage, violence against women, pedophilia, and sex trafficking are all on the rise. Each of these increases can be linked to pornography.

Association doesn't prove causation, but these trends are consistent with what would be expected based on the 1980s porn exposure study from the previous chapter. Though some of these trends have been seen before, there has never been this kind of explosive growth. The growth of these trends has been notable since the advent of internet porn in the mid-'90s and, more significantly, since the birth of streaming porn in 2006.

Why are so many young men not having sex?

Sexlessness. It is a growing phenomenon. Over the last ten years, the percentage of American men between the ages of eighteen and thirty who reported *not* having sex in the preceding year exploded from 10% to 28%.[1] In the three decades this statistic has been kept, this is by far the most significant percentage increase. At an age when young men's sex drives are highest, this generation of young men is having less sex than ever recorded. But this does not mean that these men have no sexual desire. For a growing number of pornified men, their sexual desire for real women is being replaced by a desire for images and fantasy.

Musician John Mayer raised eyebrows in an interview when he admitted preferring fantasy and masturbation to sex with a woman. In the interview, he said that during sex, he is actually masturbating in his mind and fantasizing about someone else than the person he is with.[2] Through watching porn, he has rewired his brain for what arouses him.

Like Mayer, a generation is forming their sexual tastes around voyeurism and self-sex through repeated porn use. Many porn users report the inability to climax without porn because of the rewiring of the brain through years of consuming X-rated material.[3] For instance, one frustrated teenage porn user described his first sexual experience, saying, "When I lost my virginity, it really did not feel that good. I was bored actually. I lost the erection after maybe ten minutes. She wanted more sex, but I was done."[4]

Porn's rewiring of the brain is behind the new phenomenon of PIED among young men and teenagers. In 2016, *TIME* magazine ran a cover story entitled "Why Young Men Who Grew Up With Internet Porn Are Becoming Advocates for Turning It Off." The article shared the stories of several twenty-somethings with PIED. They shared the shock of discovering porn ruined their ability to have sex with a physical partner. The article reported that before internet porn, only 5% of men under forty had ED. Today, 33% of men under forty report some erectile dysfunction.[5]

Alexander, one of the twenty-somethings featured in that article, shared about his first girlfriend as a teenager. "I thought it was normal to fantasize about porn while having sex with another person," he said, but as he continued to use pornography while he was dating, he eventually lost the ability to respond sexually to a real woman. And though Alexander is not alone, this kind of ED on such a large scale is an entirely new phenomenon among youth that has sprung up in the last fifteen years.

Dr. Abraham Morgentaler, professor of urology at Harvard Medical School, describes the men suffering from PIED as young and healthy men who can't maintain an erection when with a sexual partner.[6] These young men can, however, maintain an erection when watching porn. When a person's entire sexual history has been shaped by porn, real sex seems like an alien experience.

This is not just a phenomenon for twenty-somethings. It is impacting teenagers like Carlos. A 2016 study of Canadian adolescents showed that 45.3% admitted to problems in erectile functioning.[7] PIED can be cured after quitting porn for several months. When most people try to quit, though, they discover they're addicted.

Sexlessness and PIED are not the only negative consequences of increased porn use. With the rise in porn use, we've also seen a big jump in the hookup culture. Those who use porn regularly are more likely to view hookup sex in a positive light.[8] A national survey of over 15,000 adults asked respondents when they first had sex in their current or most recent relationship. After six months of dating? After two months? No! 32% of men under forty reported they had sex with their current partner *before* the relationship began![9]

Not only has internet porn encouraged the hookup culture, but it has also provided an alternative to real sex. A smartphone never says no. For many men, virtual women are now genuine competition for real partners.

Tolerance Leads to More

Like other addictive substances, pornography loses its potency with time. Eventually, it fails to give the same high it did at first. Because of this, users tend to watch more porn or more extreme content to get the same chemical reaction in their brains. In a survey of 1,500 young adult men, 56% said their tastes in porn had become "increasingly extreme or deviant." When people chase the high that comes with pornography, they often find themselves watching things they never thought they would. Many porn consumers eventually find themselves getting aroused by things that once disgusted them.[10] The following captures the reality for many porn users:

> I can't seem to stop myself. This has escalated over the years from age twelve... Each time I abuse porn, it gets a tiny shade more extreme. I feel absolutely disgusted.[11]

There is a spectrum of possible responses to pornography. Just as some move away from real partners because of sexual dysfunction or because they prefer porn and self-sex, others move to more extreme sexual behavior. Some act more violently toward women. Some move toward pedophilia. And is it any wonder? Two of the more popular extreme forms of porn are violent porn and child pornography.

In *Your Brain on Porn,* Gary Wilson discusses how porn pushes users to more extreme behavior. He shares the experience of a twenty-five-year-old porn user:

> I can say with absolute certainty that the fantasies I had about rape, homicide, and submission were never there before hardcore porn use from eighteen to twenty-two. When I stayed away from porn for five months, all those fantasies and urges were gone. My natural sexual taste was vanilla again—and still is. The thing with porn is you need harder and harder material, more taboo, more exciting, and more "wrong."[12]

Many users wish they were not drawn to these kinds of taboo sex. Renowned psychiatrist Dr. Norman Doidge wrote about one of his porn-addicted patients, saying:

> His feeling that sexual intercourse was a violent act upset him greatly, yet excited him. Thoughts of sexual intercourse immediately led to thoughts of violence and thoughts of violence to sex.[13]

But how does a person come to view sex as an act of violence? A study of the twenty-five most popular pornographic movies revealed that nine out of ten scenes showed violence by a man toward a woman. The study concluded that when a man acts violently toward a woman in pornography, 95% of the time one of two things happens. Either the woman expresses pleasure at the violence or she has no response at all. This teaches male viewers that women enjoy violent sex. It teaches female viewers they should like rough or violent sex, or at least, not object.[14] It is no surprise that over 100 studies have shown that pornography use increases the likelihood that a man will commit violence against a woman.[15]

Sexual violence against women has increased significantly since streaming porn.[16] And that leads to this question: can we give adolescent boys access to violent porn and not expect it to make them aggressive and sometimes violent toward women? The research suggests we cannot.

In addition to shaping views on violence toward women, porn sometimes leads to the sexualization of children, or those made to look like children. One of the most popular porn genres is of young women who are eighteen but made to look even younger. Once a user is addicted to this kind of porn, transitioning to more taboo and forbidden genres is a small step.

Robert Johnson was a husband, father, and business professional. After he divorced his wife, he began watching porn. Not long into his new habit, he saw child porn for the first time. He was initially shocked by it, but within the next year, Robert began seeking it out. Seven years later, he was arrested for possession of over 200,000 images of child pornography.[17]

Johnson is just one of the thousands of people who regularly view child pornography. The FBI's statistics show possession of child pornography is one of the fastest-growing crimes in the United States. In the past decade, child pornography arrests have increased 2,500%. The explosion of child porn has mirrored the explosion of pornography in general.[18] This is tragic because the reality is that many who view child porn eventually abuse children. Research shows 85% of those arrested for possession of child pornography admitted to sexually abusing minors.[19]

The deviance that can result from porn consumption is impacting the Church. In 2019, a headline in the *Houston Chronicle* read, "More Than 100 Southern Baptist Youth Pastors Convicted or Charged in Sex Crimes."[20] Many (if not most) of these sex crimes involved minors. These perpetrators—many of them youth pastors—didn't wake up one day deciding to be pedophiles. For the vast majority of them, it appears that a healthy, God-given sexual appetite was corrupted by years of pornography use.

Chasing the high from pornography leads many to the place where just watching isn't enough. Porn is not an excuse for this criminal behavior, but it does provide an explanation for this wickedness in the Church. Unless the Church deals with its porn problem, these headlines will continue.

Pastor Tommy Nelson, a board member of Dallas Theological Seminary, said of the porn problem among their students training to be pastors, "We don't ask the students anymore *if* they struggle with porn, we ask how bad their struggle is."[21] Because nine out of ten growing Christian college males are looking at porn, this is a safe assumption for any seminary or Bible college.[22] When many of these students go into ministry, they have a deep addiction to porn. Some have cultivated an appetite for the deviant and extreme. For many, regular porn is a gateway drug to child porn and other illicit sexual activity. The Church cannot afford to continue to ignore this issue.

Every church and every denomination has a porn problem. This porn problem is destroying Christian marriages, enslaving the next generation of Christian leaders, and helping to produce pedophile pastors. These things disgrace Christ's name. Can we allow pornography to shape the minds of the next generation and not expect there to be consequences? Will leaders in the Church step up and address the issue?

Sex Trafficking

As if all of this were not bad enough, pornography is one of the leading contributors to human sex trafficking, which is a form of modern-day slavery. This trade has expanded around the world, and in the United States, up to 300,000 Americans under the age of eighteen are lured into the commercial sex trade every year.[23] The demand for commercial sex trafficking is fueled by pornography. Put another way, pornography and sex trafficking are inextricably linked, and in many cases, they are the same thing.

The organization Rescue:Freedom surveyed women rescued from sex trafficking in nine countries. Forty-nine percent of the women who responded said their traffickers made pornographic videos of them while they were raped.[24] One female survivor was forced at gunpoint to appear in a video that the porn industry awarded as a "sex-positive production." In a later interview, she said, "Every time someone watches that film. . . they are watching me being raped."[25]

One underage girl was missing for almost a year before her mother learned that sixty pornographic videos of her had been posted to multiple pornography platforms, including Pornhub and Snapchat. Pornhub described the minor girl as a "verified model with valid ID."[26]

The porn industry and sex trafficking are very connected. This is why sex trafficking has grown as pornography has grown. Reported cases of human sex trafficking in the US increased 842% in the past ten years.[27] The average age of a trafficked victim to begin to be sold for sex in the United States is thirteen.[28]

The idea that watching porn isn't hurting anyone is a lie. Watching pornography—whether violent, child porn, or seemingly run-of-the-mill porn—creates additional demand for the enslavement and rape of girls, boys, women, and men. The collective billions of porn clicks per year help fuel the demand for sex traffickers who make money selling videos to porn sites.[29] Because rape porn is one of the popular genres of porn, traffickers who film rapes fit right in.

Decline of Marriage

Sexlessness, erectile dysfunction, pedophilia, and sex trafficking have all exploded as porn use has erupted, and so has the decline of marriage. Sociologist Dr. Mark Regnerus said:

> Marriage in the US is in open retreat. As recently as 2000, married 25-to-34-year-olds outnumbered their never-married peers by a healthy margin. By 2015 those estimates had almost reversed, with never-marrieds outnumbering marrieds. Young Americans have quickly become wary of marriage. My own research points to a more straightforward and primal explanation for the slowed pace toward marriage: For American men, sex has become rather cheap. As compared to the past, many women today expect little in return for sex in terms of time, attention, commitment, or fidelity.[30]

According to Professor Regnerus, cheap sex not only refers to the hookup culture, but it also includes pornography. He stated:

> The quality of porn and masturbation may well have reached a level significant enough to satisfy many men, such that the pursuit of real sex with real women... seems no longer a benefit worth the costs of wooing...They may not declare virtual sex "great sex," but they may conclude that it's good enough.[31]

Porn use among women also affects their view of marriage. Women who use porn are more likely to cheat on a romantic partner and less likely to support traditional marriage. Watching pornography is eroding traditional biblical views on fidelity and marriage.[32] More porn means less commitment to marriage.

Both the cheap sex of pornography and the hookup culture contribute to the decline of marriage. This decline is expected to grow significantly in the future. Researchers predict a third of Americans now in their twenties will never wed. This is more than triple the historic norm.[33]

God made sex to be incredibly enjoyable, and He designed it to be enjoyed within the specific context of marriage. In light of this, it is not surprising that married couples consistently report the most satisfying sex lives.[34] When porn interrupts the natural design of sex, the inevitable result is the decay of marriage.

The Thief

Jesus said, "The thief comes only to steal and kill and destroy, but I came that they may have life and have it abundantly" (John 10:10). Before we turn to the thief, let's consider the abundant life Jesus promises. Doesn't this apply to sex? When you follow God's plan of sex within marriage, when you avoid porn, you can expect your sex life, marital life, and spiritual life will be more fulfilling. After all, research shows that married couples have more and better sex than the singles living the hookup lifestyle.[35] When a person follows God's design for sex, they have more sex and more satisfying sex. These are the blessings of enjoying an abundant sex life the way God intended.

The thief wants nothing more than to kill your abundant life. Through porn, isn't Satan stealing, killing, and destroying our ability to enjoy sex as God intended? Porn has promised sexual fulfillment while delivering dysfunction and death. The research shows that porn users are less sexually satisfied than non-users.[36] The masses are searching for sexual fulfillment outside of God's design. At the same time, they reject marriage, which is where the most fulfilling sex is found.

To experience the abundant life that Jesus offers, including an abundant sex life, we must obey His instruction about sex. Jesus told us to avoid visual lust outside of marriage. He said, "You have heard that it was said, 'You shall not commit adultery'; but I say to you that everyone who looks at a woman with lust for her has already committed adultery with her in his heart" (Matthew 5:27-28). These words of Jesus spoken 2,000 years ago capture the timeless wisdom of God, and as we've looked at in this chapter, ignoring these words leads to dire results. As followers of Christ embrace His Words, we can experience the abundant life, establish godly marriages, and shine the light of God's truth in the midst of today's brokenness. However, many of Christ's followers find it nearly impossible to say no to the pull of porn.

4

Hijacking the Brain

Jean was a happily married forty-year-old Christian mother when she discovered pornography. After upgrading her cable service, she flipped through the channels and stumbled across a porn channel. "It was an excitement that captured me like nothing else could," she said. "When I made love to my husband for the first time, it was that kind of excitement. But this was a more heightened excitement than that because it stirred up something I didn't know was inside of me."

Night after night, Jean waited for her family to go to bed so she could sneak to watch porn. The more she watched the more she wanted. She described her obsession, saying she was "living to love these movies, these videos, the internet, anything that I could get my hands on. Anything that had to do with pornography, I was drawn to. It was taking over my life."[1]

Jean, like many other porn users, had become an addict. The physical structure of her brain was changed by prolonged porn use. As devastating as that reality is, she'd later discover some very good news. Freedom is possible. God delivered her from her addiction, and her natural brain chemistry was restored. When that happened, Jean felt like she had been freed from prison.

Without addressing the brain-altering impact of porn, it is nearly impossible to change a person's behavior. Why? Because God made our brains to respond to sexual stimuli, and if a person feeds their brain with porn, they'll only want more. The brain science of pornography helps explain how a person's own neurology can imprison them.

Chasing the High

The body's response to pornography is driven by the most complicated organ in the human body: the brain. Whether engaging in sex, watching sexual content, or masturbating, the brain releases a cocktail of chemicals that brings excitement, pleasure, and temporary satisfaction. Dopamine is among the most important of these chemicals.

When a person experiences something enjoyable that the brain wants them to remember and repeat, it releases dopamine.[2] The first time you held hands with someone you liked: dopamine. The taste of chocolate: dopamine. Sex on your honeymoon: hello, dopamine! God created people to experience pleasure, and dopamine is a key part of that. Dopamine is incredible, but unfortunately, people have learned to manipulate dopamine production.

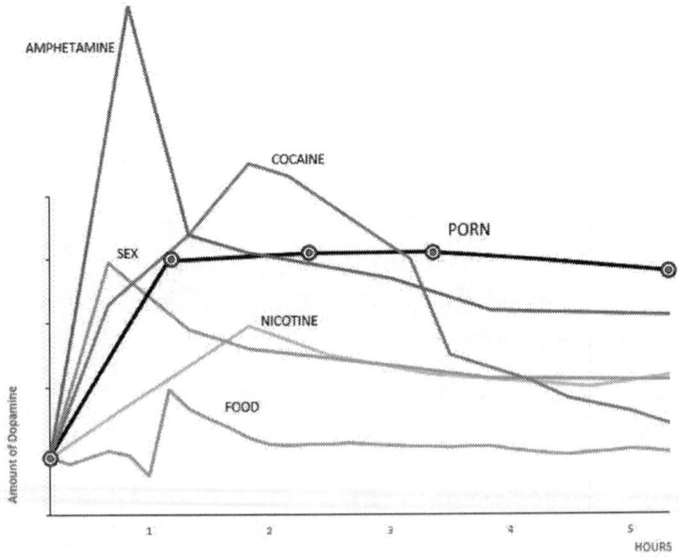

The graph shows the amount of dopamine estimated to be produced in the brain by different stimulants.[3]

Sex provides the highest natural dopamine hit. As you'll see in the above chart, there are three man-made stimulants estimated to produce more dopamine than sex: meth, cocaine, and porn. Drugs like cocaine release unnatural amounts of dopamine into the body. So does meth. So does pornography.

Dopamine ensures that the brain remembers and later craves the activities that led to the high.[4] The use of drugs like cocaine, meth, and porn is rooted in chasing that high again and again. Many times, chasing dopamine can be so consuming that people risk it all—their job, marriage, ministry, and integrity—for another hit.

As you look at the chart, notice that nothing compares to porn in sustaining a high near its peak. As a result, users might binge on porn for hours at a time. The users get a fresh hit of dopamine as they move to new and different sex scenes. Porn binges can produce up to ten times more dopamine in the brain than relational sex.[5]

I interviewed several married men who had porn addictions in the past. I asked them, "What produced a higher high: porn or sex?" The men all agreed that porn causes more of a rush, even though sex is more fulfilling. One of the men commented, "I think the more sex I have with my wife, the more satisfying it is each time. Porn gives less satisfaction each time… or at least, it takes more porn to get the same effect."

Porn is like candy: it brings a quick high, but it can't sustain you and it rots the soul. Sex with your spouse is like a five-course meal: it satisfies and nourishes your relationship. When we consider the unlimited access and the dopamine burst of porn, it's no wonder people get hooked on it. It's not just about the porn, it's about the craving for the high.

In the porn documentary *Brain Heart World*, three individuals share how the pornographic high grabbed them from the very beginning:

> I first saw porn at ten. I went from seeing the pictures to watching the videos. I had to watch it at least once or twice a day. Even when I wasn't watching it, I was regularly thinking about it and the next time I could watch it. –Sherese

> I got a glimpse of pornography when I was surfing the internet at ten. I felt a little guilt, but it felt so good, so I kept looking. I went from one picture to another. I loved how it made me feel. If I felt bad, I could watch porn and it made me feel great. I wanted more. –Ryan

> The first time I watched porn, I was hooked. I watched it three more times that day and then every day for the next six years. –Dan[6]

Different people react differently to porn. Not everyone is immediately hooked. Most people—people like Sherese, Ryan, and Dan—are. Why? Because like drugs, pornography hijacks the brain's reward system and offers rewards for behaviors which are ultimately harmful.

The Porn Pathway

As behaviors are repeated, brain neurons connect to form pathways that allow messages to travel more efficiently. The more we travel those pathways, the easier it is to do it again in the future.[7] This is why habitual behavior like riding bikes and tying shoes eventually becomes second nature.

Repetition is how all habits are built, including porn habits. When people regularly use porn, they build a strong neurological pathway. The chemicals released during porn use reinforce the neurological pathways in the brain and make them even stronger. The more the action is repeated, the less conscious thought it requires to go down that path.

Dopamine is not only released at the height of pleasure, but also in anticipation of pleasure. When a person climaxes using porn, the brain makes note of it to remind them to do that again. The next time a sexual trigger appears, the brain increases the craving by releasing dopamine, urging the user to chase the reward again. The dopamine release moves the user down that familiar path because of the rewards and pleasure at the end. Everything in them says, "I must have it." It consumes their thoughts. All they want is to be alone with porn.[8]

We are not without defenses though. The prefrontal cortex (PFC) of the brain helps manage impulse control and moral reasoning. These are the brakes that help people say no to cravings based on morals or goals. But here's the bad news. Through brain scans, scientists have discovered that the PFC appears to shrink through regular use of porn.[9] In essence, the more you use porn, the less likely you are to say *no* without significant reprogramming.

Elevated dopamine levels in the brain because of regular porn use impair the ability of the brakes (PFC). This is why it is difficult for an addict to stop watching porn even when they want to.[10] This phenomenon is true for any addiction. This doesn't excuse a person's porn use, but it does help explain how an otherwise godly person who genuinely wants to quit often can't until they get help.

Sex is powerful, and God warns of the consequences for engaging in it outside of the context for which it was designed—marriage. The Bible warns that when people sin sexually, they sin against their own bodies. "Flee from sexual immorality. All other sins a person commits are outside the body, but whoever sins sexually, sins against their own body" (1 Corinthians 6:18).

In the original language of the Bible, Greek, the word for immorality is *porneia*. It refers to any sexual activity outside of marriage. As you probably guessed, we get our English word "pornography" from this Greek word. I believe one of the ways a person sins against their own body through porn use is that their brains lock them into bondage. Their brakes grow weaker as their cravings grow stronger.

After repeated use, the porn user's brain builds a tolerance to dopamine. They need more porn or more deviant porn to get the same high. They often seek the variety through new and different images or engage in risky behavior.

The porn high is made stronger when adrenaline is added to the mix. Even worries about being caught can heighten the excitement. Where are my roommates? When will my spouse be home? I think the door is locked. The sense of danger from these questions adds risk to the equation, and thus, a kick of adrenaline. One student I coached described how fear added to his experience:

> The first time I viewed a porn site was on my parents' computer in our home office. My dad was home. I can still remember the image and how I felt. It was exhilarating, and I could feel the adrenaline pumping because I was afraid of getting caught.

Introducing fear or shock into the experience might also encourage the user to seek out more extreme or risky porn. Violating one's moral standards also increases adrenaline. A testimony from *Your Brain on Porn* illustrates:

> Without realizing, I was watching a lot of taboo and extreme porn that I never would have considered a couple of years ago. I couldn't believe I let myself get to this point. I just couldn't stop myself.[11]

What's the end result? Because porn artificially raises the baseline level of dopamine, porn users need more dopamine to get that high. Normal levels of dopamine can leave them feeling depressed, unmotivated, and antisocial. In fact, these feelings affect porn users more frequently than non-users.[12] Some porn addicts report they can't enjoy the simple pleasures of life like before. They become bored and disengaged with things they used to enjoy. One user shared his experience:

> As a child, I was highly athletic, smart, and sociable. I was always happy and had a million friends. That all changed around age eleven when I started watching porn videos and progressed to nearly every type of porn imaginable. I started having severe depression and anxiety. The next fifteen years of my life were completely miserable. I was incredibly antisocial, and I quit all the sports that I had played. As much as I hate to think about it now, I even started thinking about suicide.[13]

Not every porn user has this severe of a reaction, but a growing number of them do. Porn creates a chemical dependency in the brain. For some, this dependency is mild. For others, it is significant. It's particularly significant for our youth.

The Perfect Storm of Addiction – Adolescence and Porn

If I've learned anything from working with college students for thirty years and through my training as a sex addiction professional, it's this: the power of porn is amplified in the adolescent brain. The research confirms what I have experienced. It shows that the adolescent brain is more vulnerable to addictive substances, including porn. The effects go deeper and last longer. The young brain is much more malleable, and the habits picked up during adolescence are often the most difficult to break.[14] Adolescence is roughly defined as between the ages of ten and nineteen, a time when the brain goes through critical development.

Why are adolescent brains so deeply impacted by porn? First, the brain decreases its connections after the age of twelve. During this time, billions of nerve connections are pruned and reorganized. The pruning of unused nerve cells helps the connections that remain grow stronger and become fine-tuned. It's much like pruning a bush of the old and weak branches so that the strong branches can grow stronger.[15] The brain does this to narrow and intensify brain connections. In his book *Your Brain on Porn,* Gary Wilson shows the significance of this. He wrote:

> … once new connections form, teen brains hold tightly to these associations. In fact, research shows that our most powerful and lasting memories arise from adolescence along with our worst habits.[16]

The brain organizes its neural pathways around the strongest connections. And for a growing number of teenagers, those are their porn connections. Wilson continued explaining about the dangers for the young porn user:

> A natural shrinking of the brain's circuits to the more well-worn pathways means he has well-honed responses to life. By his twenties, he may not exactly be stuck with the sexual conditioning he falls into during adolescence, but it can be like a deep rut in his brain, less easy to ignore or reconfigure.[17]

The research shows that bad habits established early in life are hard to break. Ninety percent of Americans who are addicted to alcohol, tobacco, or drugs started using their addictive substance before they were eighteen.[18] This is why there are laws to keep addictive substances away from minors. Despite this information, today's youth have unlimited access to one of the most addictive substances on the planet—porn.

A second reason youth are more vulnerable to porn addiction is because their reward circuitry is in overdrive. In response to internet novelty, the adolescent brain produces higher spikes of dopamine than an adult or child's brain does.[19] As a result, the teen brain can deeply condition itself to internet pornography with surprising ease. This means real sex can feel like an alien experience to some people. A twenty-five-year-old who developed his porn habit during his teen years shared:

> My sexual experience is very limited, and the few times I've tried sex have been a total disappointment: no erection. Been trying to quit (porn) for five months now and finally have. I realize that I've been conditioned to the point where my sexual urges are deeply linked to a computer screen. Women don't turn me on unless they are behind my glass monitor.[20]

Imagine the obstacles he'll experience in cultivating a healthy marriage. This is the new norm for many people. This might be why the sexlessness rates tripled for eighteen-to-thirty-year-old men. It might be why marriageless rates are spiking for this same age group. When adolescents have their brains hijacked by porn, it changes the course of their life.

Pre-adolescent Porn Use? It's Becoming the Norm

A therapist I met at a sex addiction training told me that it is not uncommon for him to treat boys under the age of ten for pornography addiction. One of his clients was a nine-year-old whose parents brought him in because "he can't quit looking at porn." The parents were so desperate that they cut the family's internet access and took all their children's mobile devices.

One day the mom discovered her phone was missing. She scoured the house looking for it and found her nine-year-old son watching porn on it. He went to the corner of the house so he could get on their neighbor's Wi-Fi. He badly wanted to stop, but he couldn't. A pastor friend recently emailed me asking for resources for kids struggling with pornography. He told me that in the past few months, their church discovered several boys between eight and twelve struggling with a porn addiction.

Some sources say the average age of first exposure to porn is eleven,[21] while others say eight.[22] Regardless of the specific number, the initial exposure age is getting younger. What's more, children under the age of ten now account for 22% of online porn consumption for those under eighteen.[23] Consider Licensed Mental Health Counselor Steven Kavanagh, who writes of the dangers of exposure to porn at early ages:

> During certain critical periods of childhood, a child's brain is being programmed for sexual orientation. During this period, the mind appears to be developing a "hardwire" for what the person will be aroused by or attracted to. If there is exposure to pornography during this period, sexual deviance may become imprinted on the child's "hard drive" and become a permanent part of his or her sexual orientation.[24]

It's not just the pastors and therapists who are taking note. The government also recognizes the problem:

> Never before in the history of telecommunications media in the United States has so much indecent and obscene material been so easily accessible by so many minors in so many American homes with so few restrictions. (US Department of Justice)[25]

There is reason to expect the number of children addicted to porn to explode in the coming years. During the coronavirus pandemic of 2020, the organization Amaze, a well-funded organization with a team of staff and volunteers, launched their online sex education program for all the children learning at home. It teaches children that porn is normal "even a few times a day." Their goal? To reach five million children by 2022.[26] They know a simple truth: One child who thinks porn is normal will spread that message and share their favorite videos with their friends and classmates.

Today's youth are watching more porn, more extreme porn, at younger ages, with more frequency, and for longer periods than any generation in the past. Combine this with their susceptibility to addiction, and it is truly the perfect storm, one that's creating porn addicts by the day. Typically, the younger someone starts using porn, the deeper the addiction goes. Still, freedom is possible. I see it happen all the time. But breaking free is one of the most challenging things a person can do.

The Good News About Neuroplasticity

Although the brain locks people into addiction through repeated use of pornography, there is good news. The brain can be changed.

The brain has great neuroplasticity, meaning it can physically change as someone changes their behavior. Old neurological circuits shrink when they are not used, while new ones form with new activity and learning.[27] The brain shaped by porn can be modified and changed. Changing the brain requires reprogramming it. The longer the porn use, the harder it is to reprogram. Stopping the old habit is a good first step, but ultimately, the old pathways must be replaced with new ones.

Only recently have scientists understood that the brain can be changed throughout one's life and not just in adolescence. But what science recently discovered, the Bible has been saying for thousands of years. Romans 12:2 says, "Be transformed by the renewing of your mind." Understanding this truth in light of the addicted brain brings hope. Change and freedom are possible. Just making commitments and trying harder doesn't work. The addicted brain must be renewed.

When I first started helping others overcome their porn struggles, my efforts could be reduced to a simple formula:

Accountability + Spiritual Disciplines = Freedom

As I continued the work, I began meeting those who loved God, hated their sin, found accountability, and memorized Bible verses. Still, they could not break free. It became clear it wasn't just a moral problem. Something deeper was happening, something in the brain. When we fail to take into account the brain science of porn addiction, we potentially short-circuit recovery.

As I grew to understand this truth, I concluded that my approach was incomplete. What I thought was the case—Accountability + Spiritual Disciplines = Freedom—was actually more like this: Accountability + Spiritual Disciplines = Less Porn

I needed a new approach.

Try Harder?

Evan graduated college and became a minister. He was addicted to porn. He tried to quit but couldn't. He sold his laptop and got a flip phone. That helped for a while, but he just used his roommate's devices in the middle of the night. He wanted to quit so badly that he tried something crazy. He asked a roommate to handcuff him to his bed every night so he wouldn't sneak their devices. That didn't work either. He still found ways to watch porn, even if it meant going to an electronic store to use the display computers. Evan's situation wasn't just a moral problem. It was a brain problem.

For those with an addicted brain like Evan's, trying harder doesn't work. They wonder why freedom is elusive, but they do not understand that there are roots to every porn addiction. Among them is the addicted brain. And when I came to understand this truth, I set out to discover the most common roots of pornography addiction and how to address them. After more than a decade of research and training, I modified my approach to sobriety from pornography, which can be expressed in a more complete formula:

Accountability + Spiritual Disciplines + Address the Roots = Freedom

Addressing the addicted brain is only addressing one root of porn addiction. What are the others? As I'll discuss later in the book, they are the sexualized society, the addicted brain, isolation, negative emotions, shame, and trauma. I will show how each root can be addressed with biblically based, gospel-centered, and clinically informed solutions that bring freedom. But before we turn to those roots, we must understand how ferociously pornography is waging war against the soul, against marriages, and against the Church.

5

War Against the Soul

Alex felt guilty every time he looked at porn on the phone he received for his fourteenth birthday. He made commitments to stop, but he couldn't seem to make it more than a few weeks without bingeing again. He felt like a hypocrite, so he got more active in his church's youth group, hoping that would help his problem. It didn't.

In his shame, Alex avoided God. Hoping for relief, though, he told his youth leader. It helped some, but his addiction continued. He prayed for God to take away his lust, but without any real accountability or solutions, he struggled on. And as his porn habit continued, he began to doubt his faith. If God was real, why wasn't he answering Alex's prayers for freedom from porn?

In college, Alex found a small group with more consistent accountability, it helped, but he still struggled. One night, the small group Alex was leading discussed a passage in which Jesus talks about being free from sin. "If the Son shall make you free you shall be free indeed" (John 8:34-35). As the group discussed this promise, Alex felt even more hypocritical. How could he tell the group this freedom was real, especially when he wasn't experiencing it?

That's when the reality that he had been living a lie began to overwhelm him. He lost his desire to seek God. He stepped back from leadership and stopped pursuing Christ. The nagging questions continued in his mind. Was all of this true or was it made up? Why wouldn't Jesus give Alex freedom when He had promised to?

Alex graduated from college still doubting his faith. The apostle Peter warned of the effects of fleshly lusts, saying, "Beloved, I urge you as aliens and strangers to abstain from fleshly lusts, which wage war against the soul" (1 Peter 2:11 NASB). By nursing his porn addiction, Alex had unknowingly invited the enemy to wage war against his very soul.

Living in Denial

Two out of three Christian men watch porn regularly.[1] Many of them feel bad about it, but few of them have an urgency and commitment to break free. In fact, less than one in ten of these men seek meaningful help.[2] How can so many Christians seem content to live in sin? The answer is shame and self-deception.

Shame leads believers to hide their porn problem. Though shame haunts both men and women who use porn, the shame response is often higher with women. After all, porn is supposed to be a man's problem. Researchers like Samuel Perry suspect this causes Christian women to under-report their porn use and makes them less likely to seek help.[3] The shame of porn keeps many people from confessing their struggle and can lead to self-deception and rationalization.

Self-deception keeps many Christians stuck in their porn habits too. Some people think they can quit anytime they want. Others justify their behavior, claiming it's no big deal. The porn addict might say, "I'm not that bad," or "Everyone struggles with this," or "I'm not addicted—I just mess up once in a while." These rationalizations might help the believer live with the hypocrisy of regular porn use, but this self-deception keeps them stuck.

The Bible is clear about the deceitful nature of sin. It commands us to "exhort one another every day, as long as it is called 'today,' that none of you may be hardened by the deceitfulness of sin" (Hebrews 3:13). We are warned in this passage about hardening our hearts and becoming stubborn and unresponsive to God, His Word, and other people.

The tendency to be deceived is so great that God warns us repeatedly about it.

- "Do not be deceived: 'Bad company ruins good morals.'" (1 Corinthians 15:33)
    - Keeping the bad company of porn will change us.
- "Do not be deceived… for whatever a person sows that will they reap." (Galatians 6:7)
    - Sowing porn in our lives will have consequences.
- "Let no one say when he is tempted, 'I am being tempted by God…' each person is tempted when he is lured and enticed by his own desire. Do not be deceived." (James 1:13-16)
    - When deceived, we can blame God instead of taking responsibility.
- "Do not merely listen to the word, and so deceive yourselves. Do what it says." (James 1:22 NIV)
    - We can think knowing the truth is enough instead of obeying it.

The Scriptures are clear about the deceitfulness of sin, which includes porn use. But why does porn seem so much more deceitful than other patterns of sin?

Staying Stuck

I interviewed several pastors about how the majority of Christian men and a growing number of women seem content to stay stuck in their porn habits. I wanted to determine what factors keep people in the shadows. Here's what the pastors told me:

What keeps single men and women stuck in their porn habit?

- "Many people are addicted and cannot go a day without it. Their brains have been re-wired from the time they were in middle school. They literally feel they can't function without porn."
- "Many of them believe the lie that when they get married, their porn habit will go away. Therefore, they do not have urgency."
- "Many people do not set up boundaries or take the first steps to get out. I'm convinced many could see some victory if they would take small steps."
- "A lot of people start the fight each day feeling like they have already lost. They are hopeless. They have tried to stop and always fail."

What lies do married Christians use to rationalize their porn use?

- "At least porn isn't a real affair."
- "It's private and doesn't affect anyone else."
- "Everyone struggles."
- "It's not as bad as an alcohol or drug addiction."
- "If I admit my need for help, I risk losing my spouse."
- "I don't have the time or energy to dig into the root causes of my porn issue."

What have you seen break people out of porn's deception?

- "Realizing they want to get married or be in a serious relationship."
- "Getting married."
- "Being married and still being addicted to porn."
- "Having their first kid."
- "Finding themselves attracted to the same sex in the porn they watch."
- "Getting caught."
- "True biblical conviction."

One pastor captured the reality of a lack of true biblical conviction: "I see lots of guys saying they want out, but very few actually coming with the conviction and readiness to get out!" A porn addiction is not easy to break. If someone doesn't have deep convictions about why they are pursuing freedom, they won't find it. Weak convictions about pursuing holiness mean weak convictions about breaking free. These weak convictions undermine long-term spiritual health and growth.

More Porn = Less Spiritual Disciplines + More Doubts

Most Christians who stay stuck in a porn habit have no idea how pornography "wages war against the soul" (1 Peter 2:11), but the impact is measurable. Dr. Samuel Perry, a sociology professor at the University of Oklahoma, has done extensive research on the effects of pornography use on a person's religious commitments. He summarizes his conclusions: "Any porn use…is associated with declines in religious commitment and behavior (i.e., attending services, prayer, etc.) and an increase in religious doubts."[4]

So if the enemy wants Christians to be less committed to reading their Bible, attending church, and praying, and if he wants them to doubt more, all he has to do is get them to watch porn. The following testimonies of Christians interviewed by Dr. Perry prove this truth:

> If I viewed pornography, I hid from God. I avoided talking to him.[5]
>
> If I had remaining guilt or shameful feelings from viewing porn, I would refrain from just about any activity that reminded me of God.[6]
>
> I felt too ashamed to pray and attend worship events and read the Bible when I was using porn.[7]
>
> I think porn is an insidious little thing that can happen often enough to break the fellowship with God. I don't find myself as eager to pray or even go to church.[8]
>
> Because I feel bad (about porn use) ... I sometimes don't want to go to church ... The place you need to go, you don't actually want to go.[9]
>
> When I see the Bible, I feel guilt and try to avoid it. I'll, like, knowingly not look at my nightstand because I know the Bible's right there.[10]

Perry's research concludes there is a correlation between pornography use and religious doubt. The more porn someone watches, the more religious doubts they have.

More Porn = Less Service

Doubts not only diminish one's desire to pursue God, but they often move people to step away from spiritual service. Jesus said in Luke 10:2, "The harvest is plentiful but the workers are few." In today's porn-saturated environment, the number of workers is becoming even smaller. Perry studied over 3,000 people for six years to determine how their porn use impacted their service and leadership in their congregation.

What he discovered was stunning. If a church-going man never or rarely used porn, there was a one-in-three chance he would serve or take some type of leadership role in his congregation. If he started using porn every month, his odds of serving fell to one in ten. If he watched porn every week, there was a one-in-twenty probability that he would serve. If a man started using porn daily, his probability of serving went to almost zero. The conclusion was obvious: the more frequently someone watches porn, the less likely they are to serve in their church.[11]

A church-planting missionary who worked overseas shared how his own discouragement over his pornography use was a major reason he doubted his faith and came home:

> I don't see any victory in the area of porn—I mean is my faith real? I'm reading in the Bible, "How shall we sin anymore if Christ is in us?" Meanwhile, I cannot shake this thing, and I have no idea what in the world to do about it.[12]

Another former leader shared why he pulled back from ministry:

> A few years ago, I stopped taking opportunities to lead groups at church or disciple younger men because of where I am personally with porn. I'd really

> feel like a worthless hypocrite for teaching some young men about how to study the Bible and share their faith when I'm regularly looking at pornography and masturbating.[13]

A collegiate leader in his campus ministry that I interviewed shared how his porn habit impacted his service:

> When I looked at porn, it took away almost all of my confidence to do ministry. I did not want to be around people after I watched porn because I felt ashamed. When I did do ministry, I did not feel like I was in a position to lead someone spiritually because I sinned sexually, again. I looked at myself as a hypocrite.

The experts know this truth: porn is silently sidelining God's people from serving Him. The Freedom Fight's national survey proved this truth also. Our survey showed how porn use impacted Christian young women and their faith:

- Six out of ten said watching pornography decreased their desire to read or study God's Word.
- Almost two out of three said watching pornography decreased their desire to serve in spiritual leadership.
- More than eight in ten said they experienced self-hatred after using porn.
- More than half of these women say they have doubted their faith because of their porn use or the inability to stop.[14]

The college men from The Freedom Fight's survey were even more likely than these college women to pull back from

God's Word and from service opportunities. These realities suggest that many leaders of the next generation will seek God and His Word *less* because they seek porn *more*. If this pattern continues, the future leadership of the church is in serious trouble.

More Porn = Less Spiritual Interaction with Kids

In addition to stunting spiritual growth and service, Dr. Perry found that porn consumption is negatively associated with the time parents spend talking or reading about religion with their children. The more porn a parent watches, the less religious instruction they give their children. Findings suggest that increased pornography consumption might threaten the transmission of religious heritage from parents to children.[15]

A youth pastor recently told me a story, which demonstrates porn's impact in Christian homes. One of the students in his youth group confessed his struggle with porn to the youth pastor. The pastor asked for permission to bring the student's father into the conversation. The son agreed. The pastor met with the father and explained that the son was open to help and wanted to talk about his struggle. The pastor was excited about the meeting and how it set the father up to provide spiritual leadership at home. Three months later, the pastor was disheartened to find that the father *still* had not talked to his son. Why? The father had a porn habit of his own. His own struggle with porn kept him from helping his son at a point when his son desperately wanted leadership.

Porn is waging war against the believer's walk with God, against marriage, against parenting, and against service and leadership in the church. It should not be surprising, then, that after fifty-six years of a worldwide ministry, Josh McDowell says, "There's never been anything in history that is destroying more churches, more pastors, more marriages, and more young people than pornography." And as we've seen throughout this book, the evidence supports McDowell.

Identity Under Attack

Jesus described Satan as "a liar and the father of lies" (John 8:44). These days, he uses pornography as one of the primary methods of advancing those lies. Ultimately, the lies advanced by pornography undermine the believer's identity in Christ. Shame is different from guilt. Guilt says, "I've *done* bad," but shame says, "I *am* bad." There is a sense of worthlessness and self-loathing at the core of shame.

Mike, a young professional who ultimately lost his marriage because of his porn addiction, revealed the warfare that was taking place in his heart. "I know I'm forgiven in Christ, but the level of self-hatred I have because of some of the stuff I have watched can be overwhelming and makes me feel worthless." It is a sad reality that a growing number of believers in Christ are living out of a shame-identity instead of their true identity as a child of the King.

What is the true identity of a Christ follower?

Jesus' death and resurrection opened up the opportunity for a new life in Christ. When a person receives Christ, He takes their sin and credits them with His righteousness. They are made a part of God's family. They have a new identity as a child of God. They are new creations in Christ, holy and beloved. Their sin is forgiven and its power is broken.

If Satan can't keep believers from trusting Christ for salvation, he wants to undercut the work of the gospel in their lives. Often the devil (a name which means "accuses falsely") uses pornography as a full-frontal attack on people's identity in Christ. The power and beauty of the gospel is muted in their lives. An identity of shame can overshadow an identity in Christ. Through porn, the believer adopts an identity of shame.

Through the shame of porn use, the enemy keeps believers rationalizing their sin instead of repenting. This is why I believe porn is one of the enemy's most powerful weapons in spiritual warfare.

Each of us has immense worth and value because we were created in the image of God. God wants a relationship with us, and He demonstrated this truth by giving His Son to pay for our sins. This is true no matter how mired in porn a person might be. Those stuck in porn and the shame that results often miss out on experiencing the full reality of the love of God in their lives. God, His Word, and His love seem distant and less real for the Christian porn user drowning in the shame. Porn is waging war against the soul.

Grace Isn't a License; It Produces Fruit

The book of Jude warns against a group of "ungodly people who pervert the grace of their God into a license for immorality" (Jude 4). This is exactly what happens when a porn user claims, "God doesn't condemn me for my sin, so I don't need to worry if I mess up once in a while with porn." The twisting of grace into an excuse to sin is the opposite of what biblical grace produces. Biblical grace pushes people toward holiness. In his letter to Titus, Paul writes:

> For the grace of God has appeared, bringing salvation for all people, training us to renounce ungodliness and worldly passions, and to live self-controlled, upright, and godly lives in the present age (Titus 2:11-12).

Instead of an excuse to sin, true grace applied to porn use results in repentance and a pursuit of holiness that includes asking for help. True grace leads to recovery.

But here's the hard truth: some people who abuse grace are not true believers. They are among those who will call Jesus "Lord," on the day of judgment, but Jesus will say to them, "I never knew you; depart from Me, you workers of lawlessness" (Matthew 7:21-23).

How do you know whether you're a true follower of Christ? Ask yourself: Have I surrendered my life to Christ? Is there evidence that Jesus is in my life? Is my life marked by repentance?

Revisiting Alex

Alex, from the start of the chapter, leaned into the grace of true repentance. Eventually, he returned to church and joined a recovery group that had daily accountability. He finally understood that the freedom Jesus promised is preceded by a condition: "If you continue in My word, you are truly disciples of Mine; and you will know the truth and the truth will set you free" (John 8:31-32).

Alex learned that knowing the truth is more than knowing Bible facts—it's practicing what he learns by incorporating it into his life. Alex realized this meant replacing the lies he believed about himself with God's truth, and as he did, he began to believe what God said about his identity in Christ.

Alex began to genuinely mature in Christ like he never had before. As he did, he realized he had been living in denial about the severity of his addiction. He confessed to his small group and found strength in the daily encouragement and accountability. He also began to understand the brain science of addiction and how to renew his mind. All of this helped the shame to lift in his life. After a year in the group, Alex was free. His doubts faded and he was more committed to following Christ and serving in his church. What's more, he became excited about helping other men walk in the truth.

In his letter to the Romans, Paul describes Alex's life both before and after recovery. He wrote:

> For those who live according to the flesh set their minds on the things of the flesh, but those who live according to the Spirit set their minds on the things of the Spirit. For to set the mind on the flesh is death, but to set the mind on the Spirit is life and peace. For the mind that is set on the flesh is hostile to God, for it does not submit to God's law; indeed, it cannot. Those who are in the flesh cannot please God. (Romans 8:5-8)

When Alex indulged in porn, his mind was set on death. But when his mind was renewed by the truth of Christ, he walked in step with the Spirit and was full of life and peace.

Freedom is possible, and the earlier the believer pursues that freedom, the better. Freedom from porn bolsters faith, increases involvement in the things of God, and strengthens the relationship between God and His people. Even more, as we'll see in the next chapter, pursuing freedom protects the closest earthly relationship many of us will ever have—the relationship with our spouse.

6

Till Porn Do Us Part

Mason and Sarah were married for nineteen years. They had three children, were regulars at church, and participated in a small group. They believed in the truth of the Bible and taught the power of prayer. By all accounts, they were a model Christian family. But Mason nursed a secret. In college, he'd had a porn habit, but after they were married, Mason had led Sarah to believe it was a thing of the past. It wasn't. Because he knew his continuing struggle with pornography would crush Sarah, he tried to manage it on his own.

Over the years, though, Mason's struggle grew to the point that watching wasn't enough. He wanted something more exciting. One day, he reconnected with a college girlfriend on social media, and what started as a direct message quickly turned into a sexting relationship. Mason felt guilty and he tried to back away. He quit responding when she texted, but his old flame was persistent.

Weeks passed, and one day, when Mason had left his phone with Sarah, the old girlfriend sent a text.

"Miss me?"

Sarah was puzzled and then distraught. She pretended she was Mason hoping to gather a little more information. As she did, things became clear. She'd caught her husband red-handed.

That night, Sarah confronted Mason and he came clean. He had lied about his porn habit, a habit that led to this connection with the old girlfriend. He needed help.

Sarah's world collapsed as the man she thought she knew turned out to be someone else. Mason was overwhelmed with shame and even considered suicide. How would they make it? Neither was sure.

Sarah and Mason are not alone in their struggle. According to two studies from *Psychology Today,* more than half of the roughly one million divorces each year in the US are caused, in part, by pornography.[1] In fact, a six-year study of 3,000 people showed the sobering impact of porn on marriages. If one partner watches porn, the couple is two-to-three times more likely to divorce in the following two years than the marriages that were porn free.

And that's not all. In marriages where the husband watches porn, the couple is twice as likely to divorce in the next two years. If the wife watches porn, they were almost three times as likely to divorce.[2] This is a concerning reality when considering the significant increase in pornography consumption among thirteen–to-twenty-four-year-old women.[3]

Porn has been devastating marriages, and these trends suggest that the future will be even worse. It is no wonder that sixteen US states have declared pornography a public health crisis.[4]

Will Marriage Cure Your Porn Problem?

Jared began to habitually watch pornography in high school. He was a follower of Christ, so the guilt and desire to quit were strong. Still, his lust was stronger. He continued to struggle through college. Though he had some streaks of sobriety, Jared would always fall back into porn. He took comfort in the fact that he was still a virgin and used this as a rationalization to continue watching pornography. He told himself regularly that once he got married and was having sex, he would give up porn. This hope became a conviction. He used it to justify his porn habit and to rationalize lying to his girlfriend about what he was doing. He told himself, "There is no reason to tell her about it now because it's going to be a non-issue once we're married."

His girlfriend became his wife. Not long into their marriage, Jared discovered that even though he was having sex with his wife, his hunger for porn was as strong as ever. He said, "Sex with my wife was good, but it was different than what I was used to." A couple of months after getting married, Jared started using porn again. He discovered that marriage did not fix his porn problem.

The idea that sex will fix someone's problem with pornography is a lie. When brain pathways have been built upon voyeurism and self-stimulation, real sex cannot fulfill the craving. Real sex is a different experience and is registered through a different neural pathway. This is why married men who have wives willing to meet their sexual desires *still* struggle with their desire to watch pornography. As author Dannah Gresh pointed out, "the lure of porn is never quenched by marital sex because porn has almost nothing to do with real love and real sex. It's as counterfeit as a counterfeit can be."[5]

Porn builds expectations that can never be met. Many men have wrong expectations about sex in marriage. They think they will have sex any time they want. Those who watch porn have even higher expectations. Porn suggests that everyone wants sex all the time. Real marriage, though, does not work this way.

Men are like a microwave when it comes to sex—they are ready to go instantly. A woman is more like an oven. It typically takes her time to warm up sexually. For men, sex is mostly a physical event. For a woman, it involves the emotions to a greater degree. The pornified man who is hypersexualized often experiences frustration and disappointment in marriage. One husband shared:

> Because I was watching porn regularly, I was thinking about sex all the time and trying to have sex with my wife all the time. This led to frustration and fights when she didn't want it as much as I did. I realize now how unrealistic my expectations were. When I stopped using porn, I quit thinking about sex all the time and I am content with just talking with my wife instead of always trying to move toward sex.

Porn does a disservice to wives by training men to expect sex whenever the urge hits. A man raised on porn who is used to getting sexual satisfaction whenever he wants it sets himself up for disappointment in marriage. He can't have sex whenever he wants. This can make it tempting to go back to what is easy and familiar—porn. One pastor I recently talked to said of the young couples in his church:

> Porn is undercutting a strong healthy sex life in marriage. I have noticed something when the husband and wife struggle to get on the same page sexually. Instead of working at it, they often go back to porn to get sexual release. It's easier than putting in the work required to build a great sex life with their spouse.

Marriage won't fix a porn problem. But a porn problem can ruin a marriage and sex life.

Cardboard Cutouts

In 1973, Dutch biologist Nicolaus Tinbergen won the Nobel Peace Prize for his research on supernormal stimulus. A supernormal stimulus is an exaggerated version of an ordinary stimulus. Using butterflies, he showed how male butterflies were attracted to the size and brightness of female butterflies' wings. For his research, Tinbergen created cardboard cutouts of butterfly wings that were bigger and brighter than the real wings. The result? The male butterflies tried to mate with the cardboard cutouts. Even when the female butterflies were reintroduced into the environment, the male butterflies ignored them and continued to try and mate with the fake butterflies. The butterflies were offered something real, but they wanted the cardboard.

What's true of butterflies seems to be true of people. Pornography is a supernormal stimulus. It hijacks the mind and creates an appetite for the false over the real. People learn to be more stimulated by fake sex than real sex.[6]

Porn causes people to cultivate an appetite for new and different sexual partners. Porn users begin to grow bored with their spouses. Though they could be enjoying the increasing satisfaction of healthy marital sex, they instead chase the cardboard of pornography. Porn cultivates an appetite in the user for harder forms of pornography or other partners or for self-sex. And when it comes time to have sex with their spouse, the natural comparisons between porn and the user's spouse only adds to the discontent. Over time, this discontentment erodes the marriage.

Sexual relationships outside of marriage are also diminished by porn. Jonathan described how porn use impacted his relationship with his girlfriend. "It's just an unfulfilling cycle. You become dissatisfied with the person you're with. How can you not?" Another young professional, Anthony, echoed, "If you're looking at porn every single day, you're gonna want something else. You're not gonna want what you've got. There's no way you could be happy with it."[7] People who grew up watching pornography have cultivated an insatiable appetite for new and different sexual partners. Their need for variety makes it difficult for them to grow in physical intimacy with one person.

Pornography, for many, is a gateway drug to adultery. It normalizes hookup culture. Porn addicts' brains have rewarded this behavior for years. Is it any surprise, then, that couples who watch porn are 318% more likely to commit adultery?[8] These secret, forbidden interactions with a real person can add a hit of adrenaline to the high of porn. The Bible describes this phenomenon. "For the lips of a forbidden woman drip honey, and her speech is smoother than oil" (Proverbs 5:3).

The taboo nature of adulterous sex adds to the excitement of it. Hookup and adultery services and apps have exploded since streaming porn became readily available. Ashley Madison is a website for married couples looking to cheat on their spouse. In 2019, they reached 65-million users, and they claimed to create one million affairs a month. During the pandemic of 2020, they saw an increase of up to 17,000 new daily users.[9]

After a while, the virtual adultery of pornography isn't enough for many. Often those who've spent years chasing a sexual high to satisfy their cravings will start watching and doing things they never thought they would. And often, they find their spouse just doesn't do it for them anymore.

War Against Marriages

The Bible compares the union between a husband and wife to the relationship between Christ and the Church. This is one reason why marriage is a prime target of the enemy. One of the easiest ways to attack a marriage in the age of high-speed internet is through pornography.

Studies show that as porn is consumed more frequently, a person's commitment to their romantic partner decreases substantially.[10] Men who view pornography often report lower sexual satisfaction too.[11] Why? Bonding hormones are released during sex. When people watch porn and masturbate, that is what they bond with.

This is one reason people are drawn to porn. It brings people comfort when they are down or stressed. It never rejects them. It is always there for them. The bonding hormones released during climax create an emotional attachment to the people in porn. This secondary attachment undermines attachment to your real relationships.

Over time, people turn to porn instead of doing the work of loving, serving, and romancing their spouse. Instead of putting in the work to resolve a conflict, it becomes easier to ignore tension and turn to porn. Porn becomes a cheap substitute for real, healthy, marital sex. Blogger John Doyel shares how a husband's porn addiction impacts the sexual relationship he has with his wife. He said,

> Then instead of sex with your spouse being this deep and intimate uniting of your bodies and creating an emotional and spiritual oneness… it becomes only mildly satisfying, and you feel you are getting more from internet sex than actual sex with your spouse. That is when erectile dysfunction comes knocking at the door, because you feel she is not enough. The investment it takes to create within her a real desire for you is so much more difficult than five minutes in the bathroom with your smartphone.[12]

The cheap sex of porn undercuts marital sex and strikes at the heart of a healthy marriage.

Numerous studies show that people who do not consume porn are significantly happier in relationships than those who do.[13] This is particularly true for Christian marriages because porn use often causes great shame for Christians. One man expressed what many Christian husbands who use porn feel:

> You feel that shame and you feel dirty. I mean, it's tough to even look in a mirror, much less to look in someone else's eyes, much less to look in a spouse's eyes, and feel anything but fake and dirty, so the weight of that with God and the weight of that with a spouse, it is so devastating.[14]

In my experience, people who feel this way often isolate themselves from their spouse. And many times, their spouse feels the isolation and accompanying loneliness without knowing why.

Dr. John Gottman founded the world-renowned Gottman Institute, a research center devoted to the study of relationships. Although in the past Dr. Gottman once claimed pornography did not harm couples, he has changed his stance. He wrote an open letter retracting his earlier position, in which he stated:

> Use of pornography by one partner leads the couple to have far less sex and ultimately reduces relationship satisfaction. We are led to unconditionally conclude that for many reasons, pornography poses a serious threat to couple intimacy and relationship harmony.[15]

Can Porn Add Sizzle to Your Marriage?

Porn is a $100-billion industry. And with so much at stake, the porn industry has done its best to cast doubt on legitimate research. They have fought to keep porn and sex addiction from being recognized as a real condition. They've claimed pornography benefits some marriages too. Their research often comprises testimonies of couples sharing how porn use has made their sex lives spicier.

The anecdotal evidence they use is deceitful at best. Their goal is not to win the scientific argument, because they can't. They hope to cast doubt on real research and declare it inconclusive. This is the same strategy the tobacco industry used to suppress the research showing the harmful effects of smoking.[16]

All the peer-reviewed research on the impact of pornography on marriages demonstrates that porn use is never linked to positive marital outcomes.[17] Psychologist Mary Layden has counseled women who have shared how in the beginning porn did spice up their sex lives. But then reality hit. These women later shared:

- "I noticed he was only focused on the women in the videos and not me."
- "He was just using me as a masturbation machine as he fantasized about other women."
- "I realized it was all about him and his sexual fulfillment."[18]

One wife wrote her ex-husband to explain how porn impacted their sex lives:

> There were words for what we did, but it was never making love. And without the extreme visuals, the videos playing in the background – you looking at

> them rather than me – you could never find satisfaction. So there could never be compromise (it always had to be your way). It made me feel that I was less than. There was never intimacy in what we did and in the end, I stopped wanting sex. Not that you wanted it with me anyway.[19]

Marital sex is a guard against immorality. The Bible instructs both the husband and the wife to be available sexually to one another for this reason. 1 Corinthians 7:2-3 says, "Because of the temptation to sexual immorality, each man should have his own wife and each woman her own husband. The husband should give to his wife her conjugal rights, and likewise the wife to her husband."

It is misguided, however, to believe a spouse can satisfy the cravings of a partner who has cultivated an appetite for pornography. Some believe just that, though. They try to satisfy their partner's porn lust by engaging in more extreme sexual fantasies. This behavior, however, actually makes a porn addiction worse. Sex addiction counselor Invia Betjoseph warned of this perspective, saying, "Asking his wife to heighten the sexual arousal experience serves only to strengthen the unhealthy neural pathways that perpetuate the addiction. Neither the addict nor his wife wants this outcome."[20]

The more couples try to fulfill each other's pornographic fantasies, the worse things in their relationship can become. Mutually pleasurable lovemaking can be reduced to self-sex as the couple is no longer engaged with reality. It is common for men having sex with their wives to be unable to climax without fantasizing about porn. Urologist Dr. Harry Fisch said,

> When a man chronically watches porn and gets off on it… the sensory stimulation he gets from the virtual world makes it much more difficult for him to get aroused, stay aroused, and be happily aroused

> by the real live woman in his life. In other words, his frequent, porn-fueled masturbation leads to sexual dysfunction with a partner. If he can only have an orgasm when watching porn, and if he becomes accustomed to having orgasms only in a certain way or while watching a certain thing, he's in trouble… Porn isn't just risky business; it's a killer for your sex life.[21]

One man explained his rude awakening to this reality.

> After years of masturbating five or more times a week to pornography, sex was embarrassing. Not only was there not enough friction, but it felt like the wrong type of stimulation. Six months without porn, and I now have no performance issues of any kind. Sex is now twenty times more fulfilling than masturbation.[22]

When someone is caught up in the fantasy world of porn sex, they have less sex and less satisfying sex. Sex is an important part of a healthy marriage, and porn is destructive to both sex and marriage.[23]

Sixty percent of committed Christian college men say that pornography is their primary sex educator.[24] Porn offers them a distorted view of what sex is about. Besides cultivating a taste for voyeurism and masturbation, men who watch porn are taught to see more extreme sexual behavior as normal. This distorted porn education often robs them of sexual and marital fulfillment.

The Importance of Christian Marriage

Mason and Sarah, from the opening story, fought for their marriage. Mason was grateful he was caught before he met up with his old flame. He got into a recovery group and counseling. He was honest with Sarah and started to rebuild trust. He got a flip phone until he gained a level of sobriety and Sarah was comfortable with him getting a smartphone.

Mason's recovery group helped him realize he wasn't alone. His shame began to lift. He has since committed himself to regular accountability and has even led a recovery group. Mason is using his redemption story to bring hope and healing to others. He and Sarah have become a walking vision of a redemptive marriage.

In John 17:21, Jesus prayed that His disciples "may all be one… so that the world may believe that you have sent me." The oneness of believers is a witness to the world that Jesus is real, and the ultimate oneness God created on earth is the marriage union. Marriage is also a picture of Christ's relationship with the Church. Broken Christian marriages and families have a significant and lasting negative impact on all involved. Everyone loses. But even aside from the tragic relational results, broken Christian homes also destroy the witness of Christ to the watching world.

Christian marriages are failing at an unprecedented rate because of porn use.[25] If the Christian family continues to wither under this assault, the impact on the Church and its influence will be devastating. By God's grace, we have a chance to address the problem before it's too late. But the Church has significant obstacles to overcome to effectively confront this issue.

7

Pastors and Porn

If the data and stories included in this book have shown anything, it's that porn is capturing the hearts and minds of the masses. Because of its pervasiveness and destructiveness, a growing number of Christian leaders are calling porn the greatest threat to the Church. In light of the historic danger porn poses to Christian growth, Christian marriages, Christian parenting, and Christian service, one would expect spiritual leaders to address the issue and provide solutions. Instead, most churches are silent on the topic.[1] Why?

There seem to be three primary obstacles that contribute to this crisis of silence. As we look at the obstacles and corresponding solutions, it is important to remember that we are in a spiritual battle and our leaders are under major attack from a relentless enemy. They need our prayers and encouragement.

Obstacle #1: Pastors Themselves Are Stuck

During the 1999 NFL draft, Antwan got a call from the San Francisco 49ers. They wanted to know if he would join the team if they drafted him later that day. For much of his life, Antwan had dreamed of playing professional sports. Though it would have made perfect sense for Antwan to accept the offer, he did the unthinkable. He declined the offer. He and his wife knew

God was leading them to plant a church, which they launched after six years of ministry and seminary training.

Soon after the church started, men began to confide in Antwan about their porn struggles. The topic made Antwan curious. Antwan later said, "One day I was in my home office and out of curiosity, I typed 'porn' into my search engine. That one decision changed my life forever." In the ensuing days, he moved from sexual images to videos. He told himself he could stop whenever he wanted, but as weeks turned into months, he realized he could not. Years passed. He continued to watch pornography.

Porn was the thing Antwan enjoyed most. He considered confessing but was ashamed. He later said, "I wanted to get help and open up, but I was afraid. I was so afraid of how it would make me look. Here I am, a pastor of this growing, new church, and I'm constantly watching porn?" Every time he thought of confessing, he found an excuse not to.

Antwan was living a lie and grew unhappy with who he'd become. He said, "I was preaching sermons every week, all the while knowing I was not living what I was preaching. I felt like the biggest hypocrite. My porn addiction paralyzed me from loving my wife, from teaching my kids, from truly investing in my church and community."

Antwan's wife eventually caught him. She was shocked and devastated. They tried marriage counseling, but it did not work. Eventually, Antwan lost it all: his church, his wife, his family, and his reputation. Recalling his story, Antwan said:

> Looking back, it was all because of my pride. I was so afraid of how I would look to people that it cost me everything, and I still ended up looking about as bad as a man could look—not because I came clean but because I did not. My biggest problem was that I had lost fellowship with God. I had learned to suppress so much and silence my con-

> science that it was time for me to reconnect with the only One who could truly bring healing.

Antwan's road to recovery began when he confessed to a friend and mentor. He said of his recovery, "It was probably the hardest thing I've ever had to do in my life, but God healed me."

No matter how dedicated, focused, and committed you are, no one is immune from pornography's hooks. Two separate anonymous surveys showed half of pastors struggle with pornography.[2] Like Antwan, they are caught in this plague. They feel hypocritical to even address the porn issue when they themselves are stuck.

Obstacle #2: Pastors Are Often Unaware of the Significance of the Issue

Over half of pastors say porn addiction is the most damaging issue in their congregation.[3] Still, only 7% of pastors provide solutions to help their people break free from porn.[4] Many of the pastors who see porn as a major problem are stuck in it themselves and, like Antwan, are unable to address it. Pastors who could address it, but don't, often don't see it as a significant enough issue to prioritize.

Pastors are unaware in large part because the damage is under the surface and they are busy. Many of them have no idea how pervasive and destructive porn is in their congregation. Those who do usually don't know how to effectively address the issue. Addressing porn in the church is not easy, and solutions are not simple. Pastors can view addressing porn as a distraction from the real mission of the Church instead of the opportunity for deep discipleship that it actually is.

The Word of God is sufficient, but it can sometimes be shallowly applied to the porn problem when a deeper heart application is needed. In the book of Jeremiah, God rebuked the spiritual leaders of Israel, saying, "They have healed the brokenness of My people superficially, saying, 'Peace, peace,' But there is no peace" (Jeremiah 6:14).

The clichés of 'peace, peace' didn't change the reality in the days of the Old Testament prophets, and cliché Christian answers won't cure a porn addiction. In fact, superficial answers can do more harm than good. Implying that more accountability and stronger spiritual disciplines alone will free people from pornography can lead struggling people to feel hopeless. A basic understanding of the pornography issue will help spiritual leaders effectively apply the Word of God in a more helpful and relevant way.

I got a call recently from a man in my church. He was distraught after attending a church-based recovery program. The program has been a great resource for people to find freedom from all kinds of addictions except pornography. That night, his group of seven men each shared about how they had experienced freedom from drugs, alcohol, and eating disorders, but none of them could break free from pornography. He was blindsided by this discovery.

Porn or sex addiction is one of the most challenging addictions to break. We will see why when we address the roots of addiction. Freedom will require a holistic approach as well as a greater surrender to God, His Word, and one another.

Obstacle #3: The Shame Factor

Pornography is a topic that often causes people shame. It is uncomfortable to talk about. Some well-meaning pastors have addressed porn in their churches, rebuked those who are indulging in it, and called the strugglers in their congregation to repentance, often without providing real solutions that help bring freedom. And though people must be called to repentance, those in the audience who have repeatedly tried to quit often leave these messages filled with shame and hopelessness.

A pastor I know recently shared a powerful sermon on pornography, and at the conclusion, said "If you struggle in this area, we have a booth in the back where you can sign up for a group." How many people do you think visited the booth? Zero! The shame of being seen as the one struggling with porn was too powerful.

If a church offers a group to help people out of their pornography addiction, it can be daunting for a person to attend. Those who struggle don't know who else will be there. They don't know who they will be disclosing their secret sin to. As a result, they often won't go unless they are in crisis. This leads many pastors to wrongly conclude that porn must not be a problem since so few people get help when it's offered. Experts estimate less than 10% of Christians who are addicted to porn seek recovery.[5] Shame is a big reason.

If the Church is going to engage in this spiritual battle, it must address these three obstacles. Here are possible solutions that churches have utilized.

Solution #1: Leaders Get Help

Leaders need to come out of the shadows, confess, and lead the Church in repentance. It won't be easy. A pastor might be afraid of what others will think. They might fear losing their jobs. They are likely saddled with their own deep shame too.

A young associate pastor recently shared how shame and fear took hold in his life. His boss, a Dallas pastor, stood in front of his congregation and declared, "If I ever look at pornography I will resign as your pastor." The bold declaration received approval from the older members of the congregation. But the twenty-five-year-old new youth pastor was distraught. He had struggled with porn for years and had considered sharing his problem with the pastor. Now he felt he couldn't, so he continued struggling in isolation.

A Barna Group survey asked, "Should a pastor be fired or asked to resign if they are found to be using porn?" Only 8% of pastors said yes, while over 40% of members said yes.[6] This low number for pastors suggests that pastors are struggling themselves. Pastor John Piper said of this survey, "Both figures are appallingly low."

Piper went on to say that a pastor should indeed resign if he has "an ongoing habit of watching pornography."[7] His stance represents the punishment culture that characterizes the Church. The unintended consequence is that it encourages hiding instead of repentance. When there is a fear of being fired for porn use, pastors will likely stay in the shadows, trying to get free on their own. And if the leaders do, so will the people.

Regardless of the culture in a given church, the responsibility falls on the pastor in sin to step out of the shadows and get help, even if his leadership has created a punitive atmosphere. No one gets free on their own. The first step toward freedom is confession, and that confession must happen in community. God says, "Therefore confess your sins to one another and pray for one another that you may be healed" (James 5:16).

To find freedom, those in an addiction must repent. In the book of James, the author writes,

> You adulteresses, do you not know that friendship with the world is hostility toward God? Therefore whoever wishes to be a friend of the world makes himself an enemy of God … Therefore it says, 'God is opposed to the proud, but gives grace to the humble.' Submit therefore to God. (James 4:4-7)

God longs to give greater grace when people humble themselves and repent. What kind of grace? The grace that drives the devil away and brings the struggler closer to God. James continues,

> Resist the devil and he will flee from you. Draw near to God and He will draw near to you. Cleanse your hands, you sinners; and purify your hearts, you double-minded. Be miserable and mourn and weep; let your laughter be turned into mourning and your joy to gloom. Humble yourselves in the presence of the Lord, and He will exalt you.
> (James 4:7-10)

Drawing near to God begins with cleansing hands and purifying hearts. How can spiritual leaders expect the men and women in the church to repent from pornography if they do not model that repentance first? Revival starts with repentance, especially the repentance of the leadership.

Pastor John Doyel tried to manage his porn addiction. His lust grew into multiple affairs, which is when it was finally exposed. He said, "Had I been a better man with more courage, I would have sought help earlier instead of allowing my sexual addiction to grow deeper and darker for over eight years."[8] For those struggling, God's grace gives the opportunity to confess and get help.

Another former pastor, Kenny Smith, shared his story:

> I tried for most of my life to break free of this struggle by confessing to God and praying for deliverance over and over. It wasn't until my wife discovered my addiction that I finally reached out for help. Coming out of isolation is essential for healing.

Smith tried unsuccessfully for forty-five years to stop his porn habit. He was unsuccessful until he confessed and got help. He continued:

> Today, I walk in freedom from this addiction and freedom from shame, and so can you if you get the help that you need. Take the first step. Tell someone today. It will probably be the scariest thing you ever do but also the most courageous. Living in freedom is worth whatever it costs to get there.[9]

Solution #2: Get Equipped

For over thirty years I have been a leader in Student Mobilization, a college ministry focused on evangelism, discipleship, and missions. My calling is to fulfill the Great Commission and make disciples of all nations. I viewed addressing the porn issue as a distraction from the real work of the ministry. However, when our team determined that the greatest obstacle to our ministry of making disciples was pornography, we knew we had to act. We realized if we make disciples but do not adequately address their porn habit, we set them up for long-term failure. The porn epidemic revealed a hole in our discipleship that undermined everything else we built into students' lives.

As we began addressing pornography head-on, we discovered how God can use the process to plant His truth more deeply into the lives of His people. As new disciples found the freedom the gospel promises, they experienced "truth in their innermost being" (Psalm 51:6). Their excitement for the King and His Kingdom grew. Their desire to serve in church and be a spiritual leader increased. And over time, they proved to be faithful and fruitful. When leaders apply God's Word to the deepest parts of someone's heart and mind, they can experience the power and relevance of God's Word like never before.

If a pastor or spiritual leader is going to make disciples in today's culture, they must get equipped to apply God's truth to pornified hearts and minds. This is one reason for this book.

Solution #3: De-Shame the Topic

Since pursuing freedom leads to deeper discipleship, churches need to provide a path to get there. The churches I follow with the most effective programs have de-shamed the topic of pornography addiction. Often, staff members participate in the program. Many times, they model authenticity and share their own porn story.

Pastors can de-shame the topic of pornography addiction by introducing it as an equipping issue instead of a recovery issue. An equipping issue is for everyone in the church, not just those who are struggling with a particular issue. A recovery issue is only for people with problems. Starting with an equipping focus de-shames the topic and gives people permission to get educated without having to first indict themselves. When people learn about the brain science of porn addiction that we covered in chapter four, it is very de-shaming. When the issue is de-shamed, people are more willing to come out of the shadows to get help.

When addressing porn is presented with an equipping focus, both the struggler and the non-struggler will show up. I can attest to churches that have done six-to-ten-week equipping groups, and while they are educating people, these groups de-shame the topic. At the end of the equipping groups, these same churches then offer recovery groups. The equipping groups provide an intermediary step from the Sunday morning congregation to a recovery group. Once a porn struggle is de-shamed and a pathway to freedom is given, many more people are willing to get help.

De-shaming the topic is especially important for Christian women. The shame for women often prevents them from opening up about their struggle even more than it does for men.[10] Leaders must offer separate equipping groups for women, even if they don't have a resident expert. Women leaders can be fellow learners as they explore content together.

In fact, when a group is led by a fellow learner, it helps de-shame the process and creates the safety to pursue freedom. I suggest content for an equipping group in the appendix.

A Word to Church and Ministry Leaders

Porn use is at epidemic levels among the next generation of Christian leaders, and many church leaders openly acknowledge this reality. Still, most of these new pastors are stepping into churches that have a punishment culture. Those with an ongoing porn struggle will be fired. This sets them up to live a double life and to compartmentalize their porn use and their ministry. And this compartmentalization, when coupled with the pressures of ministry, often increases stress, and fuels porn consumption. And as porn consumption increases, so does their fear of being fired. It's a vicious cycle, and in it, the whole church suffers.

Dr. Ted Roberts has worked for more than twenty years helping pastors and denominational leaders navigate porn addiction. He suggests that churches adopt the following policy because it reflects a restorative spirit.

Restorative Policy:

> As long as you haven't done anything illegal or with another person and as long as you are committed to recovery, you can get help for your porn addiction without the fear of punishment. The goal is restoration.[11]

This policy de-shames the restoration process. What's more, it embodies Paul's words to the church in Galatia: "Brothers, if anyone is caught in any transgression, you who are spiritual should restore him in a spirit of gentleness" (Galatians 6:1).

Each case is different, and each leadership team must determine what is best for their church. A church cannot guarantee that restoration will always mean a full return to the previous position, but that is the goal. Once a pastor is in recovery, it may become clear that the ministry isn't the healthiest place for them. Without a restorative policy clearly communicated, it is easy for pastors to assume there is a culture of punishment, which encourages secrecy and hiding.

There is a spectrum of severity in porn addiction. So some ministers might stay engaged in ministry while they focus on recovery. Others may need to take a leave of absence to get more intensive help. A restorative policy allows church leadership to make those decisions on a case-by-case basis.

Finally, to remove all doubt, a restorative policy should only apply to those who have not done anything inappropriate with another person. Abuse allegations and instances of sexual misconduct involving another person must be reported immediately.

Some say it is a compromise of the biblical standards of leadership to establish a restorative culture. But when half of churches currently do not have leadership meeting the biblical standard because their pastor is using porn, the opposite is true. A restorative culture encourages pastors to repent. It enables them to start moving toward the biblical standards of holiness expected of leadership. A restorative culture requires the pastor to be committed to recovery. It allows people to get help. It doesn't create an enabling environment for leaders to stay stuck in their sin.[12]

Get off the Beach

On June 6, 1944, the largest land invasion in history happened on the beaches of Normandy, France. This was the first crucial step to liberating Europe from the Nazis. During preparation for the invasion, Colonel George Taylor was obsessed with getting his men off the beach as quickly as possible after landing. To Taylor, staying on the beach was a place of sure death. Getting off the beach meant advancing on the enemy, taking the hill, and clearing a path for the forces coming behind them.

When Colonel Taylor's platoon hit Omaha Beach, they were under heavy fire. Machine gun fire trapped his men behind sand dunes. The soldiers were shell-shocked and confused. They were stuck on the beach. Taylor became desperate to lead his men off the beach. He stood up and yelled, "There are two kinds of men on this beach: those who are already dead and those who are about to die. Now let's get out of here." He was pointing to the ridge to make a path for the troops that were coming behind them.

Taylor's words galvanized his men into action. The soldiers escaped the beach. They took the hill, cleared out the Nazis, and made the first path from Omaha Beach inland. Getting off the beach was the first crucial step to liberating Europe from the Nazis.[13]

There are two kinds of pastors who struggle with porn. The first kind are those who stay on the beach and die. They destroy their life, family, and ministry (or they're about to). The second kind are the pastors who flee the beach and live. They get help and repent. Mercy, grace, and freedom await those who get off the beach. For the sake of those coming behind you, get off the beach and charge the hill!

Nick Stumbo was a pastor on staff with a thriving church in Kelso, Washington. He had a wife, three children, good friends, and a porn addiction. He battled it for fifteen years. He confessed it to trusted friends through the years, but nothing changed. It was slowly killing his marriage and ministry.[14]

He wanted a solution, but he didn't know of any. Nick lied to himself. He said of this self-denial, "I convinced myself that I was doing okay. Sure, it cropped up from time to time, but surely I wasn't as bad as others. I thought that if I just kept believing and praying, sooner or later it would go away. Well, it didn't."

At an annual meeting, his denomination presented the restoration policy mentioned earlier. They offered to help any struggling pastors. They didn't just offer the assurance he wouldn't lose his job; they promised a partnership with Pure Desire ministries to help him find freedom. Pastor Stumbo's self-denial ran deep. He still wasn't ready.

He later explained, "The shame in my life had created such great lies of rationalization and minimization that I convinced myself I didn't need this much help." He prayed for deliverance and wanted to be free, but his self-deception kept him in the shadows. Finally, Nick's wife urged him to get help, and he listened to her. After a year of a recovery group and counseling, Pastor Stumbo was free.

Nick shared his story with his church. He said, "I confessed my struggle with pornography to the church. I asked their forgiveness for failing them as a leader. More importantly, I asked for their help in starting a ministry for men and women who struggled in a similar way."

The response and encouragement the Stumbos received was overwhelming. Eventually, Nick launched a ministry in his church that began to flourish. A restoration policy led to repentance and freedom for the pastor and for his people too.

The pastor or spiritual leader struggling with porn cannot wait until his or her church adopts a restorative culture. True spiritual leaders must make the first move. Nick's partial confessions to his leadership opened the church to the idea of a restorative culture. And once that culture of restoration set in, they were able to provide resources for their congregation.

When leaders confess, it paves the way for the church to confess. When the pastor stays stuck, the church stays stuck. This was true in Pastor Stumbo's case. Within five years of his confession, almost one-third of the men and one-fifth of the women in the church completed a porn recovery program.

Repentance came because there was a restorative culture. Nick Stumbo showed us what it looks like for a pastor to get off the beach and charge the hill. May God give us more of his kind!

Most church pastors aren't addressing the issue of pornography like Nick did. As a result, we are failing to address one of the biggest threats to the faith since the establishment of the church. It will take supernatural power to charge the hill of confession and repentance. It will take courage to change the way we deal with pornography in the church.

It is worth it. God is worth it. Repentance is worth it. Those coming behind us in the next generation are worth it. And liberating the church from the dominion of porn is worth it. But if we're to achieve true liberation, we need a deeper understanding of the roots driving the porn epidemic.

Section Two

The Truths That Set Us Free

(Addressing the roots of porn addiction)

8

Faith and Works

Sarah was embarrassed about her porn addiction and wanted to quit. She attended a recovery group to help and made adjustments that lasted for a while, but Sarah never embraced the core practices of the program. Still, she saw some improvement. She was porn-free for almost six months. Because her adjustments never became a lifestyle, however, her addiction returned when her job got stressful. She returned to porn to medicate.

Sarah's freedom from porn was short-lived because she never dealt with the roots of her unwanted sexual behavior. Why didn't she pull those roots? It cost more than she was willing to pay. She wasn't willing to fully confess and get real. She was content with superficial change.

As we saw in the last chapter, God rebuked his leaders for this kind of shallow change: "They have healed the brokenness of My people superficially, saying, 'Peace, peace,' But there is no peace" (Jeremiah 6:14). Had Sarah committed to deeper change—change that gets below the surface and addresses the root causes—she could have found real freedom.

All changes are not the same. When it comes to changing behavior, there are two approaches: first-order change and second-order change.

First-Order Change:

- Gives the allusion of change and can even have some results. The problem is that these changes do not last.
- Is an attempt to control behavior by trying harder. It is concrete action taken to quickly solve a problem. It is a quick fix.

Second-Order Change:

- Happens when core beliefs are altered that anchor changes in lifestyle.
- Takes place as people establish new structures, new relationships, and new practices in their lives. It is the adoption of a new mindset and lifestyle.

Sex addiction recovery expert Dr. Ted Roberts said in his experience only 2% of people receive the miracle of instant deliverance from a porn addiction. He said, "The rest get a miracle every day in the process of finding freedom."[1] Certified sex addiction therapist Dr. Mark Laaser said, "Healing is a lifetime journey, not a one-time event. There is a direct correlation to the work that people put into their recovery and how permanent and stable the healing is."[2] Though neither come out and say it outright, the good doctors' implication couldn't be any clearer. Without a commitment to second-order change, none of us—Sarah included—will find freedom.

Porn is not an easy addiction to break. It requires growth in key areas of people's lives. To get free from porn, people must outgrow porn. God will deliver on His promise to give freedom, but He wants to do so much more in the process. He wants to use the journey toward freedom to make His people more like Christ.

Faith and Action

Some people say that freedom is possible if they have enough faith. Others approach breaking free of a porn problem as if it's all about diligence. The truth is, finding freedom from a porn addiction takes both faith and works. After all, when faith and works operate in conjunction, core beliefs and actions change. Put another way, trust in God and committed action bring second-order change.

In his letter to the Romans, Paul wrote,

> For the death He died He died to sin, once for all, but the life He lives He lives to God. So you also must consider yourselves dead to sin and alive to God in Christ Jesus. (Romans 6:10-11)

Jesus' victory over sin is shared with all, but to access that freedom, believers must *believe* they are dead to sin, which means "to count it as done." When people believe that the power of sin is broken in a specific situation, they can experience victory over that particular sin. Liberating spiritual power is released when people put their faith in the promises of God. The apostle Peter explained it this way:

> He has granted to us His precious and magnificent promises, so that by them you may become partakers of the divine nature, having escaped the corruption that is in the world by lust. (2 Peter 1:4)

By faith in God's promises, we participate in the divine nature. We become like Christ. It is this Christlikeness that results in freedom from lust. God's promises enable us to live godly lives and escape lust. It starts by trusting His promises so that we may experience what He promised.

After years of fighting and failing to break free from porn and masturbation, Austin accepted that he would eventually always give in. Austin said, "When tempted to act out, I would fight it. If the urge persisted, I told myself it's going to happen eventually so I might as well get it over with." Austin had a turning point when he studied Romans 6.

Austin realized that he truly didn't believe that the power of sin had been broken. In fact, he believed he could not resist the temptation. So he memorized Romans 6:10-11, and whenever he was tempted, he recalled that passage. He said, "I claimed this promise and prayed for faith to believe that Jesus's death and resurrection had broken the power of this sin in my life. I started to believe it. I started claiming it when tempted."

That simple act of faith unleashed power for Austin to resist that he had never had before. Austin pointed to believing the promises of God as the single most helpful step in finding freedom, yet many other men and women have claimed that same promise, and it never led to their freedom. What made Austin's experience different? There was something else also at work in Austin's life. Peter addressed it as he continued his teaching.

Peter goes on to explain that more than just faith is required to experience the fullness of victory that God promises. Important qualities must accompany one's faith. He says:

> Make every effort to supplement your faith with virtue, and virtue with knowledge, and knowledge with self-control, and self-control with steadfastness, and steadfastness with godliness, and godliness with brotherly affection, and brotherly affection with love. For if these qualities are yours and are increasing, they keep you from being inef-

fective or unfruitful in the knowledge of our Lord Jesus Christ. (2 Peter 1:5-8)

Peter says these qualities make a person effective and fruitful. This was true of Austin.

In addition to believing that the power of sin had been broken, he put his faith into action by pursuing the qualities that Peter said believers should add to their faith. How?

- *Knowledge* – Austin's knowledge grew when he studied Romans chapter 6 and sought to apply it to his life. Growing in his understanding of the truth about the power of sin being broken made a world of difference.
- *Self-control* – He quoted Romans 6:10-11 each time the temptation hit. He also checked in with his accountability regularly.
- *Steadfastness* – Austin didn't give up when he stumbled. He kept confessing, repenting, believing, and pursuing.
- *Virtue and godliness* – Austin was convicted to adopt biblical standards for his media and movies. This diminished his temptations significantly.
- *Brotherly affection with love* – Austin had two accountability partners he confessed everything to. This group encouraged and challenged one another in their pursuit of holiness.

Each of these qualities made Austin's faith more effective and led to lasting freedom.

Peter warns followers of Christ that their lives will be "ineffective and unfruitful" when their faith is not accompanied by these qualities. Unfortunately, the words "ineffective" and "unfruitful" describe most believers stuck in a porn habit. They aren't chasing after virtue and knowledge. They aren't acting in self-control and steadfastness. They aren't pursuing godliness. They aren't learning how to live in brotherly affection and true love.

Cultivating these qualities in conjunction with faith is critical to walk in the freedom Jesus promises. Salvation from the penalty of sin is by faith alone, but breaking free from the power of sin to live in godliness takes faith plus our work. Not only does Peter say people should possess these qualities, but he also writes that these should be increasing in their lives.

The best porn addiction recovery programs have the balanced approach Peter describes between faith and works. Dr. Samuel Perry says most Christian approaches to overcoming porn are heavy on theology but light on practical application. These programs are not very effective at helping people find freedom.[3] Programs like this typically talk about believing the gospel and the promises of God but lack practical input to help someone make their faith effective and fruitful. On the other end of the spectrum are the programs which focus mostly on people's effort. This results in behavior modification without deep heart change rooted in the gospel.

Six Roots of a Porn Addiction

God desires the faith that enables freedom to also be a faith that diligently pursues freedom. This reality undergirds The Freedom Fight's approach. The Freedom Fight is a biblically based, gospel-centered program that is holistic and application-oriented. The Freedom Fight reminds people that Jesus fought and won the victory on their behalf. It also helps them discover the *why* behind their pornography addiction and address it. And if there's one thing I've discovered through my work with

The Freedom Fight, it's that the *why* of porn addictions can be traced back to six roots.

Each of the six factors driving a pornography or sex addiction is most effectively addressed from a biblical, gospel-centered, and scientific approach. All truth is God's truth, and science helps clarify where God's truth should be applied. Most programs address two or three of these roots. Only the most effective programs address all six.

So what are those roots, what is the truth about them, and how should we put our faith into action? We'll talk about that more in the chapters to come, but consider this overview.

Root 1: The Sexualized Society

Sexual temptation is everywhere. To address this root, a person must identify triggers, establish boundaries in accordance with God's Word, and act on those boundaries.

The Lies

Sexual satisfaction and fulfillment are found outside of God's design. A person will miss out if they pursue holiness. Sexual sin isn't that big of a deal.

The Truth

Holiness is God's best and His will for His children (1 Peter 1:13-17). A person needs to be radical in cutting off an opportunity for the flesh (Matthew 5:27-30).

The Application Steps

Commit to detox. Identify sexual and environmental triggers, establish boundaries, and find accountability. Deepen convictions to pursue holiness.

Root 2: The Addicted Brain

People's brains are changed by porn, but they can build new neurological pathways. Repetition gets the porn addict locked into this addiction, and repetition of new pathways will help get them out.

The Lies

What someone watches won't really affect them. True freedom isn't possible. Porn causes unfixable problems that won't change.

The Truth

Porn has rewired people's brains and changed them. Transformation and freedom are possible through renewing their minds (Romans 12:2).

The Application Steps

People must renew their minds and build new brain pathways when tempted (we teach a specific tool for this).

Root 3: Isolation

"The opposite of addiction isn't sobriety, it's connection."[4] Sex addiction is classified as an intimacy disorder, and it causes us to isolate from God and from one another. When a person feels disconnected from others, it makes them more susceptible to the fake intimacy of porn.

The Lies

People need to protect themselves by pulling back from relationships. People believe they can't be honest because they think that if people really knew them, they wouldn't accept them. They think they can handle their addiction on their own.

The Truth

Isolation is foolish and harmful (Proverbs 18:1). Confession brings healing (James 5:16). People need others to help them find freedom (2 Timothy 2:22).

The Application Steps

Establish authentic accountability. When triggered, move out of isolation and connect with people. Pursue a deepening relationship with God and others.

Root 4: Negative Emotions

Most people don't realize they have emotional triggers they have learned to medicate with porn. Growing in self-awareness and learning to process emotions with God and others will help them see a relapse coming instead of being blindsided by it.

The Lies

People believe they just need to suppress their feelings and emotions and move on. They think they can handle their emotions on their own.

The Truth

Inviting God into one's anxiety is an important spiritual discipline (Psalm 139:23-24). The person who identifies and shares their emotions with others is much less triggered by those emotions.

The Application Steps

Regularly process emotions with God and others and grow in emotional awareness. Identify emotional triggers.

Root 5: Shame

Shame is a deep sense of worthlessness. Shame leads to relapse and relapse leads to shame. It's a vicious cycle. Shame becomes an identity that results in self-hatred. When someone shares their shame and receives acceptance from others, it causes the shame to lift. Learning to replace a shame identity with an identity in Christ is a powerful step toward freedom.

The Lies

Many people believe they are worthless. They think God is done with them. They think that their addiction is just who they are.

The Truth

Every person is made in the image of God (Genesis 1:2-27). They have infinite worth and value. In Christ, they are chosen, holy, and beloved (Colossians 3:12). A person's identity and significance is received in Christ, not achieved in their own effort.

Application Steps

Learn to live out of your identity in Christ. Meditate on who you are in Christ. Be aware of negative self-talk. Confess and share openly with a trusted person or group.

Root 6: Trauma

Trauma, dysfunction, or abuse can be a major source of shame. The shame from trauma often fuels the negative emotions people feel compelled to medicate. Not every porn addict has major trauma, but even minor trauma can deepen the addiction.

The Lies

People often believe their trauma is their fault. They believe their lives will be limited by their trauma and their wounds. They believe the trauma is who they are and that they can't change.

The Truth

Trauma plants lies in a person's mind about themselves. Replacing the lies implanted by trauma with God's truth brings freedom (2 Corinthians 10:3-5, John 8:32).

The Application Steps

Identify key traumatic events in your life and the lies implanted because of them. Learn to take every thought captive when you repeat lies to yourself through negative self-talk. Replace the lies with God's truth.

For lasting change to take place--second-order change—we must take action anchored in changed beliefs and convictions. That is why replacing lies with the truth is essential. People must understand the dynamics at work and how each application step is anchored to biblical convictions. When action steps are connected to deep conviction, it enables changes and new habits to become a lifestyle. Helping people break free from porn provides a unique opportunity to deposit God's truth deep into their hearts and minds.

Pulling the Roots, Finding Freedom

Failing to address the roots of porn addiction is like mowing a yard full of weeds. It might look great at first, but the weeds always come back if the roots aren't killed. Acknowledging and confronting these roots requires growth and development in key areas of one's life. What areas? Consider how addressing the roots of addiction leads to personal growth in specific areas.

Root of Addiction	**Growth Area**
The Sexualized Society	Pursue holiness
The Addicted Brain	Renew the mind
Isolation	Develop authentic relationships
Negative Emotions	Process emotions and grow in emotional intelligence
Shame	Live out of an identity in Christ
Trauma	Replace lies deposited by trauma with truth

When the roots of addiction are addressed, the people of God grow in significant ways. Before His truth sets us free, it changes us. Because it changes us, the freedom will last.

At the age of twenty-two, Brandon had just finished his second Freedom Fight group and had been free from porn for two years. The first year was so helpful, he wanted to make sure the changes became a lifestyle, so he did the program again. Freedom from his six-year addiction felt phenomenal. He was more real and authentic in his relationships. He developed new daily habits like meditating on Scripture, checking in with accountability, and deepening other spiritual disciplines.

His growth in emotional awareness had surprising benefits for his recovery and his relationships. The depth of relationships he had with the other men in his group was nothing like he had ever experienced. He understood the concept of living out of his identity in Christ, but now he was actually doing it. As a result, his confidence to be a spiritual leader was at an all-time high. He became passionate about sharing Jesus with those around him. He led three of his friends to Christ and continued to disciple them. Brandon then began to lead two Freedom Fight groups. He was excited to help other men outgrow porn and find freedom like he did.

Austin, Brandon, and Sarah all found freedom from their pornography addiction, but Sarah's "freedom" was short-lived. She was content with first-order change instead of the lasting change of addressing the roots of the addiction. The freedom that Austin and Brandon found came through both faith and action. They believed God's promises, worked to understand how the roots of pornography reached into their lives, and took action to pull up the roots. The freedom they experienced is available to all of us, though it will require a little digging. They knew they had to outgrow porn by developing in certain areas of their lives. True freedom will take a better understanding of how the roots operate in your life or in the lives of those you are helping. So let's take a deeper look at the roots of addiction and how to overcome them.

9

Sexualized Society

Parker had just experienced the summer of his life. He had spent nine weeks at a Christian training program growing in His relationship with Christ, his character, and his leadership. It was the first time in six years he had gone more than a couple of weeks without watching porn or masturbating. He was free! Or, at least, that's what he thought.

Before returning to college at Iowa State, Parker spent three weeks at home, and during those weeks he relapsed several times. He wondered how he'd felt so free only a few days before, but now he found himself mired in the same old patterns. Would he always struggle with porn?

After returning to college, Parker met with his mentor. Together, they walked through what led to his relapses. At the summer project, he was with people constantly. At home, he was alone more often than not. At the summer project, he slept in a room with others and went to bed at a decent hour. At home, he went to bed late, and while in bed, he'd scroll through social media. He'd come across something sexual, and from there, he'd progress to porn use.

It wasn't just the night times that crept up on him, though. He realized he often relapsed after working out. When he wasn't diligent to guard his eyes, he would find himself checking out the women. He'd carry the images of those women home with him and would continue to think sexually about them. Often, this led him straight back to porn. He knew that to kick the habit, he'd need a plan that included accountability. He committed to this kind of accountability with his mentor and started down the path to freedom. Until Parker started trying to pursue freedom from his sexual addiction, he didn't realize just how sexualized society is.

Sex Is Everywhere

For someone to experience lasting freedom, the six roots of porn addiction must be addressed. The first and most obvious of these roots is the sexualized society. Beyond the pornography statistics we looked at earlier, it is important to recognize how deeply sexualized our culture has become.

Sexualization is everywhere: in children's TV shows, in movies, in ads, in video games, in retail, in marketing campaigns, throughout social media. An endless amount of porn is available in everyday places: Snapchat, Twitter, and emails.[1] Girls are often pressured by society to be more sexually attractive, to wear tighter, more revealing clothing, post sexier images, and sext.[2]

Movies and TV shows deliver sex now more than ever. Kids under seventeen are *not* allowed to see Rated R or NC-17 in theatres, but they do on Netflix all the time. Netflix's mature rating (MA) often exceeds the R rating and includes graphic sexual content that used to be reserved for NC-17.[3]

Today, 61% of Netflix's content has this mature rating.[4] What used to be considered pornography now describes much of their content available to any kid with a mobile device. Millions of people, including children whose families don't even have Netflix, just use a friend's account to watch all the shows their friends are talking about.[5]

The appetite for sexualized media is growing. In 2013, only 31% of Americans believed that pornography was morally acceptable. Now almost half do, including 67% of men ages eighteen to forty-nine.[6] Even the news is sexualized. Major news outlets regularly run news articles highlighting a supermodel or celebrity in her bikini. Since when is that news? Since it gets clicks and attracts advertisers.

Sex sells. The sex-crazed society is all around us. The 2020 Super Bowl halftime show reflected our sexualized society. On the same stage that showed women in stripper outfits pole dancing, children were also performing. Our culture celebrates and worships sexual immorality, and the conditioning starts young.

When Parker returned to campus, he had a new awareness of just how pervasive sex was all around him. When he went to his fraternity parties, everyone was bumping and grinding. Besides the regular hookups that Parker could easily find through the normal course of college life, he had a plethora of hookup apps to choose from. Through these, he could connect with someone in a matter of minutes who was ready to have sex with him. The revealing clothes that women wore on campus and in the gym were hard to miss. Now that he was trying to avoid it, it seemed like sex was everywhere.

When Parker understood that the sexualized society often led him down the wrong path, it led him to consider the words of Jesus: "For the gate is wide and the way is easy that leads to destruction, and those who enter by it are many. For the gate is narrow and the way is hard that leads to life, and those who find it are few" (Matthew 7:13-14). Parker realized his desire for freedom and his commitment to pursue it would require walking down the narrow path of holiness.

Holiness

The Bible's answer to the sexualized society is holiness. The resolve needed to swim against the current of our culture must be anchored to a desire for holiness. If not, the changes won't last. What does it mean to grow in holiness?

The pursuit of holiness begins by understanding God's holiness. Throughout the Bible, we see God's holiness proclaimed. In Isaiah 6:3, an angel stands before God's throne and declares, "Holy, holy, holy is the Lord of hosts; the whole earth is full of his glory!"

Again, in Revelation 4:8, four angelic beings are singing in heaven day and night without ceasing, saying, "Holy, holy, holy, is the Lord God Almighty, who was and is and is to come!" In both scenes, these supernatural creatures, awesome and majestic in their own right, are overwhelmed by one aspect of God's character, His holiness. This is the only quality of God ever repeated three times in a row, and it happens twice in the Bible. God apparently wants us to understand His holiness.

To be holy means to be set apart, and who besides God is set apart in all His ways? God is truly holy. Theologian A.W. Tozer says of God's holiness,

> Holy is the way God is. To be holy, He does not conform to a standard. He is that standard. He is absolutely holy with an infinite, incomprehensible fullness of purity that is incapable of being other than it is. Because He is holy, His attributes are holy; that is, whatever we think of as belonging to God must be thought of as holy.[7]

God calls us to be like Him in holiness. He commands, "I am the Lord your God; consecrate yourselves and be holy, because I am holy" (Leviticus 11:44). Pursuing holiness means taking steps to be more like God and to separate from sin. It means living a life that is separate and set apart. It means abstaining from every evil, including lust. Pursuing holiness is pursuing God's best for us.

Without a vision of God's holiness and a desire to be like Him, addressing the root of the sexualized society can become a list of do's and don'ts. But when we have a relationship with God and a biblical vision for holiness, boundaries become an opportunity to walk more closely with Jesus and to become who we were created to be. It's a path that leads to the purpose to which we have been called. And in the realm of sexuality, it leads us away from the sexualized society and closer to intimacy with our spouse (or future spouse) and, ultimately, with God.

What does it look like to pursue holiness? Let's make it practical. While reading the following verses, consider what it might look like to pursue holiness in terms of media consumption.

- "Take *every* thought captive to the obedience of Christ." (2 Corinthians 10:5, emphasis mine)
- "Get rid of *all* moral filth." (James 1:21-22, emphasis added)
- "Make *no* provision for the flesh in regard to its lusts." (Romans 13:14, emphasis added)
- "But sexual immorality and *all* impurity… must not even be named among you, as is proper among saints." (Ephesians 5:3, emphasis added)
- "Examine everything carefully… abstain from *every* form of evil." (1 Thessalonians 5:21-22, emphasis added)
- "I will set *no* worthless thing before my eyes." (Psalm 101:3, emphasis added)

Notice the comprehensive words in these verses: "all," "no," and "every." These words show how far we should go in our pursuit of holiness. How would applying these verses change our media habits? For those whose pursuit of holiness is rooted in a love of God and desire for God's best, then their motivation will be a "want to" not a "have to." They will desire to separate themselves from sin because they have a deep conviction to pursue holiness instead of the fruits of the sexualized society.

A Radical Commitment

In 2003, Aron Ralston, an avid outdoorsman, went on a solo climb in the mountains of Utah. A few hours into the climb, there was a rockslide, and Aron ended up with his arm pinned beneath a boulder. Unable to free himself, he waited for someone to find him.

A few days went by. No one came. He rationed his water, but it ran out. He grew so thirsty that he drank his own urine. After five days of being trapped, he felt he was at the end. He recorded himself on his camera saying goodbye to his friends and family. He went to sleep for what he thought was the last time.

When he awoke, Ralston had a radical idea. He could cut off his arm. There was only one problem. How would he get through the bone? He considered his options and realized that once he'd cut through skin and muscle and down to the bone, he could use leverage to break the bone and free himself. That's exactly what he did. Once free, Ralston repelled down with one arm to reach the hiking trail below. When he arrived at the trail, he was discovered and taken to the hospital. He survived, but only because he did whatever it took to find freedom.[8]

This is the kind of mentality Jesus invokes after teaching about avoiding lust. He says,

> You have heard that it was said, "You shall not commit adultery." But I say to you that everyone who looks at a woman with lustful intent has al-

> ready committed adultery with her in his heart. If your right eye causes you to sin, tear it out and throw it away. (Matthew 5:27-29)

Jesus makes it clear that freedom from lust requires total commitment.

This is especially true when beginning a detox. I tell the men I coach that a 95% commitment to freedom is like repairing 95% of the leaks in a boat. It's not enough. You must go all in. What does "all in" look like when breaking an addictive cycle? Many alcoholics who join Alcoholics Anonymous (AA) commit to what they call 90 in 90. They attend an AA meeting every day for ninety days. They immerse themselves in accountability and recovery. It's a "whatever it takes" mindset, and it leads many into long-term recovery. This same kind of mindset is required for any recovery, including recovery from pornography addiction.

Joel Hesch is the founder of Proven Men Recovery Ministry. He admitted that while he was addicted, he was torn. Part of him wanted out of his sex addiction, but part of him did not. He says,

> I had not really wanted to be well for twenty years. I merely wanted the struggle to go away. I hated the guilt and shame but secretly loved the pleasurable parts of fantasy and masturbation. Deep inside, I knew that I didn't want to give God control of the part of my life that would keep fantasy as an escape option.[9]

If you or someone you love finds themselves where Joel is, freedom won't be possible. Until there is true repentance and a willingness to do whatever it takes to leave the sin of pornography behind, you will be trapped. Effort alone will not bring freedom. A lack of effort and commitment, however, is a sure path to relapse.

Detox

The first step to addressing the root of a sexualized society is detox. Just like an alcoholic needs to quit drinking so he can start the healing process, the porn or sex addict needs to avoid the sexual temptations of the sexualized society to avoid relapse. It is important for someone starting detox to clearly define a relapse. A relapse is engaging in unwanted sexual behavior such as viewing porn, masturbation, or hooking up. (In the appendix, I unpack the biblical, clinical, and practical reasons why masturbation is considered a relapse.)

Detox allows the brain to reset. As you might recall from Chapter 4, regular porn use elevates dopamine levels in the brain to unnatural heights. Detox from porn allows the chemical levels in the brain to return to normal, and many sex addiction therapists indicate ninety days is a good initial detox goal. This may seem impossible to one mired in porn use, but taking it one day at a time with a committed accountability partner or group is key.

It should be noted that detox will likely result in certain withdrawal symptoms. During the first few weeks, a person may become depressed because they are used to the high from the chemicals. They may experience the classic symptoms of detox and withdrawal: boredom, lack of interest and motivation, and the desire to isolate. Some may even experience hopelessness and suicidal thoughts. The first few weeks are typically the most challenging.

Used to operating with higher levels of dopamine, the porn addict's brain craves the neurochemical during detox. Raising levels of dopamine naturally can help diminish porn cravings.

So during detox, it's important to engage in activities that naturally raise dopamine levels.

Things like exercise, good sleeping and eating habits, spiritual disciplines (Bible reading, prayer, etc.), and enjoying friends and family increase dopamine output and are the kind of activities that help during detox. Detox will be challenging and will require a total commitment. And when I say total commitment, I don't just mean a commitment to abstain from viewing porn. I mean a commitment to avoid sexual triggers.

The Triggers

A person must not only be committed to their detox, they must be strategic. A strategic detox begins with identifying triggers—the situations or images that initially stir up sexual desire. These stimuli turn thoughts sexual and lead down the path to relapse. This includes avoiding places where you meet sexual temptation—a club, certain gyms, or Twitter.

In the opening story, Parker began to identify his triggers: social media, sexualized media, objectifying immodestly dressed women, being alone in his room with his phone, and dwelling on impure thoughts. All of these fed his craving and desire to act out. Often, he would feed his flesh throughout the day by checking out girls and entertaining sexual thoughts. His cravings would grow. When he returned to his room at night, Parker was ready to act out sexually. Usually, he did.

After falling hard in his first attempts at sobriety, Parker knew he needed strong boundaries. He decided to cut out social media and sexualized media. Instead of indulging his lust by staring at and objectifying women, he bounced his eyes from the woman to the ground.

Before he made a radical commitment to purity, Parker didn't think he lusted that much. But through the process of detox, he kept a "lust log" in which he recorded each time he lusted or dwelled on a sexual thought. After a week, Parker realized how subconscious his lusting had become. By recognizing lust, though, he began to "take every thought captive" (2 Corinthians 10:5) and keep urges in check.

Parker didn't try to detox alone. He knew he could not keep these boundaries without accountability, and he needed more than just his mentor. He gathered up the courage to ask a friend, and when he did, Parker's friend admitted that he also struggled and needed help. The two of them began meeting weekly to talk about how they were doing with maintaining their boundaries. They texted during the week when they needed prayer. This relationship took Parker's detox to a new level.

But even with accountability, each person must identify and disclose their sexual triggers. Then, each must chart a course of action to avoid triggers and hold the other accountable to it. What are the most common triggers and resulting boundaries? In every Freedom Fight group I have led, participants list the same key triggers: the internet, social media, sexualized movies, and immodestly dressed women. Steps I've seen men take to avoid triggers are:

- Restrict or cut internet access on their smartphone.
- Buy a flip phone with no internet access.
- Install filtering and accountability software on all devices.
- Sell, give away, or remove a laptop.
- Sell, give away, or remove gaming systems.
- Remove their bedroom door so they can't be truly alone in their room.
- Delete and block numbers of old hookup partners.

Not all of these may apply to everyone, but they are examples of the kind of commitment needed for a successful detox. A young woman in one of our female groups recently recognized that the sexual lyrics of her rap music started the sexual fantasies which led her to crave porn. Simply removing certain songs from her playlist made a difference.

Environmental Triggers

Ivan Pavlov was a Russian scientist studying digestion in dogs in the 1890s. He discovered something unexpected. He was working to find what triggered the dogs to salivate, assuming that when they saw the food, they would be triggered. He discovered it wasn't just the food.

The people who fed the dogs wore lab coats. The dogs started salivating any time they saw the lab coat, even when no food was in sight. Pavlov took the experiment one step further. He started ringing a bell every time the dogs were fed. When they rang the bell, the dogs would drool, whether or not food was present.[10] One of the chemicals responsible for initiating drooling is dopamine, which is released to increase the craving.[11]

What does this mean for the porn addict? Environmental cues that have been a part of a person's sexual acting out can *subconsciously* trigger dopamine in the brain, so they crave porn. Some porn addicts say an urge hits them out of nowhere. Many times, however, they may have just encountered an environmental trigger.

Some might get aroused when their computer turns on or when they enter a bathroom stall or simply turn on a shower because their sexual acting out has been connected to these activities. These environmental stimuli are like the lab coat and bell triggering the dogs to salivate. They release dopamine, which causes the craving to begin.

University students who used porn in high school tend to relapse significantly more when they go back home for the holidays. The sights, sounds, and smells of a familiar place of acting out notify the brain, "Hey, remember what happens here?" These triggers signal the brain to start releasing dopamine to increase porn cravings. Once people identify environmental triggers, they can put up boundaries and set up accountability.

Boundaries and accountability are essential. It is necessary to create a plan and communicate that plan with accountability. I know a college student who never went home during detox unless he took a friend with him. Some people have even communicated with their parents the need to make sure all the computers are password protected. When people know their own triggers, they can set boundaries and get accountability for those boundaries.

Routines That Trigger

Routines are also a form of environmental triggers. A routine consists of doing certain things to get ready to act out sexually. They are steps people take to '"set the table" to act out. It could be locking the door or getting in bed with a phone and scrolling through social media. It could be going into the bathroom with a phone. It might be locking the door to the bathroom and taking a shower.

Whatever steps or routines someone has developed as their pattern of acting becomes like the lab coat or bell in Pavlov's experiment. These routines have been so closely associated with acting out they themselves become triggers that cause dopamine to be released. This makes someone crave acting out even more. Their brain gives a hit of dopamine to encourage them to keep going down the pathway toward orgasm.

Understanding triggers and routines puts people in a position to stop the behavior. The whole process looks like this: the addiction cycle begins with a trigger that moves a person's mind toward sexual thoughts and fantasies. If it is not stopped there, it progresses to routines where the person sets the table to act out. Acting out leads to shame. To restart the cycle, shame can trigger the desire to medicate with fantasy.[12]

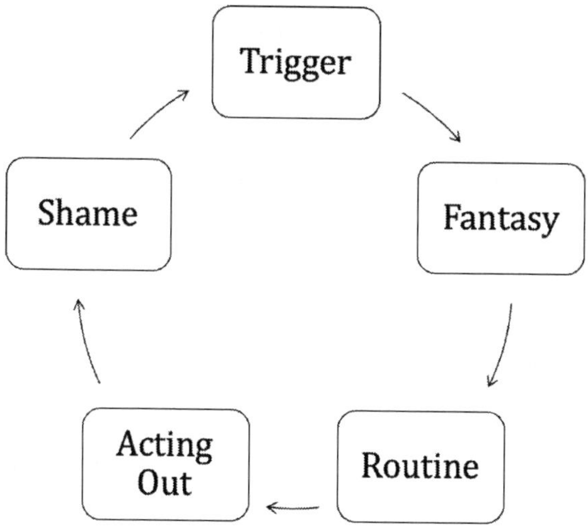

The cycle gains momentum as it moves toward acting out. It's like a boulder rolling down a hill. If people don't stop this process early, it becomes almost impossible to stop.

Those who focus on stopping the process at the trigger and fantasy stage have much more success than those who try to stop it later in the cycle. When Jesus described evil thoughts, He included sexual fantasies. He said, "For out of the heart come evil thoughts, murder, adultery, sexual immorality" (Matthew 15:19). Adultery and sexual immorality cover any sexual activity outside of marriage. Learning to take sexual thoughts captive to the obedience of Christ is essential. When people identify and remove the triggers that put these thoughts in their minds, they can stop the cycle before it starts.

If someone is going to experience freedom, not only do their actions need to change, but their beliefs about those actions need to shift also. When it comes to temptation, the human mindset seems to be "how close to the edge can I get." This mindset will undermine recovery, especially during detox.

Look at the biblical attitude followers of Christ should have regarding temptation:

- Pray that you do not enter into temptation (Matthew 26:41).
- Flee sexual immorality (1 Corinthians 6:18).
- Flee youthful lusts (2 Timothy 2:22).

"Pray against and flee temptation!" This is the mentality someone must have for a successful detox. Don't flirt with temptation—flee it. Adopting this biblical mindset will make all the difference in recovery.

Anticipation and Accountability

Unless God instantly delivers a person, no one gets free from a porn or sex addiction immediately or without accountability.

Sophia's biggest temptations were fantasy and masturbation. She also, on occasion, hooked up with guys. These had been a part of her life since her freshman year in high school. She gained a heart for purity after she started following Christ during her sophomore year in college. She joined a small group that helped her think through her *triggers* and the *boundaries* to help her avoid them. This was her list of boundaries.

- No sexualized media.
- No sexual fantasy thoughts.
- Limit social media (i.e., no Snapchat or dating apps).
- No media in bed.
- No communication with certain guys.
- Keep the phone in another room at night and sleep with the door open.

Sophia's recovery took a significant jump forward when she learned to anticipate problems and reach out to her accountability partners for help. She would send texts like:

- "I've been struggling with my thoughts about a past hookup. Can you pray for me? I'll check back in later today."
- "Brad keeps texting me. I'm enjoying the attention but need to stop replying. I'll update you tomorrow!"

Sophia realized the power of breaking isolation and reaching out for help. This helped her resist where she usually would have given in.

Andy's recovery also jumped forward when he learned to anticipate and reach out to his accountability. These were the kinds of preemptive texts he sent his accountability partners.

- "I'm going to work out. I will check in after to let you know how I did at bouncing my eyes."
- "Been tempted today and getting ready to take a shower. I'll text when done."

When Andy went home for breaks, he tried to bring a friend. If he couldn't, he made a plan that included boundaries and calling his accountability every day. Just knowing he was going to talk to his accountability daily helped keep temptations in check.

Those who are successful, like Sophia and Andy, identify triggers and routines that move them toward relapse. Then they set up boundaries. Once boundaries are established, they set up accountability to help them maintain those boundaries. But reaching out to their accountability, even preemptively, made the biggest difference.

Beware of the Drift

The pull of the sexualized society is strong. There is a growing trend among the younger generation of Christians to move away from biblical standards of purity. Nick Stumbo has noticed this pattern. He is the executive director of Pure Desire Ministries, an organization that helps pastors and ministry leaders break free from sexual bondage.

Nick commented on this trend among ministry leaders to water down the biblical standards for purity. He said, "These pastors, typically 35 and under, excuse their 'occasional' porn use with rationalizations like 'I overeat once in a while too, so it's not that big of a deal.'" Stumbo shared how some ministries have adopted the mindset that porn use is so pervasive that they just have to accept it. Many young leaders have been pornified to the point that holiness is a relative term. And so is freedom. To those who've given in to the sexualized society, freedom means "acting out only occasionally."[13]

This compromise on God's standard for holiness keeps many people stuck in porn. They are unable to break free from porn because they continually feed their flesh through sexualized media. Their fleshly appetites grow. Imagine for a minute someone pleading with God for freedom from porn while being unwilling to adopt God's standard for holiness in their media. How can such a person expect to find freedom?

As we saw earlier, God's goal is to make us like Jesus, and this change happens by renewing our minds. This is why God gives standards in His Word about what we feed our minds. Someone can't expect to have freedom from porn if they ignore God's standard for holiness.

If people don't grow in their convictions for holiness, then the tendency is to conform to our sexualized society. Left to ourselves, we tend to drift. Theologian D.A. Carson writes:

> People do not drift toward holiness. Apart from grace-driven effort, people do not gravitate toward godliness, prayer, and obedience to Scripture, faith, and delight in the Lord. We drift toward compromise and call it tolerance; we drift toward disobedience and call it freedom; we drift toward superstition and call it faith; we cherish the indiscipline of lost self-control and call it relaxation; we slouch toward prayerlessness and delude ourselves into thinking we have escaped legalism; we slide toward godlessness and convince ourselves we have been liberated.[14]

Those who enter into a relationship with God through Jesus Christ are given a vision for holiness. Holiness is the path to the abundant life Christ promises. To pursue holiness is to pursue freedom and God's best for our lives.

Action Steps Summary

- Meditate on God's holiness (Isaiah 6:3 and Revelation 4:8) and ask Him to give you a vision for personal holiness.
- Commit to detox and go on lockdown.*
- Define a relapse.
- Identify physical and environmental triggers.
- Set up boundaries for triggers and routines.
- Ask at least one person to be an accountability partner.

*(see appendix for related resources)

10

The Addicted Brain

Navy SEALs are highly trained to operate effectively under the worst conditions. In combat stress, fatigue, and fear, SEALs are taught a technique called "combat breathing." It enables them to remain calm and make clear-headed decisions when they are in combat situations, such as "Operation Red Wings," which was a 2005 Navy SEAL mission in the Afghan mountains.

The four-man SEAL team was searching for a notorious militia leader, Ahmad Shah. Before they located him, dozens of Taliban fighters attacked the team. They were hopelessly outnumbered, and a deadly battle began. The enemy fired waves of bullets and rocket-propelled grenades as the SEALs rushed down the mountain seeking a better defensive position.

Shortly after the battle began, two of the SEALs were killed. The two remaining soldiers fought hard, killing many of the Taliban fighters, but the enemy still advanced. One of the remaining SEALs was killed. Marcus Luttrell was the lone survivor. A grenade exploded near him, throwing him down a ravine. Still alive, Marcus made his way to a cave, hiding from the enemy. When the Taliban fighters had moved on, Marcus crawled for miles with a broken back, finally making it to safety.[1]

Combat breathing is also helpful in the fight for sexual purity. As we'll see in this chapter, it is part of a tool to help people overcome sexual temptation. This tool is based on brain science and biblical principles and has proven to be powerful in helping people break free from sexual sin. But before we unpack this tool, we need to look more closely at how the brain is hijacked by pornography.

Hijacking the Rewards System

The second root that drives porn addiction is the addicted brain. I introduced the reward system of the brain earlier, but now let's dive a little deeper into how it gets hijacked.

The limbic system is a complex network of nerves in the center of the brain that contains the pleasure center. It is involved in behaviors related to one's survival (*i.e.*, the fight or flight response). The limbic system is sometimes called the emotional brain and operates with a safety-first focus. When someone touches a hot stove, their limbic system doesn't wait for the brain to analyze the situation. It moves them to pull their hand away before they can consciously think.[2]

The limbic system works in the human brain to assign value and attach emotion to behavior. It rewards the behavior that it wants you to remember and repeat with dopamine. It attaches specific emotions to experiences so that we'll pursue what felt good and avoid what felt bad.[3] And this system gives the highest reward it can for an orgasm. When someone gratifies himself while watching porn, the brain makes note of this very positive experience to remind them to repeat it. As they do, those connections grow stronger and the porn rut in their brain deepens.

There is a check on the impulsiveness of the limbic system. It is the prefrontal cortex (PFC), also known as the logical brain. This region of the brain is responsible for the executive functions: logic, reasoning, determining good from bad, and impulse control. The PFC is the system that allows people to choose not to act against their moral beliefs or future goals. This part of the brain, the braking system, is not fully developed until someone is twenty-five.[4]

The limbic system regularly overrides the PFC for the sake of survival or one's well-being. After someone repeatedly acts out sexually, especially as a way to medicate pain, the limbic system begins to treat porn or other unwanted sexual behaviors as a survival issue, a way to cure the pain. And the next time he feels bad, the limbic system seeks relief and knows where to find it.

What's more, in these situations, the limbic system regularly overpowers the PFC.[5] The brain is designed to automate processes so it can operate efficiently. When a person uses porn repeatedly to bring relief to negative emotions, the brain starts to automate this process. The brain's positive response to this relief helps establish the dominance of the limbic system over the PFC.[6]

What ignites the limbic system? When a person encounters a sexual or emotional trigger, dopamine pushes the gas on the limbic system, encouraging the person to take the porn pathway of pleasure and satisfaction. At the same time, the PFC is impaired, the part of the brain that makes moral and logical decisions (the brakes). The repetition of actions rewires peoples' brains in a way that keeps them in bondage to the pleasure-producing chemicals. Meanwhile, the willpower potential of the PFC that would enable a person to stop erodes with each episode.[7]

The American Society for Addiction Medicine (ASAM) asserts that addiction is fundamentally a disease of the brain's reward system. The hijacking of that system causes people to crave pleasure from sources that are ultimately harmful—drugs, alcohol, and pornography, to name a few.[8]

But what ASAM calls disease, the Bible calls being in bondage to sin and "carrying out the desires of the mind" (Ephesians 2:3). The cravings of the addicted brain take over and feel impossible to resist. Understanding the biology of the brain helps those caught in addiction renew their mind more effectively.

Fixing the Brakes

The phenomenon of a person's PFC not operating effectively is known as hypofrontality. It is the erosion of their willpower. Prolonged porn use saturates the PFC with dopamine, although it cannot absorb these elevated levels effectively. When the PFC absorbs dopamine less efficiently, it operates less effectively. The brakes are weakened.[9]

Hypofrontality helps explain how many people continue to make bad decisions even in the face of great personal cost. They have lost the ability to restrain themselves. Quitting porn use and unwanted sexual behavior can reverse the problem of hypofrontality, but it takes time. When elevated dopamine levels return to normal, the brain begins healing and absorbing dopamine effectively again. When this happens, impulse control and moral reasoning begin to return to normal levels. This is why detox is so important. It helps addicts heal their brains by repairing the brakes.[10]

Detox is not easy, though. Deprived of the usual sexual stimuli, the brain will crave relief. And in the early days of detox, your brain's brakes will still be weak. This is why The Freedom Fight created BRACE, a tool to help those fighting for sobriety build new pathways in their brain.

The BRACE Method

BRACE is an acronym, a shorthand method for remembering the steps necessary to address sexual triggers and provide biblical and practical steps to resist temptation. This step-by-step practice keeps the addicted brain from running the show.

B. Breathe deeply.

Every time the Navy SEALs go into battle, they work to keep their limbic system from overpowering the PFC. During battle, a Navy SEAL's limbic system is primed for fight or flight. They are trained, though, to re-engage their PFC so they can remain calm and think clearly, which helps them make logical decisions. This is where they use combat breathing.

In combat breathing, soldiers take deep, diaphragmatic breaths. This slow-breathing technique sends more oxygen to their PFC, improving the brain's ability to make decisions and control impulsive behavior.

To practice combat breathing, inhale through your nose slowly for four seconds. (Your stomach should expand). Hold your breath for four seconds. Then exhale slowly through your mouth for four seconds (or however long you need to completely empty your lungs) and your stomach retracts.

Once you start breathing deeply, move to the second step of the BRACE method: Remembering the truth.

R. Remember the truth.

Remembering the truth reminds us of who God is, our identity in Him, and the consequences of our sin. All of these help reengage the PFC, where your higher reasoning takes place based on morals, values, and consequences.

Memorizing God's Word can help you recall the truth and His promises in times of temptation. Three helpful verses to memorize are:

- "The pure in heart will see God." (Matthew 5:8)
- "Consider yourselves dead to sin but alive to God." (Romans 6:10-11)

- "You are no longer a slave but a son." (Galatians 4:7)
- "God created man in His own image." (Genesis 1:27)

Meditating on a Bible verse refocuses your mind on truth. It helps you remember:

- Sin hurts your closeness with Christ.
- The power of sin has been broken.
- You are a son, not a slave.
- You were made in God's image and have infinite worth and value.

These truths engage the PFC and renew right thinking. In the heat of the moment when people are tempted to lie to themselves saying, "I can't resist" or "it doesn't really matter if I take a quick peek," remembering the truth pulls them back to reality.

Emma, a twenty-one-year-old college junior, received a text from an old hookup who wanted to see her again. She wanted to see him too. Feeling insecure in the moment, she wanted to be desired, but she knew where things would lead if they were to meet up. After receiving the text, she immediately started breathing deeply. Then she turned to the truth of who she is in Christ and re-centered.

By remembering the promises of God, Emma experienced the truth of Scripture: "He has granted to us His precious and magnificent promises, so that by them you may become partakers of the divine nature, having escaped the corruption that is in the world by lust" (2 Peter 1:4). Through remembering the promises, she escaped lust. She experienced the truth of Psalm 119:9,11: "How can a young person stay on the path to purity?"

By living according to your word. I have hidden your word in my heart, that I might not sin against you" (NIV).

After spending thirty–sixty seconds breathing deeply and meditating on the truth, move to the next step in the BRACE method.

A. Ask God for help.

Ask God to help you believe the truth you are meditating on. It is not enough to know the promises of God; they must be believed. You must believe them in order for them to affect your behavior, but so often, belief can be difficult in the midst of temptation. And when belief is difficult, we must ask God for help.

God will help us when we are tempted. When we ask for help, we are claiming this promise of God: "No temptation has overtaken you that is not common to man. God is faithful, and he will not let you be tempted beyond your ability, but with the temptation he will also provide the way of escape, that you may be able to endure it" (1 Corinthians 10:13). Ask God to give you the courage to reach out for help, and then move to the next step.

C. Call an accountability partner.

With your body regulated and firmly rooted in the truth, engage accountability. Call your accountability partner and let them know you are tempted. If they do not answer, send a text. You must reach out for help. Knowing that someone will ask you about it later helps you resist the temptation. Making the call often makes the difference of whether you act out or not.

The "Call" in BRACE is based on the principle in 2 Timothy 2:22: "Flee youthful passions and pursue righteousness… *along with those* who call on the Lord from a pure heart." Not only are we to flee youthful lusts and pursue godliness, but we are to do so with others. Community is crucial. Break isolation with a call.

Tyler, a twenty-seven-year-old bachelor, came home exhausted from a long day at work. He walked into his empty apartment and his mind immediately turned to thoughts of porn. But after years of porn use, he was ready to break free. He had begun practicing BRACE regularly in the weeks leading up to that moment of temptation, so as soon as he was tempted, he began breathing deeply and meditating on John 8:36, which reads, "So if the Son sets you free, you will be free indeed." He called his accountability partner and let him know he was struggling. His friend encouraged Tyler to finish the process of BRACE and text later to follow up. Tyler typically isolated himself when he was tempted, but that began to change when he started using BRACE. It was a major step forward in his path toward healing.

E. Escape the situation.

The final step in the BRACE method is to Escape. Fleeing temptation means leaving isolation. Being around others in a public area diffuses temptation. Escape to healthy outlets like hanging out with friends, working out, walking, or reading.

Tyler would have continued to be tempted if he had stayed in his apartment that day. Instead, he went to a coffee shop until his roommates were home. In a public place, his temptation faded. He escaped sexual sin.

Those seeking freedom must remember that repetition of porn pathways got them into their addiction and repetition of new pathways will help get them out. In sixty seconds, someone can start training their brain to have a new response to temptation.

How BRACE Renews the Mind

Tom is a Christian businessman in his mid-fifties. He started using BRACE when he went through The Freedom Fight program. He was shocked by the results. He says, "The victory I was shooting for was to not allow myself to engage in sexual fantasy that would culminate in masturbation." The more he practiced, the more he began to use it automatically when tempted. Tom says, "For me, this has been a forty-year battle. I am on a 300-plus-day streak of sobriety, which in my world, is unbelievable." Tom's *forty years* of bondage has ended. *Forty* years of a temptation leading to acting out has ended. *Forty* years of shame is over. Repetition got Tom into his addiction, and repetition also got him out.

BRACE doesn't just help people avoid their unhealthy behaviors. It allows them to build new brain pathways. Each time someone uses BRACE instead of turning to porn, they reinforce a new, healthy pathway. Instead of giving in to the temptations of a hijacked brain, they build neural pathways, which lead to wise choices and freedom. By practicing BRACE, people are "transformed by renewing their minds" (Romans 12:2).

Compare the old pathway of porn with the new pathway of BRACE:

Old Porn Pathway	**New BRACE Pathway**
Repress the truth	Remember the truth
Rely on your own strength	Ask God for help
Seek isolation	Call to break isolation
Stay in tempting situation	Escape tempting situation

The old porn pathway moves a person away from truth, God, and others and leads them to indulge in sin. The new pathway moves people toward truth, God, and others and enables them to avoid sin. The old porn pathway has been traveled so many times that it becomes a subconscious response. The new BRACE pathway is a practical way to renew one's mind and experience transformation. Each stage is important since the process builds on itself. Practicing BRACE even when you are *not* tempted will enable you to use it more effectively when you *are* tempted.

Habit expert James Clear points out an important truth about behavior change, saying, "Habits form based on frequency, not time. One of the most common questions I hear is, 'How long does it take to build a new habit?' But what people really should be asking is... how many repetitions are required to make a habit automatic?"[11]

BRACE helps you build new pathways through repetition. Allow any sexual temptation or thought to move you to practice BRACE. When tempted, use it as an opportunity to help you get another repetition of the new pathway. When it comes to changing your brain and behavior, repetition matters.

Those who struggle with porn should practice BRACE three times a day even if they are not tempted. To practice, a person should think of a common trigger, but nothing explicit. Then they practice BRACE, which they can do in less than sixty seconds. Each time they resist and practice BRACE, it reinforces the new pathway. To maximize BRACE, people must:

- Use it every time they are triggered or tempted.
- Establish with their accountability that a BRACE call is only to talk briefly about a temptation. (No other topics will be discussed).
- Text instead of call when practicing.

James Clear says, "Each time you repeat an action, you are activating a particular neural circuit associated with that habit. This means that simply putting in your reps is one of the most crucial steps you can take to encoding a new habit."[12]

Meditating Changes People

BRACE is a powerful tool. We surveyed Freedom Fight users to evaluate the life change they experienced through the program. The survey included both current and former Freedom Fight users. Before starting The Freedom Fight, 49% of users watched porn three or more times a week, and 18% were using porn daily or multiple times a day. However, after going through the program (or most of it), only 3% used porn three times a week or more. None used it daily.

When someone starts using BRACE for tempting thoughts or triggers, they begin to saturate their minds with the Word of God. Transformation happens when someone replaces meditating on porn with meditating on the Word of God. What a person meditates on changes them.

> This Book of the Law shall not depart from your mouth, but you shall meditate on it day and night, so that you may be careful to do according to all that is written in it. For then you will make your way prosperous, and then you will have good success. (Joshua 1:8)

> My word… shall not return to me empty, but it shall accomplish that which I purpose, and shall succeed in the thing for which I sent it. (Isaiah 55:11)

The first verse tells us that we should soak our minds in God's Word so we will obey it and have success. The second verse promises that God's Word will do the work in our lives that God desires. His Word is powerful, and research shows its impact. A study by psychologist Dr. Paul Meier revealed that "those who practice almost daily Scripture meditation are significantly healthier and happier than those who do not."[13]

A Habit Contract Creates Space for BRACE

Ever heard of a habit contract? It's a tool that has proven to be effective in helping people break their bad habits. As we've seen, the brain is designed to crave those things that bring pleasure, but it is also designed to avoid behavior that leads to negative consequences. And behavioral experts tell us the best way to break a bad habit is to experience some negative consequences as soon as possible after the behavior you want to change. Some of these experts suggest making a "habit contract," an agreement with negative consequences whenever you engage in a specific bad habit.[14]

The apostle Paul reflected this mentality when he said, "But I discipline my body and keep it under control" (1 Corinthians 9:27). The word Paul uses for discipline literally means "discipline with hardship." Negative consequences can be a way to discipline your body and grow in holiness. The brain has been rewarding porn use for years, which makes it difficult to give up. Negative consequences quickly applied after porn use can begin to give the brain a reason to pause at the neurological level.

Dr. Ted Roberts, founder of Pure Desire Ministries, has utilized this principle to help men break their porn addictions. He suggests accountability partners get a copy of a porn user's "relapse contract," which assigns specific negative consequences to a specific relapse. Dr. Roberts also urges married men to bring their wives into the process, but *only after* he has had six months of sobriety. Establishing sobriety alleviates the potential trauma to the wife if there are regular relapses. Once the wife is involved, she can help him come up with his consequences. Sleeping on the couch is a common one.

In my years of coaching porn addicts, I've heard numerous examples of consequences for relapsing. Examples of consequences I've seen on a relapse contract include:

- Fasting from food, sports, social media, or entertainment for an extended amount of time
- Running three miles if they aren't a runner, but only if the doctor allows
- Going without the device they viewed porn on for a month
- Wearing mismatched or out-of-style clothing for the day
- Immediately confessing to an accountability partner in a phone call or in person

Each person needs to choose their own consequences that they think will best deter their unwanted behavior. Whatever the consequences are, though, it needs to come quickly after the behavior to be as effective as possible. Confession to accountability partners can serve as a negative consequence. I have seen a correlation between those who stay stuck in their porn struggle and how long they delay confessing a relapse. Those who are most serious about finding freedom typically confess as soon as they can after acting out. Those who wait too long are more likely not to confess at all.

The relapse contract clarifies what a relapse is and what the corresponding negative consequences will be. If the person seeking freedom doesn't write it out and share it with their accountability partner, then it is too easy not to follow through. Put a timeframe on how soon the consequence needs to be enforced after acting out. Within twenty-four hours is suggested. The goal is for the brain to connect acting out with the negative consequence so the porn user might pause before using. In that pause, there is a clear opportunity to use BRACE.

If you like the idea of using a relapse contract, I've provided an example. Just personalize the consequences and you'll be on your way.

Relapse Contract

The following members, in the spirit of finding freedom, are committing to certain consequences after a relapse. The goal is not to feel condemnation, but to invoke a natural consequence to "discipline ourselves for godliness" (1 Timothy 4:7).

We all agree that the following behaviors constitute a relapse: purposefully viewing any nudity or sexualized media, masturbating, hooking up, cyber sex of any kind, any sex contact with someone other than your spouse.

We commit to confess and send a crash report to the group within 24 hours of a relapse.

I commit to being fully honest and transparent with the group and to fulfill my self-assigned consequence of running 3 miles within 48 hours of a relapse.
Signature ______________________.

I commit to being fully honest and transparent with the group and to fulfill my self-assigned consequence of starting a fast for at least 24 hours within 48 hours of a relapse.
Signature ______________________.

I commit to being fully honest and transparent with the group and to fulfill my self-assigned consequence of abstaining from playing Xbox by getting rid of its power cord for 30 days within 48 hours of a relapse. Signature ______________________.

As a member of the group I commit to holding my brothers in Christ accountable and to spur them on in both times of weakness and wellness.

Signature ______________________. Signature ______________________.

Signature ______________________. Signature ______________________.

What Happens When I Crash?

When an airplane crashes, investigators immediately seek to recover the black box. The black box records all the flight data and even the pilots' conversations. This information is invaluable in helping investigators determine the cause of the crash.[15]

Learning what caused a crash is critical because it can help prevent future crashes. This principle can apply to a porn relapse. A relapse of unwanted sexual behavior is a sort of "crash." When people fill out a "crash report" after their relapse, it helps them track where they went wrong and what triggered them so they can avoid future crashes. They answer specific questions about the relapse, like what, when, why, how, and where they went off track. This information helps them see patterns and decisions that led to their crash.

Crash reports aren't meant to be private. The report is meant to be shared with the accountability structures you've created through BRACE. There are three benefits of sharing the crash report with accountability. First, sending the crash report helps people learn and make progress in their recovery. It allows others to see their data and share their feedback.

When Anna's group discussed her crash report, one group member made the simple observation that Anna's last few relapses had all been on the weekend when she was alone in her apartment. Another group member pointed out that Anna didn't check in with anyone during those weekends. Anna took the feedback and came up with a weekend plan to address these issues. This small adjustment made a huge difference in her recovery and aligned her behavior with the freedom she so desperately wanted.

Secondly, a crash report equips others. When Anna's group read her crash report, they learned from her relapse things they could apply to their own lives. They were each more aware of the issues that tripped Anna up and applied them in their own life. A smart person learns from their own mistakes. A *wise* person learns from the mistakes of others. Anna was serving others, not just herself, by filling out a crash report.

The third benefit of a crash report is it provides a negative consequence. No one wants to confess a relapse and then detail what happened to their accountability partners. This was humbling for Anna but also very healing. "Confess your sins to one another and pray for one another that you may be healed." (James 5:16). When the crash report is filled out and sent to someone's accountability, it reminds the brain that acting out isn't good. The crash report has proven helpful for a person's recovery on all three fronts.

So if your brain has been hijacked by porn, try reprogramming it. Begin using the BRACE method when temptation comes. Use negative consequences to help build new pathways in the brain. Create crash reports to learn from a stumble and share it with others. All three of these steps address the addicted brain. Use them and see if God doesn't transform you by the renewing of your mind (Romans 12:2).

Action Steps Summary

- Choose verses, truth statements, and promises to use with BRACE.*
- Use BRACE when tempted and practice regularly.
- Make a relapse contract with consequences.
- Fill out a crash report within twenty-four hours of a relapse.*

*(see appendix for related resources)

11

Isolation

In Johann Hari's book *Chasing the Scream,* he chronicles a debate about what causes addictions that raged within the scientific community in the 1970s. Some experts argued that addictions were caused solely by the chemicals the body got hooked on. A major experiment reinforced this idea. The researchers put a rat alone in a cage with two bottles. One had normal water and the other had morphine-drugged water. The rat almost always chose the drugged water until it became addicted and eventually died. The theory that the *drug's chemicals* caused addictive behavior seemed validated.

Later in the same decade, however, psychologist Bruce Alexander did another experiment. He thought that perhaps the rat chose drugs because it was bored and lonely in its isolated cage. So Alexander constructed what he called Rat Park. Rat Park provided plenty of activities, friends, and mates—everything a rat could want. Though the rats who lived in Rat Park were still given access to drugged water, they chose the normal water instead. The experiment concluded, "The rats in Rat Park rarely used drugged water, none ever used it compulsively, and none of them overdosed."[1]

The researchers took the Rat Park experiment one step further. They placed rats in isolated cages for fifty-seven days. Over that time, the lonely rats drank the drugged water compulsively and developed a strong addiction. The scientists then moved these addicted rats into Rat Park. As the rats spent more time in Rat Park, they gradually reduced their drug use. Eventually, all of the rats gave the drugs up completely and were drug-free for the rest of their lives.[2] The conclusion? There is power and healing in community.

We see these kinds of experiments with humans all the time. Severely injured patients are given a medical form of heroin stronger than most street drugs for months at a time. Yet typically, the patient just stops the drugs when they are discharged, especially if they are going home to a life where they're surrounded by a loving family. In contrast, using heroin for similar amounts of time often turn street users who were alone and unhappy into addicts.[3]

People were made to connect and bond even more than rats were. When people don't have community, when they are isolated, it creates an environment conducive for addictions to take root. Hari recognizes this, writing, "The opposite of addiction isn't sobriety, it's connection."[4]

The importance of connection is especially true for sex addiction, which is classified as an intimacy disorder. Today's media age creates a world where people connect without true connection. The lack of connection fosters the type of isolating environment where a porn or sex addiction thrives.[5]

Sex addiction authority Dr. Patrick Carnes surveyed over 600 recovered sex addicts. He identified the two most important factors they said helped them find freedom. The number-one factor was reliance on God or a higher power. The second factor was small group connection.[6] A small group brings acceptance, safety, accountability, encouragement, and processing that can't be found any other way. If a lack of close connection with others contributes to an addiction, then it makes sense that connecting with God and others would be an essential part of recovery.

Hiding from God and Others

The first two roots in porn or sex addiction are the *sexualized society* and the *addicted brain*. The third root is *isolation*. From the beginning, sin has caused people to isolate from God and one another. After Adam and Eve sinned, the Bible says, "Then the eyes of both were opened, and they knew that they were naked. And they sewed fig leaves together and made themselves loincloths" (Genesis 3:7). Adam and Eve immediately hid from one another by covering themselves. And sin causes us to cover up from one another not just physically, but also emotionally. We hide who we really are.

Adam and Eve didn't just hide from each other, though. The biblical account continues, "And they heard the sound of the Lord God walking in the garden in the cool of the day, and the man and his wife hid themselves from the presence of the Lord God" (Genesis 3:8). Sin leads us to isolate from one another and from God. But just as God called Adam out of hiding, He does the same to us. He wants us to leave the shadows so we can be in an authentic relationship with Him and others.

The Bible says choosing isolation is a foolish thing to do. "Whoever isolates himself seeks his own desire; he breaks out against all sound judgment" (Proverbs 18:1). Still, when we're left to ourselves, we are prone to self-deception and isolation. Former pastor John Doyel describes how isolation kept him stuck. He says:

> I continued downward in my levels of sexual sin to where it cost me my career as a pastor and almost killed my marriage. For a man who had every reason in the world to stop. … I did not. Even though I was repenting in private before God, my isolation, shame, and fear kept me there.[7]

Don't believe the lie Doyel believed that *private* repentance with God is enough. People who struggle with sexual sin and addiction must break from their isolation and come into community by confessing their sin to others. James 5:16 says, "Confess your sins to one another and pray for one another, that you may be healed." The tendency to isolate from God and others because of sexual sin is the opposite of what we are told to do. And it is the opposite of the intimacy we were made for.

True Fulfillment and Intimacy

We all long for fulfillment and true intimacy. When that thirst is not met, we try to quench it on our own. Jesus tells us our thirst for ultimate fulfillment is found in Him. He said, "If anyone thirsts, let him come to me and drink. Whoever believes in me, as the Scripture has said, out of his heart will flow rivers of living water" (John 7:37-38). Jesus makes a mind-blowing claim. He asserts that when we thirst for fulfillment, we are really thirsting for Him.

A personal relationship with Christ begins when we trust in His death on the cross as payment for our sins and invite Him to live His life through us. Even if a person has taken previous steps toward Christ, they won't experience the intimacy they want until they commit fully to Him.

This is such a significant decision that Jesus refers to our total commitment to Him as being "born again." He said, "Unless one is born again he cannot see the kingdom of God" (John 3:3). When we have this spiritual birth, Christ comes into our lives to make us a new person. The apostle Paul put it this way: "Therefore, if anyone is in Christ, he is a new creation. The old has passed away; behold, the new has come" (2 Corinthians 5:17).

Once we come to know Christ, we grow in that relationship by spending time with Him, as we would with any good relationship. What does spending time with Him look like? Seeking God in a daily walk through His Word and spending time in prayer. Living a life of worship. Seeking God with other believers in a church.

Surprisingly, God says a close connection with Him isn't all we need. We need companionship and community. After creating a perfect world where God Himself was Adam's companion, God said, "It is not good that the man should be alone" (Genesis 2:18). In a perfect world with a perfect God and perfect man, God recognized our need for human companionship.

And Jesus implicitly said as much too. When asked what the greatest command was, he said, "You shall love the Lord your God with all your heart, and with all your soul, and with all your mind, and with all your strength. And the second is this: you shall love your neighbor as yourself" (Mark 12:30-31). He recognized that we were to be in community with neighbors.

Sex addiction therapists are trained to get their porn-addicted clients into small groups as soon as possible. They know that when an addict develops real connections with real people, it accelerates the healing process. And Christian sex addiction therapists know this truth: We often can't experience God's love and acceptance until we have experienced love and acceptance from other people. But as our capacity to experience God's love increases, as we learn to accept love from others, our capacity to express this love increases too. Put another way, where pornography isolates us from intimacy, connection with God and others increases our capacity to experience intimacy.

Bonding with Porn

God did not create us for isolation. He created us for connection. He wired our brains for it. And one of the primary ways we've been wired for connection is through sex. Oxytocin is the hormone that helps us bond with others. It is often called "the cuddle hormone" because it is released during skin-to-skin contact with other people. But this oxytocin released during porn use or a hookup increases a person's compulsion to bond during the sexual behavior. Oxytocin is released in even greater amounts during a climax. So for the porn user, this can result in bonding to porn by creating an emotional attachment.[8]

Behavioral therapist Andrea Kuszewski calls the dopamine-oxytocin combo released in the brain during orgasm a "biochemical love potion." This is why after having sex, a couple is more inclined to form an emotional attachment. The biochemical love potion is also released when a person uses porn. When someone watches porn, they are "bonding with it," Kuszewski says. She goes on to explain that "those chemicals make you want to keep coming back to have that feeling." This is why people develop a neurological attachment to porn. Some people refer to this as "dating porn."[9]

A man in recovery anonymously posted his story of how he bonded with porn. He wrote, "When I started seriously considering a *life without porn,* something in me literally panicked. The thoughts that ran through my mind were: *Wait. No more porn? I don't really feel like I'm ready for this.*" Once he started his recovery, this bond was still there. He continued:

> I heard this quote recently. "Letting go of porn is like letting go of an old friend." It struck me as really true. This has been the biggest hardship in my journey. It's difficult to admit that some part of me really does miss using porn sometimes.

This realization was puzzling for him. He shared, "I realized that I actually started *missing* porn. This disturbed me. How could I miss something that has worked to ruin my life? But the feelings were there—they were real."[10]

The draw to porn can seem mysterious. The bond with porn is both chemical and emotional. Though addicts often genuinely want porn out of their lives, they still find themselves seeking out reasons to continue using it. Why? Because porn has been there for them. Porn has comforted them. Porn has exhilarated them when they've been down. Porn has been their friend, their lover, and even their god. Addicts don't realize how much they have bonded to porn until they try to give it up.

Melodie's bond to porn made it difficult for her to quit. Her dad left her family when she was young. She felt rejected and longed for attention from a man. Porn was a fantasy world she could enter to feel loved and desired. Her draw to porn was not just about physical pleasure. She loved porn because of the comfort and connection she experienced by imagining being the woman in porn whom she saw being desired by men.

Melodie said, "Porn quenched my thirst for intimacy, but only temporarily. I developed an attachment to the videos and the actors in the videos, though I didn't know it at the time." Subconsciously, Melody was being drawn to the fake intimacy pornography provided. The bond to porn is real and can make it difficult to give up.[11]

Remember, God puts sexual sin in a unique category. "Flee from sexual immorality. Every other sin a person commits is outside the body, but the sexually immoral person sins against his own body" (1 Corinthians 6:18). God created sex to be a bonding experience. I believe one of the ways we sin against ourselves through sexual immorality is that we bond to things or people we later wish we weren't bonded to.

Often a porn addict has their favorite porn clip that they climax to over and over. They look at many clips, but they return to the one they have bonded to. And for the married addict, bonding to porn can undermine bonding to their spouse. While having sex with their spouse, many porn addicts will replay their favorite porn clip in their minds. What should be a bonding moment between husband and wife is actually a continuation of their bonding to the porn clip. Fortunately, this can be changed as the porn user starts being present and disciplined in their mind while having sex with their spouse. The result of this shift in focus is better sex, better bonding with their spouse, and a better marriage—marriage the way God intended.

We all have a thirst for intimacy, and porn is a cheap substitute to meet this need. When a desperately thirsty man comes to the ocean, he shouldn't drink the water because the salt within will only make him more thirsty. Porn promises to be a thirst quencher for intimacy, but it is a short-term solution that will only make the person thirstier. True intimacy will be impossible as long as the porn user is bonded to their porn.

Porn and Isolation

Not only does porn lead to isolation, but isolation makes porn more tempting. When a person has less bonding and intimacy in their life, the fake intimacy of porn becomes more appealing to them.[12] If someone is isolated from real people, they can *feel* a kind of *connection* through sexual fantasy. Those who are connected to real people don't feel the lack of intimacy as acutely, and so, porn doesn't have the same emotional temptation.

Sadly, today's younger generations are the loneliest in US history.[13] A recent survey showed 30% of Millennials (born from 1981–1996) say they are lonely and 22% say they have no friends. Gen Z (born from the late 1990s to the 2010s) is even lonelier. [14]

Pornography provides a fantasy place someone can go to feel accepted and desired by others. Porn and hookups provide fake intimacy that makes them more tempting beyond just sexual pleasure. If there was a lack of intimacy in someone's family growing up, they may be more susceptible to the draw of artificial intimacy. Isolation makes people hungrier for the intimacy they really want.

Secular author and political activist Naomi Wolf, who has traveled all over the country to talk with university students about relationships, observed the connection between loneliness and porn. She said, "When I ask about loneliness, a deep, sad silence descends on audiences of young men and young women alike… They know they are lonely together … and that [porn] is a big part of that loneliness. What they don't know is how to get out."[15]

The relational isolation Wolf observed among university students usually started in their early teen years. That was Brett's story. His porn addiction began in seventh grade. He watched porn daily, sometimes for four or five hours at a time. Porn became his escape when his relationships struggled. He said, "I can remember getting into fights with my parents and going to my room and scrolling through porn websites for hours."

When Brett isolated himself from his family, he found comfort in porn. He continued, "Porn was my source of happiness, and when I was down, it comforted me. It became my family in a way. All this time with porn disconnected me from my real family. Even when I was with my family, my mind was clouded with thoughts of *When can I watch porn next*?

The shame of what Brett was watching kept him from engaging with his sister and parents. He says, "Porn was stealing my joy because I knew what I was doing was wrong. Even when I wanted to connect with my family, I just didn't have any joy to give, so I wasn't enjoyable to be around."

Brett only found freedom once he went to college, started following Christ, and joined a recovery group. Reflecting on his addiction, Brett said, "At the time, I had no idea how porn was hurting my relationships with my family. I am still trying to mend those relationships today." Porn robbed him of the ability to cultivate real intimacy with the real people in his life.

The majority of Christian college students using porn say porn negatively impacts their relationships because it isolates them from others.[16] And this isn't just because people use porn alone. Generally, the shame that results leads the user to deceive those closest to them. People lie about and hide their porn use. They view others as objects as a result of their porn use. And in their guilt and shame, they often isolate themselves from others during and after their porn use. It's not surprising that porn use harms relationships.

In an extensive study on how pornography use impacts relationship quality, dozens of national surveys were analyzed using thirty-one different measures. Porn was *never* shown to have a positive impact on relationships in thirty of the thirty-one measures.

One measure was inconclusive, namely, whether couples who watched more porn were less likely to *talk* about separation.[17] The fact that couples who watch porn might talk about separation less didn't change the reality that couples who watched porn were two to three times more likely to divorce than the couples who didn't watch it.[18] Porn is toxic for relationships, and the data overwhelmingly confirms this reality.

Ironically, porn offers a fake intimacy to fill the relational void it helps create. When someone feels rejected, porn can transport the viewer to a place where they are desired, pursued, and accepted. Being wanted by another in the fantasy of porn speaks deeply to a person's desire for significance, worth, and love. The lack of intimacy many people feel today can be filled temporarily by the fake intimacy of porn or a hookup.

Amanda, a collegiate campus minister, described how she saw isolation and loneliness impact the Christian women at her university. Amanda said, "When these women feel lonely and insecure, they are more susceptible to a hookup. The attention they get from guys makes them feel desired and special." During these moments of loneliness, these coeds must practice BRACE to focus on truth and break isolation.

Amanda continues, "When these women meditate on truth statements about who they are in Christ, it brings them back to reality. They're reminded of God's love for them. When they break isolation, their accountability can encourage them with truth. Fake intimacy loses its power when they take a few minutes to connect in true intimacy with God and others."

A recent study in the *Journal of Sex and Marital Therapy* reported a strong association between loneliness and pornography use. Put simply, if a person is chronically lonely, they're far more likely to use porn on a regular basis.[19] Still, it's hard to know which comes first, isolation or porn use, because porn and isolation feed one another. Porn leads to isolation and isolation leads to porn. No wonder those who use porn report more loneliness.[20] During their addiction, many porn users can't see how significantly porn isolates them from others, but after they've used it, their loneliness returns even stronger.

To combat isolation and porn use, it's important to develop authentic relationships. This is one of the reasons BRACE has proven to be such a powerful tool. The person who uses it regularly breaks isolation regularly. It fosters authentic relationships.

Noah and his friends jokingly called their Freedom Fight group Rat Park because of how instrumental the group was in helping them walk in freedom. They held each other accountable for practicing BRACE. They confessed their relapses and celebrated victories, including being honest and open about their struggle. They took time out of their lives when a member reached out for help. They practiced calling and following up too. And as a result, the group experienced a depth of relationship Noah had never had before. And this depth of relationship helped him overcome.

During Noah's junior year, he was at his fraternity party with some friends. At the end of the party, he walked a girl home to make sure she was safe. When they reached her apartment, she propositioned him. Noah said,

> Hooking up was my main struggle, so when she came on to me, my brain just shut off and I was rattled. Before Christ, this was my fantasy, but I love Jesus and am pursuing purity. I literally couldn't think of anything besides to just get out of there. So I just started walking away and was totally spiraling, honestly considering getting after it with this gorgeous girl.
>
> So out of training and practicing BRACE, I took out my phone and just started calling the guys from Rat Park. When I got one of the guys on the phone, he talked me off the ledge. I drove to his house and stayed the night so I wouldn't be alone.

Community gave Noah a place to go when he needed help. It helped him stay strong when he was weak.

When someone who's seeking freedom understands that isolation moves them toward acting out, they will recognize the need to move toward community. If they are going on a business trip by themselves, they see the need to make a plan to break isolation with some strategically placed phone calls. If they are going back home to a triggering environment, they plan to regularly break isolation by reaching out to their accountability group. A meetup over coffee or a simple two-minute call can be powerful weapons against the root of isolation.

Live in Reality

It is not enough to simply attend a small group or have an accountability partner. These relationships must be open and authentic. Lying, minimizing, or rationalizing behavior will kill authentic relationships and, over time, lead to more isolation. So the one in recovery must be honest and real instead of hiding the truth and creating a false reality.

Each person needs someone with whom they can share everything without fear of being shamed. Dr. Ted Roberts, who has helped men find freedom from porn for over thirty years, says, "You are only as sick as your secrets." The Bible tells us that confession starts the healing process. The apostle James writes, "Confess your sins to one another and pray for one another that you may be healed" (James 5:16). There must be a radical commitment to be honest with oneself, God, and at least one other person. There must be a radical commitment to taking off masks.

A sex addiction therapist told me about one of his clients, a middle-aged businessman with a porn addiction. Though the businessman was in a small group and met regularly with the therapist, he made little progress. The client could not go ten days without a relapse even after over a year of treatment.

One day the man finally confessed his secret fully. He had watched child pornography. The shame and self-hatred this secret brought him was unbearable. After receiving empathy and reassurance from his therapist, he also confessed to his small group. They showed him grace, though they did not condone his actions. The empathy he received from them helped lift his shame. He was able to receive God's forgiveness and forgive himself. This was the turning point in his recovery. If you want freedom, you must live in reality.

Taking off the mask and learning to be real doesn't come naturally to most people. It's easy for someone to put up barriers subconsciously and keep people at a distance. They isolate themselves from authentic relationships. Sometimes, because of trauma, people establish these barriers early in life. People who have experienced trauma often feel the need to protect themselves. Wounds become walls, which ultimately keep them away from an important source of healing—authentic relationships.[21]

Wearing a mask starts subtly. People hide who they are because they fear rejection. They keep things on the surface or pretend to be someone they're not. If their facade is rejected, the pain doesn't go as deep as it would if they were rejected after being real. This mentality keeps them in isolation. There is no intimacy without authenticity.

A small group with authenticity and acceptance becomes a place of healing. When someone is real and then accepted, the shame begins to fade. With authenticity and acceptance, the lies like, "If they really knew you, they wouldn't accept you," or "you can't be honest—you'll lose their respect" begin to fall apart. Take Steve Kuhn, for instance. In an article about wearing facades, he wrote:

> Sure, my friends may have enjoyed being with "good-Christian-Steve," my family may have been proud of "successful-family-man-Steve," and my wife may have loved "faithful-Steve-who-wasn't-cheating-on-her," but if any of those people got to know the *real* me, they'd reject me in a heartbeat. Or so I thought.
>
> The result, sadly, was that no matter how much anyone tried to love me, I knew they were only loving fake versions of me that didn't exist. The *real* me was hidden away where no love could ever reach it, parched with a loneliness that was never being quenched.[22]

A breakthrough occurs when the porn addict finds that they are loved and accepted, and that the others in their community want them to find recovery. In other words, they discover the truth, and a key aspect of spiritual warfare is replacing lies with the truth. As Paul wrote, "We use God's mighty weapons... to knock down the strongholds of human reasoning and to destroy false arguments" (2 Corinthians 10:4 NLT).

If we are going to live in reality, to take off our masks, to expose the lies and experience the truth, we must cultivate authentic relationships. A small group enables people to become the true version of themselves. Addiction counselor Michael Dye said,

> All of these barriers people build support the same belief: something bad will happen if you drop your guard and become vulnerable by trusting others and God. Jesus said, "You will know the truth and the truth will set you free."[23]

When people wear masks, it distorts who God made them to be. God loves it when we are real and when truth defines who we are. David describes God as "delight(ing) in truth in the inward being" (Psalm 51:6). When someone commits to authentically live their walk with God, their relationships and their recovery all deepen because they are based on truth. God delights in it. Learning to be real with a small group or close friend is an essential step to breaking free and to being the person God created them to be. And once freedom is gained, it can be shared with others.

Authentic Living Means Authentic Giving

Jesus said, "It is more blessed to give than to receive" (Acts 20:35). Just *living* in authentic community isn't the goal. The goal is *giving* in authentic community. When reflecting on the key factors for a successful recovery, Dr. Patrick Carnes said, "Service to others is how things get better."[24] Those who show up to a recovery group intent on helping others in their recovery will go further faster in their own journey toward healing.

Addiction turns a person inward. The addict becomes self-focused. Their behavior is about them—their cravings, their struggles, and even their progress. Being self-focused can lead to further isolation. But when a porn addict enters recovery and realizes the power of community, she'll want to help others find that community. This turn outward often helps boost her own recovery too.

God wants us to shift our focus off of ourselves and onto Him and others. When Jesus defined greatness, He defined it in terms of serving others. He said, "Whoever wishes to become great among you shall be your servant; and whoever wishes to be first among you shall be slave of all" (Mark 10:43-44). This is another reason authentic community is so important. It gives you the chance to serve others in their recovery.

The New Testament gives fifty-nine commands about how we must relate to one another. We are commanded, among other things, to love, serve, encourage, pray for, spur on, honor, accept, not lie to, and confess to one another. And when an authentic recovery group embodies these qualities, it becomes a place of healing.

I recently saw this in one of my groups. In the beginning, Ben was the only member who regularly called to check on the rest of the men. He prayed for them. He encouraged them in their progress or when they confessed or were vulnerable. By the end, though, Ben had influenced the group. They were each more others-focused also. Ben found freedom before the rest, and his others-centeredness helped propel his progress. His servant mindset helped his recovery and lifted the quality of the whole group. He was definitely more blessed by giving.

We have been blessed by God so we can bless others. The Bible says God "comforts us in all our affliction, so that we may be able to comfort those who are in any affliction with the comfort with which we ourselves are comforted by God" (1 Corinthians 1:3-4). God gives freedom so we can help others find freedom too. Those who embrace this vision early will see it enhance their recovery and bring freedom to others.

The root of isolation is addressed head-on by forging authentic relationships. Growing in true intimacy will help them outgrow the fake intimacy of porn, hooking up, or fantasy. To outgrow porn, a person must deepen their relationships with God and others. "The opposite of addiction isn't sobriety, it's connection."

Action Steps Summary

- Confess to a trusted friend or accountability partner.
- Break isolation and join a small group.
- Surrender your life to Christ and pursue a relationship with Him.*
- Pursue intimacy with others in authentic relationships.
- Commit to being a giver in your relationships.

*(see appendix for related resources)

12

Negative Emotions

After his third relapse in a month, Rob was distraught as he sat across from his accountability partner. Though Rob was motivated to end his addiction, he still made little progress. He wanted to marry the woman he was dating, but his group leader encouraged him to establish six months of sobriety before he got engaged. Rob knew he couldn't bring his addiction into his marriage. Still, he couldn't seem to shake off his porn habit.

Even though he joined a recovery group and had strong boundaries for his triggers, Rob continued to struggle. He explained his most recent relapse to his group as an "intense urge that hit him out of nowhere." As he walked through his crash report, Rob realized each recent relapse was a response to stress. For the first time, Rob began to understand that he had emotional triggers.

Rob used porn to medicate his negative feelings. He started checking in daily with his accountability partner, which enabled him to process his emotions instead of numbing them. Emotional triggers are challenging because they are invisible and easy to miss. Identifying and diffusing emotional triggers is essential for freedom, and Rob couldn't find that freedom until he learned to identify his own.

Addiction researcher Maia Szalavitz wrote, "In order to develop an addiction, you have to repeatedly take the drug for emotional relief to the point where it feels as though you can't live without it… Until your brain learns that the drug is critical to your emotional stability, addiction cannot be established."[1]

Pornography is a powerful drug. Few drugs can be binged on for hours at a time like porn, which creates massive amounts of dopamine in the brain. Dr. Michael Barta, who specializes in treating porn and sex addiction with a neurobiological approach, says, "Pornography can produce up to ten times more dopamine in the brain as relational sex."[2] And like other drugs, porn is often used to medicate the pain and discomforts of life. When negative emotions trigger the brain's limbic system, people begin to seek relief from their negative feelings. This entire process usually happens subconsciously.

Negative emotions are a significant root of porn addiction that must be addressed for freedom to be realized. Outgrowing porn involves growing in self-awareness and learning to process feelings instead of medicating them. And when someone sexually acts out to medicate emotional pain instead of dealing with the unwanted emotions, their behavior stops being about sex and instead becomes about meeting the needs of the addicted brain.

Once this brain pathway of porn medication has been well-traveled in response to negative feelings, the emotions themselves become the trigger for use. When someone is feeling isolated, stressed, or angry, the emotion signals the brain to start craving the unwanted sexual behavior. Acting out gives a person the jolt of dopamine they crave. Pornography provides a powerful, albeit temporary, solution that takes away the discomfort.

Hannah, a high school student, showed how subtle this process can be:

> I got addicted to porn as a high school freshman. I looked like the good Christian girl… but that is not exactly what was going on. I could go two months and think I was free but then something would go

> bad and I would fall back into it as a nightly thing. I was so distressed over what I had done but then I would go do it again... I got down on myself, and in those moments is when I would run to pornography.[3]

For Hannah, porn was a medicating tool. She turned to it for comfort just like other people sometimes turn to comfort food.

A former pastor, John, said of his experience with porn:

> I learned at an early age to use porn to make myself feel good. After serving as a youth pastor for six years and a senior pastor for twenty years, this would come back to destroy my ministry. As I strained under the weight of pastoring a large church and trying to prioritize my marriage and four kids, I began using porn more and more to escape. I needed to get my fix—although it did not fix anything.[4]

The brain's chemicals bring relief, but when those chemicals are used to medicate negative feelings, the brain becomes addicted to those chemicals. The more someone uses porn to medicate their pain, the deeper their addiction to pornography will grow.

Self-Awareness and Emotional Intelligence

Self-awareness is the knowledge of one's own character, feelings, motives, and desires.[5] Not only is someone who is self-aware conscious of their emotions, but they also understand how those feelings influence their behavior. When it comes to unwanted sexual behavior, self-awareness allows a person to know their emotional triggers and how those triggers move them toward relapse.

Emotional intelligence, a subset of self-awareness, is the measure of someone's capacity to be aware of, control, and express their feelings, as well as the skill to effectively handle interpersonal relationships. Simply put, self-awareness allows us to see who we are. Emotional intelligence enables us to relate and adapt accordingly.

It is self-awareness when a man knows that after a long day of work, a loud and chaotic environment at home causes him stress. The ability to communicate those feelings and to navigate them effectively with his wife and kids is emotional intelligence.

Outgrowing porn requires deepening emotional intelligence by growing in self-awareness. Those who are not aware of their feelings will be blindsided by them. When someone grows in self-awareness, they see the patterns that, if continued, will lead to relapse. In this way, they will see a relapse coming from over a week away. It takes time and practice to develop self-awareness. Proverbs 14:8 says, "The wisdom of the prudent is to give thought to their ways" (NIV). Someone grows in emotional intelligence by evaluating their ways: they think about how their emotions influence their behavior and try to understand why they do certain things.

The Big Picture of Relapse

Restoration and relapse are two different ends of the spiritual and emotional health spectrum. Restoration is the place of lifestyle balance, trust in God, and emotional health. Relapse, on the other hand, is engaging in unwanted sexual behavior. Understanding what moves a person from restoration back toward relapse is an important step toward freedom.

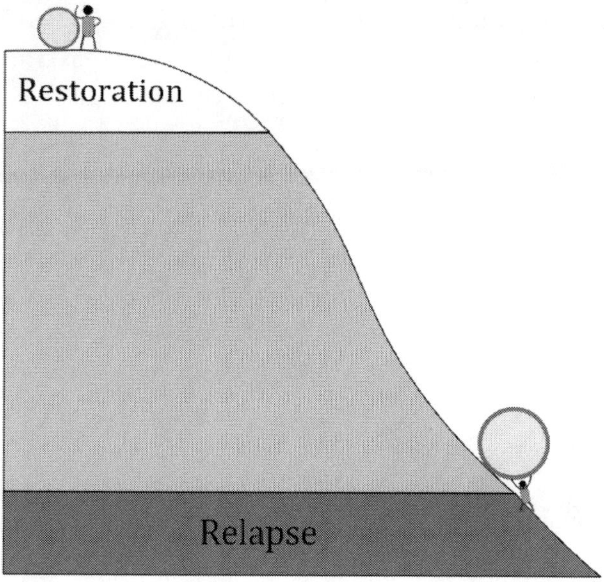

A relapse doesn't just happen. There are spiritual, emotional, and lifestyle dynamics involved in moving someone toward relapse. Someone who has good self-awareness can see how these different dynamics influence their behavior. When self-aware people notice they are sliding into relapse, they can take steps to return to restoration. People who are unaware of their emotions don't recognize that they are moving toward acting out until it is too late.

This process is like a boulder rolling down a hill. It is much easier to stop the boulder at the top of the hill than it is to stop a boulder after it has gained momentum. Those who are unaware of their emotions often get blindsided by them. And when the urge to medicate hits, it feels like a boulder they have no chance of stopping. The more self-aware a person is, the sooner they can recognize when the boulder is moving downhill and can take action to return to restoration.

People travel the road to relapse when they move from processing their emotions in a healthy way to medicating them with unhealthy fixes. This descent can also be a measure of trusting God. When a person is not trusting God, porn becomes medication for negative feelings. What a person trusts in is revealed by what they turn to in order to make them feel better.

I once attended a retreat for pastors and ministry leaders led by Christian Psychologist Dr. Gary Oliver. He said, "Unidentified or unprocessed emotions can set us up for all kinds of painful emotions that we don't know how to manage... so we seek out familiar 'friends' that give us comfort—that dull and numb the pain and help us feel good for a while."[6]

At the end of the session, Dr. Oliver gave everyone in attendance a pacifier. He explained that a pacifier temporarily soothes a baby when it's upset or hungry, but it doesn't meet their real need for nourishment. If a hungry baby only has a pacifier, their growth will be stunted. Porn is a pacifier that stunts spiritual and emotional growth by numbing the underlying pain. It keeps the real hunger from ever being addressed.

Knowing Your Emotions

What's the first step in recognizing when the boulder begins rolling? Naming emotions.

Many psychologists use the slogan, "If you can name it, you can tame it."[7] In other words, identifying emotions is the first step to processing them. This is where the acronym BLASSTED might be helpful. Each letter represents common negative feelings that trigger people to reach for their drug of choice. Those negative emotions are: Bored, Lonely, Anxious, Stressed, Self-doubting, Ticked-off, Exhausted, and Depressed.

These are normal emotions for people to experience, but they become triggers after someone repeatedly numbs them through porn use or unwanted sexual behavior. People must be aware of the emotions they regularly experience and how they react to them.

- *Boredom* is the state of feeling weary because someone is unoccupied or lacks interest in their current activity.[8]
- *Loneliness* is sadness because of a lack of friends or company.[9]
- *Anxiety* is a feeling of worry, nervousness, or unease, typically about an imminent event or something with an uncertain outcome.[10]
- *Stress* is a state of mental or emotional strain or tension resulting from adverse or very demanding circumstances.[11]
- *Self-doubt* is a lack of confidence related to failure, poor performance, rejection, or low self-worth.
- *Ticked-off* represents a state of anger because of conflict or frustrating circumstances.
- *Exhausted* means being physically or mentally depleted because of overwork or inadequate sleep.
- *Depressed* is being in a state of unhappiness or hopelessness.[12]

The less aware a person is of their feelings, the more power their emotions have over them. Porn users who aren't emotionally aware find themselves getting BLASSTED. They use sexual behavior to medicate their negative feelings. When people become more aware of their emotions, they begin to see how negative emotions cause their cravings to increase. In those cravings, they will either medicate their emotions or process them in a healthy way.

What's more, the emotions that have regularly led a person to use porn in the past can trigger them to use it in the future. If family conflict while growing up regularly resulted in medicating with porn, then when they get into an argument with their roommate or boyfriend, they may have that same urge to use.

Someone moves toward self-awareness by recognizing their tendency to isolate when they are BLASSTED. In that recognition, they refuse to isolate but instead seek connection with friends or family, or they just go to a public place.

Process Emotions; Don't Medicate Them

Learning to process the BLASSTED emotions will help disarm them as triggers. If someone escapes their unwanted sexual behavior but never learns to cope with their negative feelings, they will find something else to medicate with, like food, alcohol, or social media. Escaping the pain of negative feelings isn't the goal, freedom is. True freedom comes when we learn healthy ways to process and cope with pain, not new ways to ignore or medicate it.

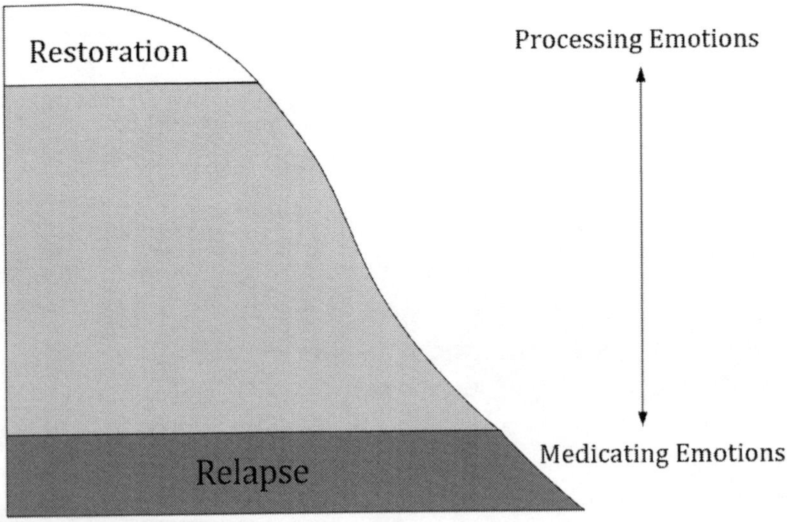

Negative emotions are similar to the check engine light in a car that informs the driver something needs their attention.

Ignoring the check engine light typically leads to bigger issues later. The same is true with your BLASSTED emotions. Left unchecked, these negative feelings can trigger a relapse.

Like a muscle, the ability to process one's emotions only develops when it is used regularly, and people who medicate their feelings instead of processing them undercut their own emotional development. Besides stunting a person's emotional development, medicating negative emotions can limit the ability to experience positive emotions.

Brené Brown says, "We can't selectively numb emotion. Numb the dark and you numb the light."[13] When people numb negative emotions, they also blunt their capacity to feel joy and love. Avoiding mental discomfort at any cost is a self-defeating strategy. When people medicate emotional pain, it ends up costing them more happiness, joy, and love than they may realize.[14]

King David, the author of many of the Psalms in the Bible, showed what it looks like to experience and express the full range of positive and negative feelings. He modeled how to process emotions with God. He confessed his sin, described his depression, expressed his loneliness, and declared his joy. David also wrote Psalms where he worshipped God for His greatness and thanked Him for His goodness.

David processed his anxiety with God, writing, "Search me, O God, and know my heart; try me and know my anxious thoughts; and see if there be any hurtful way in me, And lead me in the everlasting way" (Psalm 139:23-24, NASB). David was confused about the source of his anxiety, so he asked God to show him if it was connected to a deeper root. He invited God into his negative emotions to help him sort them out, and in doing so, he showed us the steps it takes to process emotions.

How to Effectively Process Your Emotions

If identifying and processing emotions can help users move away from porn and into healthier methods of emotional expression, how do we process them? Consider this step-by-step course of action.

1. Identify the emotion.

The first step a person takes in processing their emotions is to identify their emotions. In the above example from the Psalms, David identified his negative feeling as anxiety. When people use BLASSTED to regularly evaluate their emotions, it helps them start identifying their feelings more easily. Once their emotions are identified, people can take the next step.

2. Determine the source of the emotion.

When David was not clear about the source of his emotions, he asked for help. He asked God to help him determine if his anxiety was connected to something harmful within him, praying, "See if there is any hurtful way in me" (Psalm 139:23). We can do the same.

Sometimes negative feelings are connected to deeper issues, to hurtful ways in us. Our fear, depression, or anxiety might be related to identity struggles, shame issues, or trauma. When someone medicates their pain instead of examining what's under the negative feelings, they never discover the real issues. In this way, they trust their own coping mechanisms instead of trusting God for deeper healing.

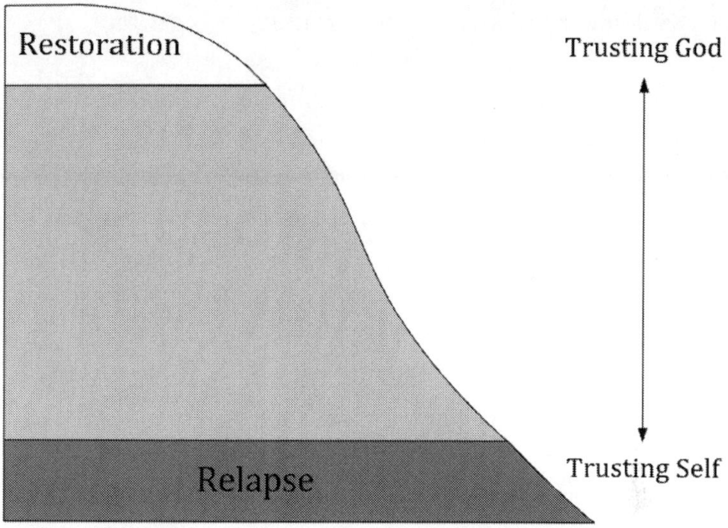

When people who are triggered turn to God, His Word, and His people instead of old coping behaviors, they are moving toward restoration. They cannot always determine the source of their BLASSTED emotions, but, like David, they can ask God for help. Doing this helps neutralize the emotion as a trigger.

3. Cast your cares on the Lord.

We are not supposed to handle our pain alone. When Paul was struggling, God encouraged him, "My grace is sufficient for you, for power is perfected in weakness." In response to God's support, Paul wrote, "Most gladly therefore I will rather boast about my weaknesses that the power of Christ may dwell in me… for when I am weak, then I am strong" (1 Corinthians 12:9-10). Paul was strong not in his own strength but in the power of Christ. However, he only received Jesus' strength by first admitting his weakness and need for Christ.

God invites us to come to Him with our cares, burdens, and issues. Psalm 55:22 says, "Cast your cares on the Lord and he will sustain you." We are commanded to cast, not carry, our cares. When we do, God promises to sustain us.

What could keep us from casting our cares on the Lord? Pride. Peter quotes the command to "cast your cares" on the Lord immediately after his exhortation to "humble yourselves under the mighty hand of God, that He may exalt you at the proper time" (1 Peter 5:6). It's the prideful person who medicates his cares instead of humbling himself and casting his worries on the Lord. God wants to carry our burdens.

4. Anticipate your emotions.

It takes emotional intelligence for someone to be able to anticipate their feelings. Emotional intelligence helps a person, who knows their emotions, effectively navigate the various situations they encounter in life. What are your emotional triggers? What situations or people set you up for negative emotions? When do you feel most vulnerable to painful or difficult emotions? When a person identifies their triggers, they can be proactive, adjust, and reach out for help.

One of the men I led in a small group recognized that self-doubt often triggered his porn use. Learning this enabled him to be proactive. One day, he had to work on a project with someone who intimidated him and caused him to doubt himself. He called his accountability partners beforehand and let them know, asking to be held accountable to report back at the end of the day. Simply articulating his vulnerability removed the power of the trigger and helped him avoid a relapse.

According to a Barna Group Survey, another prominent reason that people seek out porn use is boredom. This is especially true for younger single people.[15] When a person numbs their boredom with porn repeatedly, boredom becomes a trigger. Those people who identify boredom as a trigger can anticipate this emotion by having alternative activities ready.

When Jessica was triggered by boredom, she left her room or apartment to engage with people or to do an activity. She knew if she remained isolated, she would eventually turn to porn. She created a list of healthy responses to boredom—hanging out with friends, reading a book, exercising, or hiking. She always had something ready to do to make it easy for her to respond to her boredom in healthy ways.

5. Be aware of depleting your emotional tank.

Those who are self-aware know the things which deplete and refill their emotional tank. Emotional exhaustion brings people to a place where relapse feels inevitable. When someone goes from balance to running on empty, the resulting exhaustion can trigger a desire to medicate.

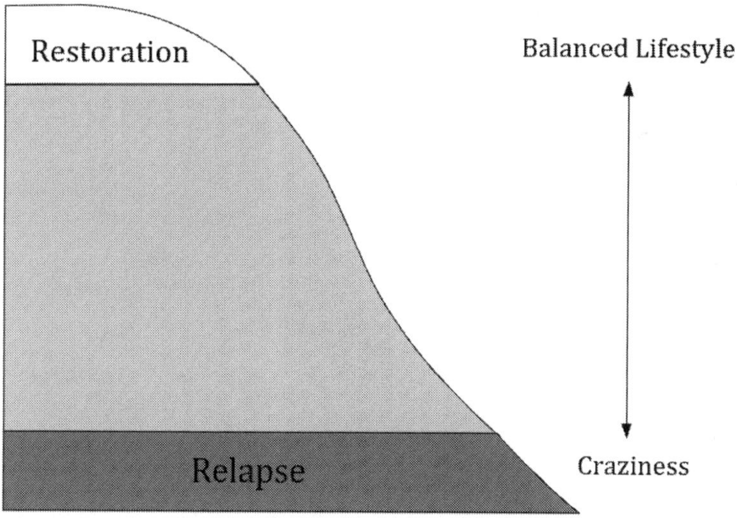

In the world of sex addiction, "craziness" refers to an out-of-control lifestyle. Craziness occurs when a person feels overwhelmed, out of balance, or has a loss of control. And prolonged seasons of craziness can deplete your emotional tank. Sex addiction expert Dr. Patrick Carnes described craziness as behavior that "first manifests itself as lapses in the routines that support self-maintenance."[16]

A person must identify the basic routines that, if missed, indicate they are moving toward craziness. These core routines could be a person's spiritual disciplines, exercise routines, sleep, or recovery group practices. When things start getting crazy, these are the first routines to go.

The men in my recovery group identified what those routines are for them. Aaron realized that when he started to skip his Bible reading, he was headed toward craziness and, therefore, toward relapse. If Ben started skipping workouts regularly, he recognized a move toward craziness. Marcus knew if he missed multiple check-ins, relapse was around the corner.

The lack of sleep and high stress of finals week often leads college students to relapse. The professional who packs their schedule with work and other responsibilities, but not adequate rest sets himself up for relapse. Each person must determine the routines that are refreshing, life-giving, and keep their life balanced.

People who are unaware of their emotions regularly head into craziness. The craziness of an unbalanced lifestyle will eventually lead to a relapse. When a person is aware of what a balanced lifestyle is for them, they can build routines that keep their emotional tank full.

6. Regularly process your emotions with others.

Evaluating emotions is helpful, but communicating that evaluation takes the processing of emotions to a deeper level. This is why regular check-ins with accountability are crucial. The most successful recovery groups have daily check-ins as a foundational practice. The check-in only takes a couple of minutes but is critical to learning how to evaluate and communicate feelings. It consists of a couple of questions and a zone check-in. What is a zone check-in?

Part of the check-in is evaluating which of three zones you might be in:

- *Recovery Zone*: This is a zone of restoration, where you are living out your priorities with lifestyle balance and healthy emotional processing. In this zone, you're trusting God and living life on His terms.
- *Danger Zone*: In this zone, you're forgetting priorities, which leads to craziness and exhaustion. You are triggered and vulnerable. If you stay in this zone too long, relapse becomes almost inevitable.
- *Relapse Zone*: In this zone, you have engaged in unwanted sexual behavior. You return to old coping behaviors to fix the problem. You trusted in your own coping mechanisms to numb your pain rather than turning to God and others for help.

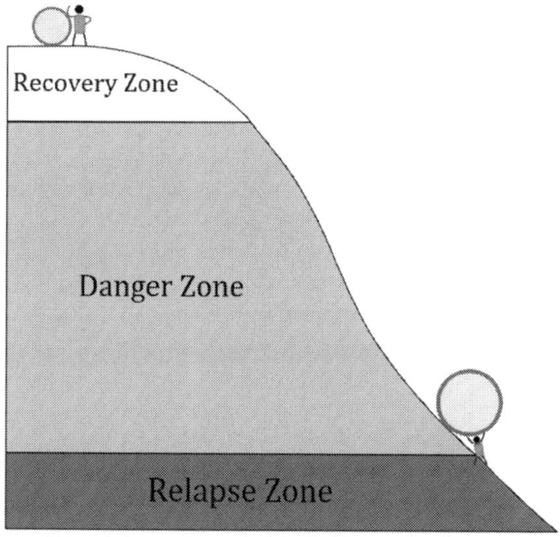

People who learn to detect early that they are moving down the zones can act to return to restoration. Those who have not learned to detect when they are moving down the scale often find themselves like the bottom figure in the diagram. The craving grows stronger while their strength to resist grows weaker.

One way to fully process your emotions with others is through regular check-ins. A person can check in with their accountability through a phone call, a text, or through the Freedom Fight app. Check-ins must be easy enough to do regularly. A check-in is a simple way to evaluate and communicate how people are doing, but it has other advantages. Psychologist Tasha Eurich says, "Evidence shows that the simple act of translating our emotions into language—versus simply experiencing them—can stop our brains from activating our… fight-or-flight command center, and this, in turn, helps us stay in control."[17]

One of the men I coach sent me this check-in text, "A socially filled day today. It was great, but my social stamina is a limited resource. I need to be proactive and aware this week, knowing that I will have a heightened desire to cope and isolate." This man is an introvert whose regular pattern was to get worn out by spending too much time with others. His exhaustion led him to isolate and numb out with media, which often resulted in porn use. In his text check-in that day, he identified the issue and what he needed to do to avoid a relapse. He developed this emotional intelligence through checking in over the last two years.

Text messages may work, but Dr. Ted Roberts, who has coached men for over thirty years, says there is something unique about verbally processing a check-in. Sharing verbally adds a different dynamic because verbally naming emotions helps diffuse them as a trigger. So in addition to sending text messages, I suggest making three check-in phone calls a week to an accountability partner.

What should that call look like? First, share which zone you are in. Then, name your emotions. Share what you're doing to avoid craziness and keep balance. The call should be short, just a couple of minutes, but it helps diffuse the BLASSTED triggers that lead to relapse. Those who walk in freedom don't medicate their negative feelings. Instead, they take the initiative to identify and process them.

To beat a porn addiction, a person must do the hard emotional work. Otherwise, in times of pain, craziness, or stress, they'll turn to porn as a form of medication. Pulling this root of a porn addiction happens by growing in emotional intelligence and self-awareness. This kind of growth results in deeper relationships with God and others. What's more, growing in this area allows us to begin work on digging up the next root of pornography addiction: Shame.

Action Steps Summary

- Commit to regular check-ins.
- Use BLASSTED to identify emotions.
- List out your emotional triggers.
- Process your emotions with God and others.
- Identify the self-care activities you need in your regular schedule.

13

Shame

Shame, it is a powerful and destructive emotion. It can cause people to end relationships, sink into depression, develop addictions, and even commit suicide.[1] Before shame can be defeated, it must be understood.

In her story, *The Prince and the Dragon,* Melinda Reinicke does a masterful job of portraying the shame a porn addict feels.

> There was once a great and noble King whose land was terrorized by a crafty dragon. Like a massive bird of prey, the scaly beast delighted in ravaging villages with his fiery breath. Hapless victims ran from their burning homes, only to be snatched into the dragon's jaws or talons. Those devoured instantly were deemed more fortunate than those carried back to the dragon's lair to be devoured at his leisure. The King led his sons and knights in many valiant battles against the dragon.
>
> Riding alone in the forest, one of the King's sons heard his name purred low and soft. In the shadows of the ferns and trees, curled among the boulders, lay the dragon. The creature's heavy-lidded eyes fastened on the prince, and the reptilian mouth stretched into a friendly smile.

"Don't be alarmed," said the dragon, as gray wisps of smoke rose lazily from his nostrils.

"I am not what your father thinks."

"What are you, then?" asked the prince, warily drawing his sword as he pulled in the reins to keep his fearful horse from bolting.

"I am pleasure," said the dragon.

"Ride on my back and you will experience more than you ever imagined. Come now. I have no harmful intentions. I seek a friend, someone to share flights with me. Have you never dreamed of flying? Never longed to soar in the clouds?"

Visions of soaring high above the forested hills drew the prince hesitantly from his horse. The dragon unfurled one great webbed wing to serve as a ramp to his ridged back. Between the spiny projections, the prince found a secure seat. Then the creature snapped his powerful wings twice and launched them into the sky. The prince's apprehension melted into awe and exhilaration.

From then on, he met the dragon often, but secretly, for how could he tell his father, brothers, or the knights that he had befriended the enemy? The prince felt separate from them all. Their concerns were no longer his concerns. Even when he wasn't with the dragon, he spent less time with those he loved and more time alone.

The skin on the prince's legs became calloused from gripping the ridged back of the dragon, and his hands grew rough and hardened. He began wearing gloves to hide the malady. After many nights of riding, he discovered scales growing on the backs of his hands as well. With dread, he realized his fate were he to continue, and so he resolved to return no more to the dragon.

But, after a fortnight, he again sought out the dragon, having been tormented with desire. And so it transpired many times over. No matter what his determination, the prince eventually found himself pulled back, as if by the cords of an invisible web. Silently, patiently, the dragon always waited.

One cold, moonless night their excursion became a foray against a sleeping village. Torching the thatched roofs with fiery blasts from his nostrils, the dragon roared with delight when the terrified victims fled from their burning homes. Swooping in, the serpent belched again and flames engulfed a cluster of screaming villages. The prince closed his eyes tightly in an attempt to shut out the carnage.

In the pre-dawn hours, when the prince crept back from his dragon trysts, the road outside his father's castle usually remained empty. But not tonight. Terrified refugees streamed into the protective walls of the castle. The prince attempted to slip through the crowd to close himself in his chambers, but some of the survivors stared and pointed toward him.

"He was there," one woman cried out, "I saw him on the back of the dragon."

Others nodded their heads in angry agreement. Horrified, the prince saw that his father, the King, was in the courtyard holding a bleeding child in his arms.

The King's face mirrored the agony of his people as his eyes found the prince's. The son fled, hoping to escape into the night, but the guards apprehended him as if he were a common thief. They brought him to the great hall where his father sat solemnly on the throne. The people on every side railed against the prince. "Banish him!" he heard one of his own brothers angrily cry out. "Burn him alive!" other voices shouted.

As the King rose from his throne, bloodstains from the wounded shone darkly on his royal robes. The crowd fell silent in expectation of his decree. The prince, who could not bear to look into his father's face, stared at the flagstones of the floor.

"Take off your gloves and your tunic," the King commanded.

The prince obeyed slowly, dreading to have his metamorphosis uncovered before the kingdom. Was his shame not already enough? He had hoped for a quick death without further humiliation. Sounds of revulsion rippled through the crowd at the sight of the prince's thick, scaled skin and the ridge growing along his spine.

The king strode toward his son, and the prince steeled himself, fully expecting a backhanded blow even though he had never been struck so by his father. Instead, his father embraced him and wept as he held him tightly. In shocked disbelief, the prince buried his face against his father's shoulder.

"Do you wish to be freed from the dragon, my son?"

The prince answered in despair, "I wished it many times, but there is no hope for me."

"Not alone," said the King. "You cannot win against the dragon alone."

"Father, I am no longer your son. I am half beast," sobbed the prince.

But his father replied, "My blood runs in your veins. My nobility has always been stamped deep within your soul."

With his face still hidden tearfully in his father's embrace, the prince heard the King instruct

> the crowd, "The dragon is crafty. Some fall victim to his wiles and some to his violence. There will be mercy for all who wish to be freed. Who else among you has ridden the dragon?"
>
> The prince lifted his head to see someone emerge from the crowd. To his amazement, he recognized an older brother, one who had been lauded throughout the kingdom for his onslaughts against the dragon in battle and for his many good deeds. Others came, some weeping, others hanging their heads in shame. The King embraced them all.
>
> "This is our most powerful weapon against the dragon," he announced. "Truth. No more hidden flights. Alone you cannot resist him."[2]

This story shows how shame is interwoven with the other roots of addiction. The prince's "rides on the dragon" led to isolation. The habit created callousness in the prince, who desperately wanted to quit but could not. Though the prince could not explain why, his addicted brain was hooked. In his shame, he kept his obsession a secret. The father gently reminded the prince that no one finds freedom on their own. The father called the prince out of the shadows and into the light of community, the only place freedom is found.

The Root of Shame

We have examined these drivers of pornography addiction: the sexualized society, the addicted brain, isolation, and negative emotions. The fifth root that must be addressed is shame. Many sex-addiction therapists believe shame is the strongest of all the drivers that lead people toward sexually acting out.

Mental health counselor Jay Stringer surveyed almost 4,000 men and women who sought professional help for sexual brokenness. He concluded, "Shame was the most consistent key driver of unwanted sexual behavior. Shame convinces us that we are unwanted, and we pursue behavior that confirms it. To find freedom, disarm the power of shame."[3] Shame is the most interconnected and influential of the roots of addiction. This is why I have devoted three chapters of this book to understanding it and how to defeat it.

Shame is different from guilt. Guilt says, "I've done bad," but shame says, "I am bad." At the core of shame is self-loathing and a sense of worthlessness. A person's shame declares some version of "I am not enough," "There is something wrong with me," "I am bad," or "I don't matter."[4] Shame researcher Brené Brown defines shame as "an intensely painful feeling or experience of believing we are flawed and therefore unworthy of acceptance and belonging."[5]

Guilt can be a healthy emotion when it shows a person their sin so that they can turn from it. Shame, however, makes people feel like they are unable to change because of an inherent personal flaw. Guilt is something people feel because they have *done* something bad. Shame is something they feel because they *are* bad.

Guilt can be good. Shame is toxic. Guilt allows people to see they need help, while shame makes them feel they don't deserve help. With guilt, a person can have the hope of a fresh start. With shame, there is hopelessness because the person is the problem. Guilt can be a springboard to an improved life. Shame is an anchor that keeps people stuck.

How Shame Connects with the Other Roots

Shame uniquely fuels a porn addiction. To appreciate the significant role shame plays in porn or sex addiction, a person must understand the interconnectedness that shame has with the other roots of addiction.

Sexualized Society

Shame fuels self-deception. Dr. Curt Thompson, the author of *Soul of Shame,* writes, "Shame has the effect of coaxing us into pretending that sin is not as bad as it seems; for if it really is that bad, and I have to face it, it would be too much and I fear I would be overwhelmed."[6] The self-deception fueled by shame undermines the pursuit of holiness. The person who rationalizes their porn use because of shame becomes an easy target for society's many temptations.

Addicted Brain

In previous chapters, we have looked at how the PFC of the brain can be hijacked, which diminishes the ability to say no. Shame also contributes to the PFC not operating effectively. When a person experiences shame, they find it nearly impossible to turn their attention to something beyond their immediate feelings. Research shows that shame activates the fear response in the brain, which means the emotional brain takes over while the logical brain (PFC) loses influence.[7] This increases the probability of a person making decisions based on emotions instead of reasoning.[8] And in that moment, it's easy to travel the porn pathway in search of relief.

Negative Emotions

Shame causes a disconnect between various functions of the mind. It limits emotional awareness, which sets the person up to medicate their emotions with porn. The cycle continues as watching porn feeds the shame.[9] The less aware people are of their negative emotions, the more likely they are to feel the need to medicate them.[10]

Dr. Curt Thompson explained, "So many of what we would term 'negative emotions' are actually rooted in shame. It is born out of a sense of 'there being something wrong' with me or of 'not being enough.' There is a sense of hopelessness and powerlessness to change. Shame is both feeding one's negative emotions while at the same time making the person less aware of them."[11] In this way, shame gives negative emotions greater power in a person's life than they would normally have. When this happens, the user will feel a greater pull to porn.

Isolation

When a person experiences shame, they tend to turn away from others because they fear being found out.[12] The natural result is isolation and disconnection.[13] The person who believes something is deeply wrong with them moves away from others. The person feeling shame often concludes that no one could ever want anything to do with them. Shame anticipates abandonment and simultaneously moves away from authenticity.[14] When shame leads people to start hiding who they are, their relational awareness lessens, which undermines relationships.[15] Abby shows what this can look like.

Abby is a Christian with a secret pornography habit. No one knows but her mentor. When she is around most people, she wants distance from them. She said, "I can only see myself as being intolerable to others, and I sense the impossibility that this feeling will ever end." She lies to her roommates and hides and keeps secrets.

Though Abby is often present physically, she is emotionally distant, not revealing who she really is. She is not vulnerable, so people respond in kind. They do not share with her because they do not know her. Abby feels the lack of connection and wonders why she doesn't have close friends. Shame leads to hiding, which leads to isolation. And in that isolation, she turns to her medication of choice—porn.

Trauma

As we'll see more in the trauma chapter, it is the shame messages delivered through trauma that makes trauma so destructive. In reality, all the roots of addiction are connected. They are woven together by shame. This constant reinforcement is how shame can move from just being a feeling to becoming an identity.

The Making of a Shame Identity

Shame is like an IV drip. Little by little, it feeds the negative emotions that trigger porn use, which, in turn, fuels the shame messages of worthlessness. And over the years, if that IV isn't interrupted, shame can become a person's identity. Part of breaking free from porn involves pulling the IV out and breaking free from shame.

Breaking free from shame requires an understanding of where this toxic emotion comes from. When a person identifies the source of their shame, they can believe the truth about their true identity instead. Five factors lead porn users to feel shame.

1. Lying to cover up porn use

The deceit an addict uses to cover up their behavior often increases their feelings of shame. Paul told his young disciple Timothy, "The goal of our instruction is love from a pure heart and a good conscience and a sincere faith." (1 Timothy 1:5). The aim of Paul's teaching was purity and integrity. Both of these qualities are undermined when the Christian uses porn and hides it. When someone violates their conscience and then lies about it, their shame is amplified.

2. Breaking commitments

Strugglers continually let themselves down when they break their commitment not to act out. They have promised God, themselves, and maybe even others that they would never look at porn again, yet they do! This constant failure brings deep-seated shame.

A performance mentality says a person is their performance. When their performance is repeated failure, then *they* are a failure. They start to believe this is who they are.

3. Immoral nature of pornography

There is a unique shame for the Christian who struggles with porn addiction. Being addicted to something is bad enough, but being addicted to something that violates biblical standards and their own morality often increases a person's shame. This is especially true for people who watch more deviant forms of porn. If a person finds themself aroused by pornography that goes against their values or even sexual preferences, their shame mounts. The self-disgust increases their shame.

One student I mentored told me the first time he watched a particular form of deviant pornography, he got physically sick, yet he was also aroused. This should come as no surprise. In his book *Your Brain on Porn,* Gary Wilson wrote, "Research shows that anxiety actually increases arousal, so dopamine rises sharply, especially in teens, when anticipating doing something forbidden."[16] Based on this reality, it is not surprising that a person would be aroused by porn that goes against their morals, values, or sexual preferences.

A person's fleshly mind is moldable and can be trained to be aroused sexually by any deviant form of sexuality. This is true even if someone is opposed to it based on their morals. The Bible describes the flesh as having "defiling passions" or "corrupt desires" (2 Peter 2:10). Someone's flesh can be corrupted so that it is aroused by repulsive images and practices. The corruptibility of a person's sexual appetite should not define them.

4. Feelings of condemnation

The word *devil* in the Bible means "false accuser," and his accusations bring condemnation and shame. And what is his goal? He wants the people of God to give up hope of ever getting free. He puts thoughts in their mind like, "You are worthless," "God is done with you," "You are never getting free from this," "There is something wrong with you," and "No one struggles like you do." And once these accusations are made, once the porn user adopts them, he can keep repeating them through negative self-talk.

Negative self-talk takes place when someone repeats the self-condemning messages of shame. But rather than rejecting us, God longs to restore us. In the book of Isaiah, the prophet wrote, "The Lord longs to be gracious to you, and therefore He waits on high to have compassion on you" (Isaiah 30:18).

Satan buries God's children in shame so they can't live in the fullness of the gospel, but Jesus died and was raised to life to offer forgiveness and a new life. A person needs to be aware of the lies of the enemy so he can replace negative self-talk with the promises of God and break a shame-based identity.

5. Trauma

For many people, a shame identity was born early in their life because of trauma. Through trauma, abuse, or dysfunction, shame messages have taken root.

Rob was a single man in his late thirties who wanted to get married. Anytime he got close with a woman, however, his anxiety increased significantly. The impact on his relationships was always the same. His anxiety made things tense, and the relationship unraveled. Rob concluded he was not good with relationships, and his shame about this failure remained until he got counseling. He then realized that his sexual abuse as a child was a major contributing factor. He had been abused by a close friend, so being close with anyone triggered his anxiety until his relationships fell apart.

Rob's anxiety was rooted in the shame, which was rooted in his abuse. Understanding the source of his shame helped him address it and live beyond the shadow of that shame. If a person doesn't follow shame to its source, they will only deal with its symptoms.

Knowing these sources of shame should enable the porn user to reject the shame messages. None of these sources of shame are because a person is worthless and hated by God. The cliché is true: God loves the sinner but hates their sin. Simply put, porn addiction is shameful, *but* the child of God is not. They are not defined by their addiction. The enemy wants to leverage shame to keep followers of Jesus from living out of their identity in Christ. If a person can't separate their identity from their addiction, they will struggle to find freedom and to live in the fullness of who they are in Christ.

Identity Shapes Habits

An addiction is almost impossible to break when a shame identity has taken root. To fully understand the destructive nature of a shame identity, it's important to remember the role of identity in behavior.

Behavioral expert James Clear teaches about the significant connection between identity and behavior. In his book *Atomic Habits,* Clear wrote, "Your behaviors are usually a reflection of your identity. What you do is an indication of the type of person you believe that you are, either consciously or subconsciously." He continued, "Research has shown that once a person believes in a particular aspect of their identity, they are more likely to act in alignment with that belief."[17] He explained how this happens: "When you have repeated a story to yourself for years, it is easy to slide into these mental grooves and accept them as a fact. In time, you begin to resist certain actions because 'that's not who I am.'"[18]

This reality underscores why the Bible warns people to be careful about every thought that comes into their minds. Thoughts change people and eventually shape identities. Identities then drive behavior. Clear says, "The more deeply a thought or action is tied to your identity, the more difficult it is to change it."[19] Shame ensures that porn use is tied to the person's identity by condemning them as worthless and sick. Shame makes a person believe *they* are their addiction.

When a shame identity has taken root, it is not uncommon for addicts to self-sabotage their recovery when they are making progress. When they are doing well, they think, "I don't deserve this," or "Who am I kidding—I'm never going to be able to break free." They relapse because it reflects who they really think they are. This is maddening to the addict and their loved ones, but shame keeps them tied to their old identity. Shame leads them to self-sabotage.[20]

Bekah, a college senior, discovered porn online in fifth grade and struggled to stop watching it ever since. She felt bad and knew it was wrong but was unable to resist the unlimited access to porn in high school and college. When she had a purity streak, she reminded herself, "I'm a porn addict and will never be free of this," or "If the people around me knew I was addicted to porn, they would run." Eventually, Bekah returned to porn. It wasn't until her shame identity was exposed and dealt with that freedom became possible for her. Bekah's identity determined her behavior.

I know men who have been seeking freedom for years, but their shame identity has taken root so deeply that they don't believe freedom is possible. Who we think we are profoundly impacts our behavior. A porn addiction is not just a *sin* problem or a *brain* problem, it's also an *identity* and *shame* problem.

In addition to shaping identity, shame keeps a person from taking responsibility. Shame, by nature, refuses to admit the truth. Shame is a type of justification where someone deflects responsibility with thoughts like, "Of course I do bad things. I'm a bad person. I can't help it. It's not my fault." This keeps the person from ever truly owning their actions, which is essential for repentance and healing.

Shame Is Love Resistant

Many followers of Christ who are struggling with porn live with a deep sense of worthlessness. Of the practicing Christian college students who watched porn last year, 89% felt self-hatred because of their porn use.[21] When someone hates themselves, it's easy for them to assume God feels the same way about them. When someone doesn't love themselves, it is hard to receive love from God or from others.

Shame is a major barrier to God's people truly embracing their identity as beloved children of God. The shame-covered Christian understands God's love intellectually, but they don't truly believe it, and they often feel emotionally numb to the love and acceptance of God. When people only have head knowledge of the love of God, it is difficult for them to build their identity around this truth. When God's love doesn't shape a believer's identity, they start looking for identity in other places.

In Luke 15, Jesus illustrates how God radically loves people even in the midst of their shameful choices. By way of parable, Jesus shares the story of a son who asks his father for his inheritance. When the son received the money, he moved away, eventually wasting all of the money on prostitutes and wild living. As a result, he lost everything and ended up homeless.

When he had to live in an actual pigpen, the son finally came to his senses.

The son felt great shame and planned to return home and do the unthinkable: ask his father to allow him to be nothing more than a servant. As soon as the Father saw his son walking back home, he ran to him. Talbot Theology Professor Matt Williams says, "In the first century a Middle Eastern man never—never—ran. If he were to run, he would have to hitch up his tunic so he would not trip. If he did this, it would show his bare legs. In that culture, it was humiliating and shameful for a man to show his bare legs."[22]

The father endured his own shame to take away his son's shame. And to be received by the father would mean to be received by the family and community. The father embraced his son, gave him a robe, handed him a ring, and threw a huge homecoming party for him. The father didn't ask for an explanation or demand answers for his son's failure. Instead, he simply celebrated his child. He never stopped loving his son even when he was far off.

God is ready to welcome the child who has strayed from Him. We are deeply valued and loved by God. Though we may have been far off because of our shameful lifestyle choices, the Lord longs to be gracious to us and welcome us back. God's love, not our shame, should shape our identity.

God has proclaimed His love for us. Romans 5:8 says, "But God demonstrates his own love for us in this: While we were still sinners, Christ died for us." God's Word must define reality for us—not our feelings, shame, or the enemy's accusations. But how do we make that a reality? Let's take a look.

Summary of Action Steps

- Identify shame in your life.
- Identify the sources of that shame.
- Identify how shame has impacted your ability to receive God's love.
- Pray that you can know and receive God's love for you.

14

Identity Defeats Shame

Brendan and Julia had two young children and lived in Cincinnati. They were active in their church for several years, but recently, they had stepped back from leadership. Julia wanted to continue serving the church, but Brendan didn't. He pulled back not just from church, but also from Julia. Life had gotten busy, he said, but that wasn't the whole truth. There was another reason his relationships were changing: his shame was driving him into hiding.

Brendan's porn habit had re-emerged. He never really quit, but he had cut back when he first installed filters and found accountability. He genuinely wanted freedom but couldn't fully find it. When Brendan confessed his porn use, he never felt the full weight of shame lift. But in reality, he never shared the whole truth about it. He never told anyone he was watching violent porn or, at times, even rape porn. Because Brendan could not bring himself to confess the whole of his sin, he struggled in silence. His daily porn habit had returned.

Over time, Brendan's appetite for violent porn grew, and he now desired to experience violent sex in real life. He didn't want to hurt anyone, at least not yet. Still, he was beginning to develop a craving to mix abusive speech and actions with sex. The seeds he started sowing as a teenager were bearing fruit. He began looking up escorts so he could act out his violent sexual compulsions.

Brendan was exhilarated by his thoughts of violence, but at the same time, he was disgusted with himself. How did he get to this point? He felt desperate and joined a men's group. Why wouldn't God answer his prayer to take these desires away? Brendan shared his struggle with porn in general terms with his new group. All the guys agreed that porn was a fight they were losing.

Brendan knew he needed to confess his violent porn compulsion and explain how it led him to want to cheat on his wife. Still, he could not bring himself to do it. He was too ashamed. In fact, he was convinced God was disgusted with *him* and not just with his sin.

Brendan's shame came from all directions: from lying and deceiving Julia, from going against his biblical values, from his desire for violent porn, and from his guilt that people viewed him as a spiritual leader. How could he ever admit he was considering prostitutes?

I am a sick pervert, he thought. *If my family and friends knew who I really was, they would be horrified and want nothing to do with me.* The overwhelming shame made Brendan feel terrible. His brain had been trained to seek emotional relief through porn, so he did. Brendan's shame drove him deeper into porn use to find relief. He believed he could never let this secret out.

A few months later at Brendan's small group, his leader shared his own porn story. He shared about the type of deviant porn he was watching. Brendan was shocked. This man was a respected leader in the church, yet he was willing to be vulnerable. His leader spoke of details that Brendan could never bring himself to share. It was incredibly relieving for Brendan to know he wasn't alone. This encouraged Brendan, but he still wasn't ready to deal with his shame. The risk was too great.

Understanding Shame

According to shame researcher Brené Brown, "When we feel shame, we are most likely to protect ourselves by blaming someone or something else, rationalizing, or hiding out." Brown continues, "In my research, I found that shame corrodes the very part of us that believes we can change and do better."[1] Unaddressed shame keeps people rationalizing instead of repenting. It keeps them feeling hopeless instead of believing freedom is possible. Shame controls the porn user.

Shame is a key reason that less than 10% of Christian men using porn truly seek help.[2] The fear of being exposed and considered inadequate keeps many Christian porn users denying and minimizing their problem. Shame can't be completely eliminated, but it can be consistently defeated and disempowered with the right approach. Addressing it requires adopting a lifestyle of vulnerability and living out of an identity in Christ.

Dr. Curt Thompson, author of *Soul of Shame*, emphasizes the importance of understanding shame for the person who wants to break free from it. He writes, "The more unaware a person is to the shame they carry, the more influence it has on their lives and emotions."[3] Shame in someone's life is fed in many ways. It's like a river fed by many tributaries.

The Mississippi River starts as a trickle flowing out of Lake Itasca in Minnesota. From a trickle, it's fed by other tributaries and turns into a river that pours more than one million cubic feet of water into the Gulf of Mexico every two seconds.[4] In the same way, multiple tributaries are feeding the river of shame. The diagram below captures this idea. The river of shame carries lies that form strongholds in people's minds. Recognizing where these lies come from is the first step to defeating them.

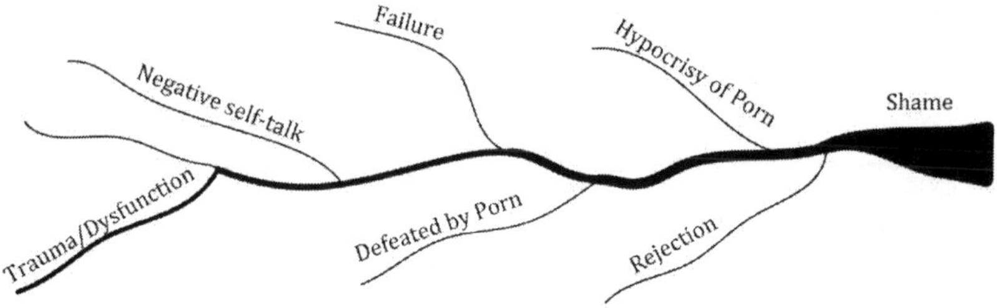

- *Negative self-talk*: We repeat and replay the shame messages, which are often delivered by the other tributaries. When we reinforce the enemy's accusations about us—*I am a failure; I can never overcome porn; I disgust God*—we come to believe them.
- *Failure*: Everyone fails at something, but when performance is a source of worth and identity, failure adds to the roar of shame. For many Christians, a failure or setback significantly feeds their river of shame.
- *Hypocrisy of Porn*: Lying and deceiving to hide a porn habit adds to the shame of being a fake. When someone violates their moral standards and enjoys it, shame multiplies. For the Christian with strong biblical standards for integrity, the hypocrisy of porn can be crushing.
- *Rejection*: Everyone faces rejection, but when our worth comes from others' opinions, rejection delivers more shame than it would otherwise.
- *Defeated by Porn*: Repeated failure to stop using porn adds to an identity of being a failure. With every stumble of using porn, this message is delivered and shame grows.

- *Trauma/dysfunction*: Traumatic events, abuse, or a dysfunctional environment can deliver powerful shame messages that shape a person's deeply held core beliefs about themselves.

Brené Brown defines shame as "the intensely painful feeling or experience of believing that we are flawed and therefore unworthy of love and belonging—something we've experienced, done, or failed to do makes us unworthy of connection."[5] The shame river delivers different forms of the message: "I'm not enough, therefore I'm unworthy of love."

Shame experts say that to defeat shame, a person must be vulnerable. They must be vulnerable about their trauma, negative self-talk, and their feelings of hypocrisy, defeat, rejection, and failure. Vulnerability requires courage. Courage requires worthiness.[6] When a person feels worthy, they have the courage to be vulnerable.[7] Followers of Christ have the ultimate source of worthiness, which comes from Christ Himself.

A Worth That Transcends Shame

The world says a person's worthiness comes from their performance and the opinions of others. If they have "success" and others think highly of them, the world declares that they have worth.

But the Scriptures show that every person has infinite worth and value because they were made in the image of God. God said, "Let us make man in our image, after our likeness... so God created man in his own image, in the image of God he created him; male and female he created them" (Genesis 1:26-27). Each of us, regardless of background, performance, or the opinions of others, have dignity and value because we reflect the image of our Creator.

As followers of Christ, we have the staggering privilege of having the worthiness of Christ credited to us. To fully appreciate this, we must understand that God requires perfection to go to heaven. The Bible is clear—only perfect and holy people make it to heaven. But this is obviously a problem. No one is perfect. No one is holy.

In the Sermon on the Mount (Matthew 5-7), Jesus told His followers that anger was equivalent to murder. He then said lusting was equivalent to adultery. Jesus had a perfect standard of what is considered holy. It's not just our actions, but it is the sin in our hearts. He said, "You therefore must be perfect, as your heavenly Father is perfect" (Matthew 5:48). How is it possible to be perfect like God?

Everyone knows that no human is perfect, but not everyone knows that God provided people perfection through Christ. God, because of His love, sent His son Jesus Christ, who lived a perfect and righteous life. Jesus died on the cross and paid the sin debt we owed because "the wages of sin is death" (Romans 6:23). God did this so He could make the greatest offer ever made—the great exchange.

The Bible says, "God made Him (Jesus) who had no sin to be sin for us, so that in Him we might become the righteousness of God" (2 Corinthians 5:21). God offers to take our sin, even our pornography addiction, and put it on Jesus. And, in exchange, God credits us with the perfect righteousness of Christ. As a result, God sees those who have placed their faith in Christ as perfectly worthy! Indeed ... the great exchange!

Paul says that salvation is "credited as righteousness" (Romans 4:5). The Bible uses the accounting term "credit" to describe what takes place. It's the same idea when the parents of a college student pay their student's tuition by crediting the student's account with money. The parents meet the financial standard of the school on behalf of the child.

In a similar way, God credits us with the righteousness of Christ when we trust Him as Savior and Lord. God went through immeasurable lengths to make the way to heaven possible. Christ is the only person who met God's perfect standard, and God credits His righteousness to all who trust in Him. Christ lived the life we could never live and then He paid the debt we could never pay.

The Bible tells us it's not enough to know or even believe this intellectually. Each person must turn from their sin and from trusting in their own works and put their trust in Christ. When a person trusts Christ, they enter into a relationship with God. When God looks at a person who receives His offer, He sees them as His child, perfectly loved and perfectly worthy because they are covered in the perfect righteousness of Christ.

When a person makes the great exchange, not only do they receive the righteousness of God, but they also receive the full identity of a child of God. When we talk in terms of salvation, we typically only speak of having our sins forgiven and getting into heaven. These are incredible gifts of God's grace, but He has given so much more.

The Bible refers to those who receive His forgiveness and righteousness as being "in Christ." Being in Christ means that what is true of Christ and His standing before God is true of all who follow Him. What are those truths? Here are a few:

- I am holy and blameless before God (Ephesians 1:4).
- I am a new creation (2 Corinthians 5:17).
- I am a temple of the Holy Spirit (1 Corinthians 6:19).
- I am beloved of God (Colossians 3:12).
- I have obtained an inheritance (Ephesians 1:11).
- I have bold access to God (Ephesians 3:12).
- I have everlasting life (John 5:24).

- I am more than a conqueror (Romans 8:37).
- I have no condemnation before God (Romans 8:1).
- I have victory over sin (Romans 6:10-13).

These truths shape our new identity. They become the new source of our significance and worth. They remind us, as Paul wrote, that in Christ, we are "a new creation: The old has passed away; behold, the new has come!" (2 Corinthians 5:17). Receiving Christ means receiving a new identity and a new source of worthiness. It means becoming a new person. Old things like where we looked for our identity and worthiness pass away. New things now define us, like where our righteousness, significance, and worth come from.

The world tells us that we must achieve our worthiness, significance, and identity. The Bible makes it clear that Christians *receive* our worthiness, significance, and identity *from* Christ. So instead of basing our identity, significance, and worth on our performance, we base it on *His* performance. Instead of basing our identity, significance, and worth on other people's opinions, we base it on *God's* opinion.

It takes time to move from living out of the old identity based on performance and the opinion of others to living out our new identity in Christ. It is one thing to know and believe these truths intellectually, but it is another thing to experience this new identity daily. And as long as the Christ-follower struggles with porn, he'll move away from Christ as the source of his identity and toward a performance-based shame identity. And this is a fact the enemy of our souls knows full well.

The Spiritual Attack of Shame

Shame from porn is a destructive weapon Satan uses to keep God's children from experiencing the fullness of their identity in Christ. So to live out of your new identity in Christ, you must be ready to defeat shame through Spiritual warfare. In his letter to the Corinthians, Paul addressed spiritual warfare. He wrote:

> For though we walk in the flesh, we are not waging war according to the flesh. For the weapons of our warfare are not of the flesh but have divine power to destroy strongholds. We destroy arguments and every lofty opinion raised against the knowledge of God, and take every thought captive to obey Christ. (2 Corinthians 10:3-5)

The thoughts, opinions, and arguments of the enemy are lies that, when believed, form strongholds. These strongholds keep us from believing the gospel and understanding our new identity. God's truth cannot take root and bear fruit in a person's life until these strongholds are destroyed. But how do we destroy them? We use "weapons" that are "divinely powerful" to destroy the strongholds. These weapons include faith, prayer, and God's Word (Ephesians 6:10-20).

Pornography is a weapon in the hand of the enemy to keep God's children from the life God has for them in Christ. Let's look at the shame river through the lens of spiritual warfare.

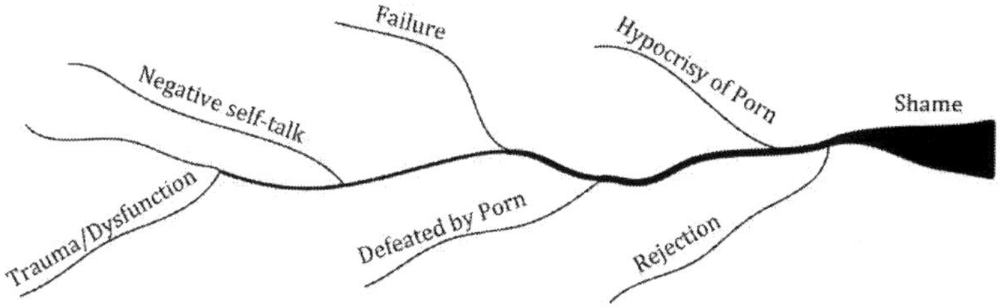

All of these tributaries are delivering different forms of the lies "I am not enough" or "I am not worth loving." Over time, these shame messages form strongholds in the mind of God's children, overshadowing their experience of the truths of the gospel.

We must fight with spiritual weapons, weapons like prayer. Paul prays that we can come to know "what are the riches of His glorious inheritance" toward us (Ephesians 1:18). Paul knows we are in a battle and we have an enemy that distracts us from the spiritual riches we have in Christ. He prays that we will know the truth of God's Word, which is an essential weapon against the lies of the enemy. Through the "shame tributaries," our enemy is delivering his message repeatedly in different forms and in different ways. His goal is to keep us from fully believing what God says about us and our new identity.

Making Thoughts Obey Christ

Paul concludes his instruction on spiritual warfare with, "Take every thought captive to obey Christ" (2 Corinthians 10:5). One way to make this practical is to record your negative self-talk.

In his book, *Treating Pornography Addiction*, Dr. Kevin Skinner shares the impact of the false self-perception of one of his clients. "He had formed so many negative beliefs about himself that they fueled his relapses. His beliefs about himself had truly kept him trapped for many years." Shame feeds the negative emotions that often trigger the porn user to act out. Until the shame is uncovered and dealt with, this cycle will continue.

This man's negative self-talk kept him in a prison of his own making. He realized how trapped he was when he wrote down his negative thoughts so he could see for himself the messages that were controlling his life. Some of the thoughts he recorded were: "Nobody has problems like me. I deserve what I get since I'm not strong enough to quit on my own. Nobody will want me. I'm a horrible person."[8]

The negative talk typically reinforces how bad and hopeless people believe they are compared to others. Getting specific about negative self-talk allows people to evaluate each statement so they can identify the lies and remind themselves of the truth. These self-accusing beliefs are thoughts that must be taken captive and destroyed by the truth.

People must identify the lies they repeat to themselves, whether about the addiction, themselves, or God. They should start their own list of negative self-talk so they can become aware of it in their own life. Once they have identified their negative self-talk, they can replace these lies with the truth about their identity in Christ.

Mia, a teacher in Colorado, had God's truth statements ready to meditate on. When she remembered past hookups or her current struggle with porn, she meditated on the truth. The more she did this, the easier it was for her to distinguish between herself and her addiction. Her *addiction* was shameful. *She* was not. Mia prayed for God to take the lies away and for faith to believe the truth.

Her ability to identify a shame attack grew stronger with time. Instead of allowing those messages to flow through her mind, she took them captive. As the truth took root in her heart, the shame decreased and so did the desire to medicate the shame with porn. Certain realities didn't become clear until she started replacing the lies with God's truth. By faith, she allowed God's Word and not her failures to define her. Her faith was another powerful weapon against the enemy's attacks.

A person won't overcome shame by ignoring it. Overcoming shame begins by acknowledging it. The addiction is shameful, but the person is not. The struggler must take responsibility for their sin and repent, but not let their sin define them. More than anything, they must live in their new identity in Christ. Prayer, faith, and God's Word are powerful weapons that enable us to defeat shame and live out of our identity in Christ. How? Consider the four practices in the next section.

Putting It All Together

1. Renew our minds.

We have been commanded, "Do not be conformed to this world but be transformed by the renewing of your mind" (Romans 12:2). The world will try to move us into performance thinking and people-pleasing. God wants our identity rooted in Christ. This transformation happens by renewing our mind with God's truth, and we do this through reading, studying, memorizing, meditating, and listening to God's Word. Using BRACE is a powerful way to saturate our minds with God's Word in a moment of temptation.

2. Allow shame to remind us when we drift.

We are accepted in Christ, secure in Christ, and significant in Christ. Shame attacks these truths. Shame is like the grooved part of the highway on the side of the road. When we veer off the road, it lets us know when we are drifting from the truth. When a person feels shame, it can be an indicator that they have a wrong basis for their identity. It may indicate they are trying to achieve or earn their identity. This is an opportunity to acknowledge wrong thinking and embrace their identity in Christ by faith.

When a person is fearful of being honest about a failure or relapse, that is an indicator they may have slipped back into a pattern of pleasing people. When they recognize they are feeling shame, they should meditate on the truth of who they are in Christ. Instead of shame reinforcing a shame identity, it can be a reminder to renew their minds with God's truth.

When shame leads a person to shade the truth or manage their image, this should be a red flag that they need to stop and evaluate what is happening. It should point out a lie that needs to be exposed and replaced with the truth, and shame lets them know it is there. People must not run from feelings of shame but rather examine the lie behind it so they can renew their minds with the truth.

3. Live our new identity by faith.

Living out of our identity in Christ requires faith that we are who He says we are. When a person's identity is in Christ, they have nothing to prove, nothing to hide, and nothing to lose. Instead of being an image manager, they are free to be real. They become bold to share their faith. This is true freedom. They received Christ by faith and will need to continue to walk by faith to live out of their new identity.

According to Paul, this describes the Christian life: "We walk by faith not by sight" (2 Corinthians 5:7). When a person is tempted not to be vulnerable because they are afraid of looking weak, they must choose to be real. This takes faith.

4. Ask God for help.

The Bible promises, "If we ask anything according to His will… we know that we have the request" (1 John 5:14-15). We can be confident that living out of our identity in Christ is God's will for our life. Therefore, when we struggle to live in that identity, when shame creeps in, we can use it as a reminder to turn to prayer. When we meditate on His truth, we can ask for the faith to believe it despite our feelings.

Brendan's Freedom

Brendan's wife, Julia, discovered his porn secret before he cheated. Brendan was mortified. He was also relieved. His relief turned to brokenness and urgency as he saw how his sin affected his wife. Knowing his marriage and family hung in the balance, he finally got serious about recovery.

Understanding the toxicity of a shame identity and how to address it was significant for Brendan. He learned the importance of living out of an identity in Christ and how shame attacked it. He started memorizing truth from Bible verses each day. He recited these Biblical truths using BRACE when he was tempted.

He meditated on truths like, "The power of porn has been broken" (based on Romans 6:10-12) and "In Christ I am loved and fully pleasing to God" (Ephesians 1:4). These truths directly countered the lies and negative messages Brendan had identified. They helped him make an important distinction that led to true repentance and the realization that though his porn habit was disgusting, he was not. His sinful actions were a disappointment to God, but he was not. Brendan was broken over his sin, but he did not let it define him.

When Brendan felt tempted to avoid confession because of how it would impact his reputation, he recognized that he was looking to others for worthiness. He meditated on the truth that, in Christ, he was blameless and fully pleasing to God. He prayed that God would enable him to believe this. His practice of replacing negative thoughts with truth and praying about his worth in God took less than five minutes throughout the day. These became opportunities to renew his mind.

It didn't take a lot of time, but the frequency of repetition made all the difference. It allowed his identity in Christ to take root. Three years after Julia discovered Brendan's sin, their marriage was better than ever. When Brendan got equipped to defeat shame, it was a turning point in his recovery.

Brendan could not defeat shame until he more fully knew God's love. In the words of Paul, Brendan needed the "strength to comprehend with all the saints what is the breadth and length and height and depth, and to know the love of Christ that surpasses knowledge, that you may be filled with all the fullness of God" (Ephesians 3:18-19). *Comprehend* literally means "to lay hold of so as to make one's own," and once Brendan did, he was never the same.

Through shame, porn wages war against the soul by diminishing our experience of the love of God in our lives. It can be defeated when we learn to believe and live out of our identity in Christ. Aside from living out of our identity in Christ, there is another powerful weapon to dismantle shame: Vulnerability.

Action Steps

- Identify which tributaries are the biggest sources of shame for you.
- Make the great exchange.
- Meditate on who you are in Christ.*
- Replace negative self-talk with the truth. (Read Romans Chapter 8)
- Pray to be able to live out of your identity in Christ.

*(see appendix for related resources)

15

Vulnerability Defeats Shame

On April 23, 1910, Teddy Roosevelt stood on a platform to address over 3,000 people in Paris. This thirty-five-page speech was one of the greatest of his career and would come to be known as "The Man in the Arena" speech. The most famous portion reads:

> It is not the critic who counts; not the man who points out how the strong man stumbles, or where the doer of deeds could have done them better. The credit belongs to the man who is actually in the arena, whose face is marred by dust and sweat and blood; who strives valiantly; who errs, who comes short again and again, because there is no effort without error and shortcoming; but who does actually strive to do the deeds; who knows great enthusiasms, the great devotions; who spends himself in a worthy cause; who at the best knows in the end the triumph of high achievement, and who at the worst, if he fails, at least fails while daring greatly, so that his place shall never be with those cold and timid souls who neither know victory nor defeat.[1]

Roosevelt reminded the people that failure is not to be feared. In fact, greatness requires risk and vulnerability.

Vulnerability means being susceptible to being wounded or hurt, and it's required for more than just greatness.[2] Vulnerability is essential for finding freedom from porn. Why? Because it's essential for overcoming shame. As we looked at in the last chapter, living out of an identity in Christ is the first solution to shame. The second is vulnerability. Vulnerability involves being open and honest with those you trust about the shameful areas of your life.

Research shows that vulnerability brings healing from shame, including trauma-based shame. In a landmark study, psychology professor James Pennebaker examined survivors of rape and incest who did not talk to other people about their trauma. The research team concluded that *not* being vulnerable to another person about their rape or incest increased the shame beyond the original trauma.[3] The lack of vulnerability multiplied the shame in a person's life. Conversely, the research concluded, when people shared their trauma stories, they experienced healing. Those who were vulnerable and shared also showed a significant reduction in stress.[4]

Shame thrives when hidden in the dark but is defeated when brought into the light. This research supports the Alcoholics Anonymous' mantra that "you are only as sick as your secrets." This reality applies not just to shame caused by trauma, but to all secrets that carry shame with them.

Vulnerability is rooted in worthiness. Those who feel worthy of love and belonging are more vulnerable.[5] As we've already discussed, there is no greater worthiness than the worthiness imparted by Christ. When someone's identity rests securely in who they are in Christ, others' opinions and the fear of rejection have less influence over them. As a result, if they're rooted in their identity in Christ, they can be more courageous and authentic.

The Bible commands vulnerability when it instructs us to confess our sins to one another. Specifically, James wrote, "Therefore, confess your sins to one another and pray for one another, that you may be healed" (James 5:16). The word "heal" in the Greek means to cure or to make whole. The process of healing toward wholeness begins when we are vulnerable about our sin with one another. Often, the shame a person carries is the result of their own sin, but sometimes it results because they were sinned against. Either way, bringing the shame into the light is where healing is found.

The Rest of Brendan's Story

In the previous chapter, we learned about Brendan's struggle. He'd been moved by his small group leader's raw confession, but he wasn't ready to share his whole struggle until his wife discovered his porn habit. After Brendan was confronted though, this leader, Jacob, was the first person he called.

Brendan had never shared the entirety of his story with anyone. He felt a burden lift when he shared it with Jacob. He shared about his rape-porn addiction and how he'd begun to consider prostitutes. Brendan's anxiety and shame turned into relief when Jacob told him he could relate. Jacob shared his own feelings of hopelessness and regret and how so much of the shame vanished when he found the courage to talk about his own addiction. Brendan had convinced himself for so long that he could never tell anyone or they would reject him.

But instead of rejection and ridicule, Brendan received acceptance and encouragement, and in that, his shame began to lift. When he confessed his sin, Brendan began to understand the depth of sin in his own heart. It became real. Until he confessed the totality of his struggle, he always convinced himself that it wasn't that bad. After his confession, he began to come to grips with his own sinfulness and need for repentance. What's more, confession led to a deeper friendship with Jacob. Each man's commitment to honesty encouraged the other to be real.

Brendan wondered what enabled Jacob to be open and honest in the group, especially when no one else in the group was being vulnerable. Jacob shared how growing in his understanding of his identity in Christ fueled his vulnerability.

Jacob explained, "Before I started living out of my identity in Christ, it was hard for me to distinguish between me and my addiction to porn. Over time of feeding on God's truth, I could see that my sin was disgusting, but I was not. I am a child of the King deeply loved by God." Jacob shared how it shaped his perspective, "I realized I had sin that I needed help to overcome, but that my struggle did not define me."

Jacob described how believing that his worth comes from God's opinion and not man's changed him. He said, "I didn't fear the rejection of others like I used to. I still have fear, but I am able to be honest in our group because I trust those men and I care more about pleasing God than impressing them." Jacob's courage to be authentic is what impressed Brendan the most. Vulnerability not only brings healing, but it is attractive to others when someone is bold enough to be real about their sin.

Jacob began to mentor Brendan specifically in living out of his identity in Christ. They studied what the Bible says about a follower of Christ. Jacob taught Brendan how to meditate on God's Word. Jacob showed him how to identify his negative self-talk and replace it with truth statements from the Scripture he memorized. Over time, Brendan's vulnerability grew as he came to believe that his worth and significance came from God and not man.

The day came for Brendan to share about his pornography struggle with the rest of his small group. He was extremely nervous but also excited about how God could use his confession. He remembered the encouragement he received from Jacob's story. He knew a big part of his shame was the secret of rape porn and prostitutes. Brendan had shared his porn story before, but he never shared those details. This time he shared it all. Then he shared his darkest secret: He'd been sexually abused as a child.

The men in the group responded with encouragement. They were grateful for Brendan's openness. Their acceptance caused his shame to lessen still further. Brendan's vulnerability was a turning point for the group. The other men came out of hiding and started opening up in the coming weeks. Brendan's vulnerability defeated his shame.

Over the next year, Brendan experienced a depth of authenticity he never had before with the men in his group. He came to see that when you are fully known, you can be fully loved. When he pretended and hid who he really was, he couldn't be fully loved. Not only did hiding keep him stuck in shame, but it also kept him from this new depth of friendship.

This realization encouraged Brendan to be more open and vulnerable in other relationships. Instead of hiding behind a facade, he sought to be real. He also opened up in his relationship with Julia. This was the major reason their marriage was doing better than ever. He was fully known and fully loved by his wife for the first time. Their depth of intimacy mirrored their depth of vulnerability. Brendan's sin and shame had been costing him much more than he realized.

The Power of Vulnerability

The apostle Paul embraced vulnerability, and he tells us why. In 2 Corinthians 12:9, God reminded Paul, "My power is made perfect in weakness." So what did Paul conclude as a result? He wrote, "Therefore I will boast all the more gladly of my weaknesses, so that the power of Christ may rest upon me."

Paul didn't treat weakness as something to hide or deceive others about. He was happy to brag about his weaknesses. Vulnerability is the way to unleash the power of Christ in our lives. When we are vulnerable and admit our weaknesses, it will put us in a position to depend more fully on Christ. On the other hand, when we deceive ourselves, when we claim we are strong on our own, we forfeit the opportunity for the power of God to work in our lives.

Does vulnerability really unleash God's power to help overcome a porn struggle? The research indicates as much. In a survey of over 3,800 men and women, those who sought out others and shared their struggle and shame had 22% less porn usage than those who did not.[6] Sharing our weaknesses actually brings strength. We see God's power unleashed through vulnerability all the time.

Our campus ministry has a nine-week summer discipleship program to train college students to grow in their walk with God, their character, and leadership. We started a manhood and womanhood night each week, where we separated the group by gender and discussed issues of biblical sexuality, including pornography. We realized that if we are trying to make disciples of Jesus but not addressing these issues head-on, we have a hole in our discipleship.

On that night, some of the staff and student leaders share their porn stories and how they overcame addiction. For most of the students, it is the first time they've heard another person's porn story. It sets a tone of vulnerability that has proven to be life-changing. I interviewed three students to find out how it impacted them to hear others be vulnerable and to be vulnerable themselves. Here are some of the responses.

How did hearing someone else's porn story impact you?

> I was pretty surprised, but at the same time, it was captivating that someone would be so willing to share what I thought was the biggest secret for any girl. It helped me not feel alone or helpless as well as relieving the shame of it. (Jessica)

I was refreshed that I wasn't alone. It made it more comfortable for me to share my experiences. It gave me hope. (Ben)

It was a little awkward and uncomfortable, but I was honestly relieved. I had felt for some time that my porn use was a problem in my life but didn't think anyone else around me felt similarly. It was relieving to hear my feelings validated by someone else. Feeling the freedom to share my struggle was one of the biggest factors in moving me toward healing. (Lucas)

How did being vulnerable and sharing your porn story help you find freedom?

It took me being open with others to bring them into this vulnerable area of my life before I started experiencing healing and freedom. Being vulnerable with the girls in my group has removed a lot of the shame. It has led to us having a group with real sisterhood and trust between us. Without being real, it was too easy to keep parts of my addiction hidden. (Jessica)

Vulnerability was a major part of me deciding to fight. Before opening up, I was just stuck, defeated, and had given up. Sharing my struggle helped diffuse the negative feelings of shame and hopelessness so I could actually start moving toward a solution. (Ben)

I had never actually admitted to someone that I watched porn regularly or that I was feeling it was a problem. Until I verbalized it to someone else, it

> was easy to convince myself it's not a big deal and that I didn't need to take action, even though I knew I needed and wanted freedom from it. If I had never shared my story with others, I know I would have never found true freedom. (Lucas)

What was encouraging about the response you received from sharing your story?

> Sharing my secrets wasn't natural or easy, but it was relieving when the girls in my group let me know they could relate. (Jessica)
>
> I was shocked at how comfortable and supportive the guys in my group were when I shared my stuff. It was super encouraging. (Ben)
>
> When the guys I shared with told me they struggled with the same things, it was relieving and it gave me the courage to open up even more. (Lucas)

Time after time, we have seen how vulnerability defeats shame and starts the healing process. Shame thrives in a person's life when they think they're alone. But when someone shares and the person on the other side of the confession responds with empathy and understanding, shame dies.[7] In those moments of being accepted by others and released from shame, it becomes easier to believe and experience God's acceptance through Christ. Receiving God's love and acceptance defeats shame even more.

And here's a sometimes-overlooked truth: vulnerability about *anything* can make an impact. John O'Brien was an associate pastor at the Avenue Church in Delray Beach, Florida. He struggled with pornography. It was his lead pastor's vulnerability that gave him the courage to be honest about his sin and get help. The lead pastor didn't struggle with porn, but he was vulnerable about the struggles he did have.

John said, "My pastor was incredibly transparent about his ongoing struggles with anxiety. His willingness to live in the light modeled transparency and encouraged me to live in the light as well." John described how his pastor lived vulnerably:

> He gives regular examples from his daily life of how self-doubt, people-pleasing, and fear of man manifests itself. Then he applies God's Word to his struggle and weaves in his new identity and potential in Christ as the solution. He also models what it looks like to share his burdens with others.

His pastor's transparency led to John coming out of the shadows and getting help for his struggle with porn. John received grace and also the expectation of repentance and recovery leading to freedom. After finding freedom, John now leads groups of men in the church to freedom as well. Shame was defeated through vulnerability.

Vulnerability Takes Practice

A lifestyle of freedom requires a lifestyle of vulnerability. Shame researcher Brené Brown says, "Shame derives its power from being unspeakable. If we cultivate enough awareness about shame to name it and speak to it, we've basically cut it off at the knees."[8] When people share about shameful things in their past, it takes away their power as triggers. But how do we move into vulnerability as a lifestyle? Here are five ways to practice vulnerability in connection with a porn struggle.

1. Commit to live in reality.

Living in reality means not hiding who you are but being open and honest. It means being yourself and not focused on managing your image. When there is something you sense you want to hide, bring it to the light. Share it with others.

When you share with your accountability, you have a choice. Either keep it on the surface or be real. When I was in college, I realized that I was an image manager. So I made a goal. I committed to share a weakness, a failure, or confess a sin at least once a week. It wasn't natural at first, but it became more normal with practice. The benefits were significant, from my relationships, to my walk with God, to leadership effectiveness. My concern and accompanying anxiety about managing my image shrunk.

2. Ask the "why" question.

When you sense your identity or image being threatened, seek to understand the source. When you feel the need to manage your image, it's an opportunity to grow. If you feel the need to hide or pretend, ask why. If you have an unhealthy competitiveness toward others or you feel offended, evaluate the reasons. Instead of ignoring these thoughts and emotions, seize the opportunity to identify the wrong thinking and renew your mind. This is how a person grows.

We must realize when the old thinking of worldly significance challenges the new thinking of significance in Christ. We need to confess and ask God to change our thinking. We can meditate on truth statements of who we are in Christ. These moments are opportunities to renew our minds with God's truth while rooting out old thinking. If we want change, we have to take advantage of all the opportunities we are given to renew our minds throughout the day. Asking why helps us identify a wrong mindset and replace it with the truth.

3. Share your porn story.

Many sex addiction therapists have their clients write out their porn story chronologically from first exposure, to addiction, to its shame-causing elements, including any trauma connected to their story. It helps to write it out, but it is even more beneficial when they share it. Sharing their whole story with a trusted friend, mentor, or counselor is an important healing step.

When a person shares their porn story, it can open opportunities to share one's faith. It demonstrates the power of Jesus to change a life. Nate, a pastor who used to struggle with porn, regularly shares a summary of his porn story as part of his testimony. When sharing how Christ changed his life he includes, "I was looking for fulfillment in porn and got addicted. I had this secret that I didn't want anyone to know about, but Christ showed me how this was drawing me away from Him… now I am walking in freedom." In these general terms, a person can share their porn story more broadly. The more shameful aspects of a person's story should be reserved for a trusted small group or friend.

4. Join a small group.

Vulnerability requires community. Shame thrives in secrecy, so people must move toward others to experience freedom. This is why small groups are essential to recovery. When people share their whole story and are still accepted, they experience safety. The safety of a group translates over time into love, acceptance, and a strong sense of belonging. Being vulnerable is how we learn a greater understanding of unconditional love. Small groups are where vulnerability thrives and where shame is disempowered.

Emily is a twenty-five-year-old physician's assistant from Texas. She only had one friend she trusted when she began to seek freedom. She took the risk and shared her porn story. This friend became her accountability when she started our program. Over time, she grew in vulnerability and got a second accountability partner. These women formed her small group. After seven years of a significant addiction to porn, Emily has been porn free for over three years. She couldn't have done it without others.

5. Check-in regularly with an accountability partner.

Check-ins provide regular opportunities to evaluate struggles, emotions, and the negative self-talk so common when people hide in their shame. When you check-in, if you have sin to confess, confess it. If you feel shame, name it. In a matter of minutes, a person can evaluate and describe how they're feeling. A check-in brings everything into the light and makes space for healing.

A check-in might look like this. "I'm doing okay. I still feel shame from my porn binge last weekend and how I lied to cover it up. I was embarrassed to admit it. I'm mentally beating myself up about it." There is a significant difference in silently having a thought versus sharing it with someone else, even through a text. When an issue is shared, its power is diffused. Evaluating and communicating shame are non-negotiables to defeat it. Like anything else that is unnatural, you only grow in vulnerability through regular practice.

Restored After Shame

The apostle Peter denied Jesus three separate times only hours after he promised he would die for Him. On one of those occasions, Peter denied Jesus not to a Roman guard or religious leader, but to a servant girl who asked him if he was a follower of Jesus. Peter, overcome with shame, returned to the only trade he knew, fishing.

But after He rose from the dead, Jesus went to the place Peter was fishing and called to him from the shore. When Peter saw Jesus, he jumped in the water and started swimming toward Him. The other disciples rowed to shore. Not Peter. He dove in and swam. He risked looking foolish as he swam in his tunic to get to the shore. He was vulnerable. He wanted to be reunited with Jesus.

Peter's vulnerability was an expression of love and remorse. He wanted to get to the source of his healing and restoration as fast as he could. He wasn't worried about his image. That's vulnerability. As a result, Jesus restored Peter (John 21:15-17). After Jesus removed Peter's shame, Jesus made him a pillar in the church. Peter's vulnerability led to his restoration and service to the King.[9]

Failure did not disqualify Peter. In fact, Peter was more usable because he was humble rather than self-sufficient. And Peter's response teaches us a lesson: Even people who have committed the worst sins are still able to be used by God when they act in vulnerability. And though certain sins can disqualify a person from positions of leadership in the church (i.e., adultery), even the most sexually broken can be restored to fruitful service in the Kingdom.

I know many former pastors who have fallen, vulnerably repented, and are now serving the Kingdom by helping others break free from sexual sin. If you love Jesus, are repentant, and free, then you have a role to play, no matter what you've done in the past.

Shame is defeated by vulnerability. But if it's going to work, we need to be completely open. We need to vulnerably confess even our darkest sins. What's more, we need to be vulnerable about the final root of pornography addiction: Trauma.

Summary of Action Steps

- Memorize 2 Corinthians 12:9.
- Commit to live in reality by being open and honest.
- Ask God to help you live vulnerably and to be aware when you hide.
- Join a recovery group.
- Share your complete porn story with one trusted person.

16

Healing Trauma with Truth

Maggie was disgusted with her out-of-control porn habit. She was a Christian *and* addicted to porn. After years of hiding and trying to quit on her own, she finally confessed and got help. A breakthrough happened for Maggie when she learned to connect the dots of her porn use to her childhood trauma.

Maggie's father left her family when she was eight. He never talked to her again. Despite living in the same town, he didn't try to have a relationship with Maggie. As far as he was concerned, she might as well not have existed. The rejection was painful. Maggie wondered what was wrong with her that her own father wanted nothing to do with her.

The pleasure of porn became a place of comfort to numb her pain. It was also a place Maggie could go to feel wanted and desired by men to fill the void of being unwanted. By putting herself in the shoes of the actresses, she was desired. But it wasn't until she came to understand the source of her pain, and how she used porn to medicate it, that she found liberation.

As she understood how her pain led to porn, Maggie started to address the source of her shame by focusing on her identity in Christ and viewing God as her heavenly Father. He never left her. He always wanted to spend time with her. He was loving and faithful. And this helped, at least for a while.

For many porn addicts, making this connection between their trauma and their porn use is enough to bring lasting freedom. But for Maggie, there was another layer to her trauma.

It remained unaddressed until Maggie was willing to be vulnerable and share her secret. She was addicted to violent, abusive, and degrading pornography. She finally confessed it to her therapist, who told her that sometimes the genre of pornography a person is attracted to can reveal a deeper issue. After multiple sessions with the therapist, it was clear Maggie was drawn to the shame, abuse, and rejection that the actresses endured in porn. Why? These were the emotions Maggie first felt when her father abandoned her.

The abusive porn allowed Maggie to relive her trauma. Trauma reenactment is a phenomenon where trauma survivors seek to relive their trauma.[1] Psychologists report that reliving trauma can be a way for abuse victims to subconsciously control their trauma. It can be a way to understand and master the traumatic experience.[2] Many trauma survivors don't feel fully alive unless they repeatedly relive their trauma.[3] For Maggie, watching violent porn was a way she could control the pain of her trauma instead of letting her pain control her. Unfortunately, as Maggie discovered, porn provided short-term relief but, ultimately, only multiplied her problems.

In her struggle, Maggie had pulled back from God because she thought He was disgusted with her. She stopped reading her Bible and praying. She felt miserable attending church. But as Maggie began to understand trauma reenactment and how it connected to her porn habit, her shame decreased significantly. This gave her the courage to be honest about her struggle, not just with pornography, but also about her trauma, and bring others in.

Until Maggie identified the trauma that fed her porn habit, she was only dealing with the symptoms. As her shame subsided, Maggie started reading her Bible and praying again. Through counseling, personal growth, and being a part of a small group, Maggie began to experience true freedom.

Maggie was stuck in her addiction until she dealt with her trauma. And this is true for so many porn addicts. It is such a prevalent issue that it's the sixth root of porn addiction.

Revisiting the River of Shame

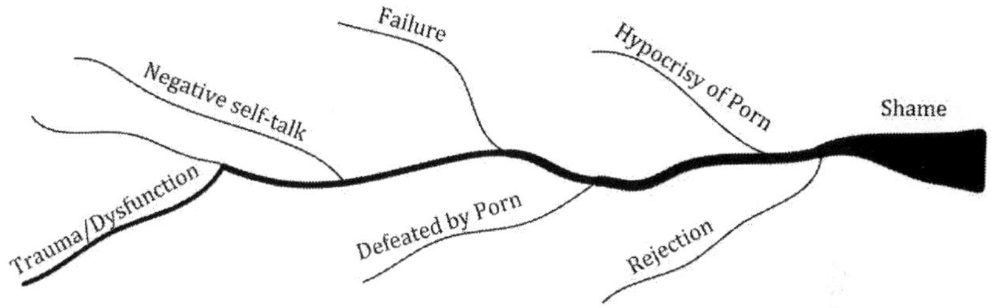

For many people, trauma becomes the first and most significant shame message in their life. This is why in the picture, I show Trauma/Dysfunction as the first and largest tributary of the river of Shame.

It's not just the pain of the traumatic event or a dysfunctional environment that weighs people down. There are messages and lies that a person takes to heart as a result of the trauma. Renown psychotherapist and Harvard professor Elvin Semrad declared, "The greatest source of a person's suffering are the lies they tell themselves."[4] What Professor Semrad observed is a biblical truth related to spiritual warfare. It should come as no surprise that trauma is another manifestation of spiritual warfare. As we have discussed, Satan's goal is to establish strongholds in a person's mind by implanting lies. Paul wrote:

> For though we walk in the flesh, we are not waging war according to the flesh. For the weapons of our warfare are not of the flesh but have divine power to destroy strongholds. We destroy arguments and every lofty opinion raised against the knowledge of

God, and take every thought captive to obey Christ. (2 Corinthians 10:3-5)

When lies are not taken captive to obey Christ, they become strongholds. A stronghold is a deeply held false belief. Strongholds determine a person's perspective of how they see themselves, God, and life in general. Shame is the most common message that trauma delivers to people. When a person feels the worthlessness that accompanies shame, they are easy to isolate and trap in addiction.

Maggie believed she was worthless and unlovable because of her father's abandonment. Those lies shaped how she viewed herself. Her trauma became a potent delivery system for the destructive lies of shame that shaped her perspective. Long after her father left, the lies remained and did their work.

These strongholds (lies) had to be destroyed for Maggie to walk in freedom. But how? First, she had to identify the lies by taking her thoughts captive and holding them up to the light of Scripture. Her small group leader helped her identify the lies of worthlessness that had taken root in her life because of her father's abandonment. She then destroyed those strongholds by meditating on the truth about her heavenly Father's love and acceptance through Christ. Over time, she began to experience what Jesus promised in John 8:32: "You will know the truth and the truth will set you free."

We've looked at how God rebuked the spiritual leaders of His people when He said, "They have healed the brokenness of My people superficially, saying, 'Peace, peace,' But there is no peace" (Jeremiah 6:14). The spiritual leaders of Jeremiah's day offered shallow solutions for deep brokenness.

Well-meaning spiritual leaders today often do the same when it comes to trauma. But as followers of Christ, we must recognize the spiritual warfare related to trauma so we don't offer superficial solutions. Helping someone overcome a porn habit is an opportunity for deep discipleship as we help them replace lies that have taken root in their heart with the truth of God's Word.

Exploring Trauma

Trauma survivors are more susceptible to addictions of all kinds, including porn addiction.[5] Sex addiction expert Dr. Patrick Carnes said, "It is clear that for sex addicts, trauma or high stress and addiction are inextricably connected. Addiction in its various forms becomes a solution to the anxiety and stress of the trauma."[6] A person may be medicating their stress and anxiety with porn, but, in many cases, trauma is fueling the negative emotions. The purpose of exploring trauma is to identify the root of the pain a person is seeking to medicate with porn.

Many people who have been stuck in their addiction have discovered they are triggered by past trauma or dysfunction they never processed. Still, understanding the lie the person accepted because of the trauma is more important than understanding the trauma itself. As a result of trauma, abuse, or dysfunction, a person can believe certain shame messages like:

- I'm a failure.
- I'm unlovable.
- There is something wrong with me.
- The trauma or abuse is my fault.
- I deserve to be addicted.

Trauma engraves these shame messages into a person's mind so that these lies eventually become their identity. Once someone believes these lies, small things can trigger big emotional reactions. One minor mistake can cause the addict to replay the "I'm a failure" message over and over. The negative emotions that result trigger a craving to medicate the pain.

Unless past trauma is identified and processed, the pain from it will continue to trigger the addict.

Before high-speed internet, almost all sex addicts had some type of abuse in their life. A survey of 650 sex addicts from 1985 to 2002 discovered that 81% had been sexually abused and 97% had been emotionally abused. And those who experience trauma at a young age are often more impacted by it, because the young brain is more malleable and influenced by trauma. This allows shame messages to go deeper.[7] This is why childhood trauma is so influential for people.

For these sex addicts, trauma was the major driver of their addiction. Childhood abuse causes less healthy bonding and insecure early attachments,[8] both of which make a person more prone to sex addiction. The shame messages that a trauma survivor has accepted about themselves often become a major contributing factor to their addiction. And this is not to excuse pornography addiction, but instead, it provides an explanation that helps bring solutions.

Trauma experts say that one of the important elements for healing trauma is having physical experiences that contradict the trauma.[9] This reality is a major reason why small groups are such a powerful tool in healing any addiction. In the context of small groups, people experience the acceptance, love, and compassion that are the opposite of what they experienced during their trauma. Dr. Ted Roberts says of small groups, "You were wounded in community and you will be healed in community."[10]

Granted, not every porn addict has trauma. Since pornography is now so widely available at younger ages, today's porn addiction isn't as clearly linked to past trauma as sex addictions used to be. There is a whole new breed of porn addicts, which is why a holistic approach is essential for recovery. Still, the porn addict who has trauma in their past, even in lesser forms, will have their addiction strengthened by it. And whether a person had a massive traumatic event or a smaller one, the pain and lies must be processed.

Understanding Your Place on the Trauma Scale

Those with little to no trauma may register a 1 or 2 on a scale of trauma while someone who comes from a very dysfunctional or abusive background may be at a 9 or 10. Most of us are probably somewhere in between.

Less Trauma **More Trauma**

1___2___3___4___5___6___7___8___9___10

Even if a person has little to no trauma, it is important to explore their pain for two reasons. First, people typically have more trauma than they think. Secondly, going through the process will equip a person to help others who do have more trauma to overcome.

A suggested exercise to help someone explore the pain of their past is to list their ten worst moments.[11] One way to gauge a worst moment is to determine if there are certain negative memories or instances of trauma. The trauma might be related to abuse that is emotional, verbal, physical, or sexual. Were there dysfunctional moments that shaped their childhood? Are there events in the past that cause great shame?

Some people are not able to point to a traumatic event but instead to a traumatic or dysfunctional environment. Maggie, in the opening story, had an environment of dysfunction versus an event that shaped her. The messages from Maggie's abandonment were clear: "I'm worthless, unlovable, and unwanted." Are there certain negative messages from your youth that you regularly repeat to yourself?

Facing pain is a major challenge for people. Sex addiction therapist Joe Dallas says, "Many guys who aren't willing to deal with their pain simply give up at this point, not because abandoning sexual sin is so hard, but because facing their own pain is too threatening."[12] If there is an event that someone has stuffed and kept a secret, it's probably one of their worst moments. We will look at how to process these traumatic events later in the chapter. But for now, know that the pain is best processed with a mentor, counselor, or in a small group.

The Trauma of the Father Wound

It is impossible to address every type of trauma experienced by people in the world. That said, there is a very specific trauma suffered by many in today's world: the father wound.

A father has such a foundational role in the development of his children, and the lack of his healthy influence will create wounds. A father's neglect, rejection, abuse, or abandonment creates certain deficiencies that may impact a child for life. These father wounds often leave a child insecure, confused, and ill-equipped for life. The impacts can be tragic.

According to research, fatherless homes contribute to many societal problems. In fact, fatherless homes account for:

- 63% of all youth suicides
- 90% of all homeless and runaway children
- 85% of all children who show behavior disorders
- 80% of rapists
- 71% of all high school dropouts
- 75% of all adolescent patients in chemical abuse centers

- 70% of youths in state-operated institutions
- 85% of all youths in prison[13]

This says nothing about the impact of neglectful or passive fathers who aren't living up to their responsibility even though they may be physically present.

For decades, Ted Roberts has helped men break free from sexual bondage. He says the majority of men he has worked with had a father wound. For many men, the father wound is the source of the pain they've been medicating through sexually acting out. The goal of identifying a father wound is not for people to blame their fathers for their current behavior but to identify a potential source of pain they are medicating with porn. If a person has a wound from their father that makes them feel like they don't measure up, it could be a "worst moment." Growing up with a distant or disinterested father may create more of a dysfunctional environment than a moment, but the effects are the same.

Eric, a forty-year-old sales manager, had a worst moment when he was ten. His baseball team lost the championship. Eric played a great game with tremendous effort. His dad told him that he let his team down because he didn't play well enough to win. What could have been a moment to celebrate individual effort instead resulted in Eric seeing himself as a failure. Well into his thirties, Eric regularly replayed the lie, "I'm a failure," which was deposited in his heart that day.

Failure and the fear of failure led to anxiety and self-doubting, both of which were Eric's most common triggers for his porn addiction. Porn became Eric's medication of choice to numb the feelings of failure and inadequacy. Until he identified this trauma as the root of his addiction, he was destined to stay stuck focusing on the symptoms. If a person repeats to themselves a negative message, its source could indicate a worst moment.

Each person is unique, and what is traumatic for one person may not be for another. Be careful not to compare. Once a person has identified their worst moments, it is vital to process them effectively.

Process the Pain

Dr. Bessel Van Der Kolk, author of *The Body Keeps the Score,* said, "We have discovered that helping victims of trauma find the words to describe what has happened to them is profoundly meaningful."[14] Learning to process trauma is an important part of finding freedom.

How do we process traumatic pain? Consider these six important principles.

1. Determine the message delivered by the trauma.

Identify what shame messages you replay to yourself because of the trauma. Drew, a software engineer in his thirties, identified a worst moment when he was called "stupid" by his father, multiple times in various ways. His trauma was more of a dysfunctional environment rather than from a single event. The message to Drew was clear. He believed he was stupid.

There can be multiple shame messages from one worst moment. For Drew, the message was "I'm stupid," but the lie that shaped Drew's life as a result of that message was, "I can't mess up and still be accepted." The fear of failure that resulted from this lie became the backdrop of Drew's life. The second message was produced once the first one was fully internalized. His belief reflected how Drew's perspective was shaped on a practical level because of the lie. It was a stronghold in Drew's life.

The shame messages a person replays need to be identified and evaluated (taken captive to the obedience of Christ). The lie planted in Eric's mind after his little league game blossomed over time as he regularly revisited it over the years. Eric shared, "Whenever moments occur in my life today that are perceived failures, like if I don't meet a work goal or I make a mistake as a husband, I go back to that moment when I first believed I was a failure. I say to myself, "Of course you failed, because you're a failure." In those wounds, Eric was drawn to medicate with porn.

Identifying the lies will help a person address them with the truth of God's Word. As a follower of Christ, Eric learned to reject the lie and choose to believe what God's Word said about him. Through prayer, faith, and study, he undid the lie that was born in trauma. He destroyed the stronghold. Whether the trauma is big or small, its impact is determined by the destructive nature of the message it implants in a person's heart. Determining this message is the first essential step.

2. Process the pain with others.

Trauma isn't measured by the size of the initial impact of the event but instead by the current impact it has on a person's mindset. Eric, who was told he was a failure by his dad at age ten, got into a physical altercation with his father when he was seventeen. Years later, Eric still claims that the episode at age ten was more traumatic because the failure message continued to impact him decades later. But as Eric processed his pain with others, he said, "It wasn't until I could articulate the lies I believed to my small group that I was able to identify how those lies still affect me as an adult. This is when I started to find victory."

Maggie's experience was similar. When she processed her pain with her counselor, she began to see the impact of her father's abandonment on her life. Maggie's small group was particularly helpful in the process. When other women in her group shared their trauma, it helped her learn more about her own experience. Processing her pain gave her insights she never had before.

Trauma expert Dr. Van Der Volk explained, "Being able to share your deepest pain and deepest feelings with another human being ... is one of the most profound experiences we can have. Communicating fully is the opposite of being traumatized."[15] And though verbally processing in a small group setting is helpful, some with more severe trauma may need professional help to process their pain. This might mean going to see a professional counselor or therapist.

3. Connect past trauma to your current porn use.

The shame messages implanted by past trauma often manifest in a person's present life. Many people never recognize when this happens. Those who follow the first two steps put themselves in a position to connect these events. As the diagram below shows, trauma delivers shame messages that feed negative emotions until a person medicates them with porn.

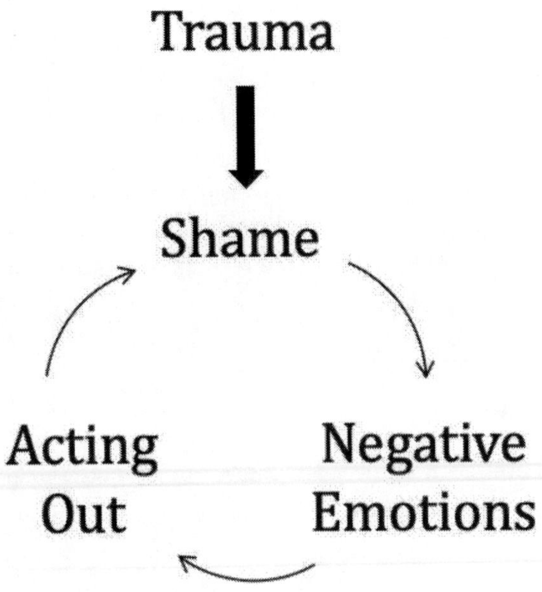

People who process their trauma in a healthy way can give a coherent explanation of how their trauma has affected them. Research is clear that the individuals who never connect the dots between their trauma and their addiction are more likely to be triggered by their past trauma.[16]

Drew, whose childhood led him to believe the lie, "I can't mess up," explained the importance of connecting the dots in his own life. He says, "My pattern was to relapse near big events or competitions because of my fear of failure. I never knew why. I just attributed it to letting my guard down." When Drew connected how the lies he believed gave him anxiety before certain events and fueled his acting out, he was able to address it effectively. Instead of being blindsided by the urge to act out, he learned to anticipate it and reach out for help. This wasn't possible until Drew connected his past trauma with his current porn use.

Eric also explains how connecting the dots was important for his recovery. "The pain of my past is pain because it produced emotions that were real in the moment. But the lies it produces about my identity aren't true. I have to be able to go back and separate the two." He continues:

> For instance, I felt rejected and hurt when my father said I failed. It is perfectly ok to feel that way as a ten-year-old. However, the lie that came from that was, "I'm always a failure." Obviously, this isn't true, and going back allowed me to discern the difference so when I have moments today when I fail, I can feel the emotion but reject the lie that keeps me in the addiction.

Eric learned to reject the identity that grew out of the shame message implanted because of trauma. He realized this because he processed with others and connected the dots. Before, when Eric failed, he embraced the "I'm a failure" stronghold. He felt terrible about who he was and ran to porn to numb the feelings. Now he knows those emotions are based on lies that he can replace with God's truth. He destroyed the stronghold.

4. Grieve your losses.

Part of processing the wounds of the past is to acknowledge and grieve your pain and loss. The Bible says, "There is a time to weep… and a time to mourn" (Ecclesiastes 3:4). People who stuff their pain instead of grieving it typically get tripped up by it later. Psychologist Dr. Lisa Firestone wrote about trauma:

> We're affected by the extent to which we haven't been able to feel the full pain and make sense of our experiences. When we don't deal with our trauma, we carry it with us. We haven't made sense of our story, and therefore, our past is still impacting our present in countless invisible ways.[17]

Grieving losses is part of processing trauma in a healthy way.

When grieving losses, we should grieve both the painful experiences we endured and the ones we missed out on. Don't minimize the pain. Acknowledge loss and process it. The purpose of grieving is not to remain in self-pity but to fully experience the pain and loss, which brings closure to the wound and helps you move forward in an emotionally healthy way.

Part of Maggie's recovery was to grieve the abandonment by her father. After she was eight, she never had a relationship with her father. This was a significant loss for her to grieve. Healthy people process their grief. This process helped Maggie see that her father leaving was not her fault. Maggie's grieving also naturally led to the need to forgive, which she did. If she didn't fully grieve her loss, she would likely not have fully forgiven her father.

5. Forgive those who hurt you.

Unforgiveness and bitterness hurts the one who refuses to forgive. It keeps them in bondage, tied to negative emotions. On the other hand, forgiving and releasing those who have hurt you brings you into alignment with Christ. The Bible commands us to "be kind to one another, tenderhearted, forgiving one another, as God in Christ forgave you" (Ephesians 4:32).

Forgiveness doesn't mean excusing the people who hurt you. You can still call sin what it is and choose forgiveness. Consider the story of Joseph from the book of Genesis. He was sold into slavery by his brothers, but several years later, when he was reunited with them, he said, "As for you, you meant evil against me, but God meant it for good in order to bring about this present result" (Genesis 50:20). Joseph called his brother's actions against him evil. He also acknowledged how God worked through the situation to bring good out of it. Joseph allowed God's truth to reframe the most traumatic event of his life.

Abuse and abandonment are evil, but, as Joseph demonstrated, they don't have to define a person. And forgiving perpetrators is an active resistance against allowing trauma to define you. Unforgiveness, on the other hand, guarantees the trauma will continue to plague you. Eric said of his trauma, "I was angry with God because other people had deliverance, but God wouldn't set me free. I had to quit blaming people, and I had to forgive my father so my bitterness wouldn't fuel more porn use." When Eric released his father by forgiving him, he was able to move forward by taking responsibility for his recovery.

For many people, extending forgiveness comes in the form of writing a letter to the offending party. The letter may or may not be given to the person depending on the circumstances. Often the letter is followed up with a conversation. In Maggie's case, her counselor didn't advise her to give her father the letter she wrote because it would open her up to more rejection and pain. She was able to forgive him even while keeping boundaries to protect herself.

6. Prepare to experience past pain.

It is vital to have support and accountability when processing the pain of the past. When a person experiences their past pain, it can trigger them and lead to relapse. People need to be prepared as they begin this process and take precautions to have extra boundaries and accountability.

There is a reason people hide their hurt. Acknowledging it brings pain. In the midst of the pain, however, God is present. He walks with us through it and desires to bring healing. "He heals the brokenhearted and binds up their wounds" (Psalm 147:3). God is "a father of the fatherless" (Psalm 68:5). God is the only one who can meet our deepest needs, so we can have wholeness in Christ regardless of our past. This reality should allow people to courageously address the pain of their past so they can move forward in a healthy way.

Mason was seven when his friend invited him over to a man's house in their neighborhood. Over the next two years, the man sexually abused the boys. Mason never told anyone. This trauma was a source of great shame. The lie implanted in Mason's heart was that the abuse was his fault. He felt responsible because he never told his parents and because he had continued to visit the man's house. Mason hated it, but still, he connected the experience with pleasure. This confusion only added to the shame of his secret. He vowed to never tell.

Mason got hooked on porn as a teenager. In college, he started following Christ. He also had occasional hookups with a guy in college. Mason was drawn to repeat his experiences from his abuse. The shame that resulted led him to medicate with porn. Porn only multiplied his shame as he regularly violated his biblical convictions about sexual purity. He tried many times to quit porn, but he could never find freedom.

Mason got married but kept his porn a secret for twenty years. When his wife discovered his porn addiction, his past all came out. Through his counselor and his recovery group, he began to process his past. He began to see his unwanted sexual behavior in light of his childhood trauma. This was key to him finding freedom. His other attempts to quit porn never lasted because he wasn't dealing with the root of his struggle.

Mason's vulnerability helped lead to freedom. He shared about the abuse and explained how he felt responsible for it. Simply voicing it to another person helped him see it more objectively. It wasn't his fault. Sharing about the hookups with the guy in college also relieved shame. He understood this behavior in light of his sexual abuse. Processing the pain allowed him to connect the dots from his trauma to his unwanted sexual behavior.

Trauma and Porn Genre

Mason's story illustrates how early childhood trauma can shape a person's arousal template. An arousal template determines what arouses a person sexually and the type of sexual experience they are drawn to. When people connect the dots from their trauma to why they are attracted to certain types of porn, they often experience freedom.

For Maggie's recovery, understanding why she was hooked on violent porn was de-shaming. She understood that she, like many trauma survivors, sought to relive the rejection of her father. Before this understanding, the shame of being addicted to violent porn kept her in bondage.

When Maggie discovered how her trauma shaped her arousal template, her shame began to lift. The truth set her free. This new understanding enabled her to live out of her identity in Christ. It became easier for her to resist the temptation to watch porn when she understood more fully where the desire was coming from. Instead of allowing those moments to lead to sin, Maggie started meditating on Bible verses related to God as her Father.

Sometimes people who have been sexually abused don't feel aroused unless they relive their abuse. They watch violent porn to relive their abusive past. This is often a subconscious desire to understand or control their trauma. It can help explain why someone might be drawn to a certain kind of porn. Until a person understands how their compulsive behavior serves them, it will be difficult to overcome.[18]

Author Jay Stringer's survey of 3,800 men and women found that women sought out violent and aggressive porn *more* than men did. This unexpected finding was confirmed by former Google data scientist Seth Stephens-Davidowitz. He wrote, "If there is a genre of porn in which violence is perpetrated against a woman, my analysis of the data shows that it almost always appeals disproportionately to women."[19]

This is surprising until we remember that trauma reenactment is the response of many trauma victims. Jay Stringer summarizes the findings when he said, "Men and women pursue violent porn for different purposes. Men tend to pursue pornography to find power *over* their shame and harm. Women tend to pursue violent pornography to *repeat* their shame and harm."[20]

God's Greater Good

It is important for followers of Christ to be honest as they process their trauma by asking questions like:

- *Where was God during my trauma event?*
- *If God loves me, why did He allow this to happen?*
- *Why doesn't He just instantly heal me?*

Processing these questions in community and in the context of Scripture is critical. The narrative of the Bible is full of suffering. Suffering is part of the human condition in a fallen world. All people, including God's people, suffer. God Himself suffered on the cross.

There are no easy answers, but the Bible places suffering in the context of God's love and greater purposes. This process requires faith. And though we will not have all of our questions answered, God's Word gives hope that He will use suffering to bring good. In the book of Romans, Paul wrote:

> And we know that for those who love God all things work together for good, for those who are called according to his purpose… Who shall separate us from the love of Christ? Shall tribulation, or distress, or persecution, or famine, or nakedness, or danger, or sword? No, in all these things we are more than conquerors through him who loved us. For I am sure that neither death nor life, nor angels nor rulers, nor things present nor things to come, nor powers, nor height nor depth, nor anything else in all creation, will be able to separate us from the love of God in Christ Jesus our Lord.
> (Romans 8:28, 35-39)

Through trauma, the enemy delivers powerful shame messages, which cast doubt on God's goodness and love. But through Jesus' trauma on the cross, God delivered His most powerful message of love: "For God so loved the world, that he gave his only Son, that whoever believes in him should not perish but have eternal life (John 3:16). The result for all who believe is, "There is therefore now no condemnation for those who are in Christ Jesus" (Romans 8:1).

Trauma is destructive because it delivers powerful shame messages that limit a person's awareness of God's love. Childhood trauma is a particularly potent root of porn addiction. Trauma that is unaddressed fuels shame and negative emotions that regularly trigger the porn or sex addict to act out. Until the trauma is identified and processed, it will keep people stuck. Trauma can also provide insights into why a person may be drawn to a specific kind of porn. If the type of porn is particularly shameful for the person, this factor adds to the grip of shame the addiction has.

The six roots of addiction dig deep into a person's soul and keep them in bondage. Adequately addressing each root requires growth and development in key areas of life. Overcoming the lies that trauma implants in a person's life happens when they replace those lies with God's truth. They can know the truth and the truth will set them free.

Summary of Action Steps

- Identify your ten worst moments.
- Identify the message those traumatic events delivered to you.
- Walk through the steps of processing your traumatic events.
- Evaluate if trauma has shaped your arousal template.
- Share these with a trusted friend, accountability partner, or counselor.

17

May It Be

On December 26, 2004, scientists detected the massive 9.1 earthquake that caused the deadliest tsunami in history. They made frantic warning calls in the moments after the earthquake. Many of those calls were met with apathy and skepticism. One such call went to a meteorologist seminar happening the same day in Thailand.

When these weather experts heard the news, they called an emergency meeting. They wrestled with whether or not to issue a public warning of a possible tsunami, even though there was no way to confirm whether a tsunami was coming. They feared repercussions from both the government and businesses if they issued a false warning. After all, it was the peak tourist season. Hotels were full and beaches were packed. If they issued a warning for people to evacuate and no tsunami came, there would be a backlash. They decided not to issue a warning, and an hour later, over 5,000 people perished in Thailand.[1]

Tsunamis are most destructive when people are unaware. And there is a tsunami coming! We see the destructive impact of porn now, but the worst is yet to come. This book is an attempt to sound the alarm and share real solutions. If the Church doesn't start addressing the issue with more conviction, the full force of the destructive tsunami will destroy marriages, families, and churches on a massive scale. When porn addiction is addressed with gospel-centered solutions, freedom results. It's not just a danger to avoid, but addressing it is an opportunity to seize. People are not just finding freedom but also significant growth and purpose.

Purpose

The goal isn't just to live a porn-free life. The fight for freedom must be coupled with a bigger purpose. If someone finds freedom but they don't have a bigger vision for their life, they usually fall back into bondage. God has called us to so much more than just freedom. Research shows that a lack of purpose is connected to pornography use. Men who say they don't have a sense of purpose are seven times more likely to pursue porn.[2]

The Scriptures show how a lack of purpose can lead to sexual sin. When King David was not living his purpose, he fell hard. Consider this passage from the Bible:

> In the spring of the year, *the time when kings go out to battle,* David sent Joab, and his servants with him, and all Israel... But David remained at Jerusalem. It happened, late one afternoon, when David arose from his couch and was walking on the roof of the king's house that he saw from the roof a woman bathing; and the woman was very beautiful.
> (2 Samuel 11:1-2, emphasis added)

David was supposed to be fighting with his men. Instead, he was back at the palace, lying on his couch and killing time. He wasn't looking for sin, but he was bored and alone, and so his eyes wandered.

David looked outside and saw a woman named Bathsheba bathing on her roof. His heart was filled with lust. What did he do with that lust? David committed adultery with Bathsheba. In his shame, he killed Bathsheba's husband and took her as his wife. This was not David's original plan, of course. The murder and resulting marriage was just a way to cover up his sin. But this attempt to hide his sin led him to do far more than he intended. It hurt more people than he intended to hurt. And if you read about the rest of David's life, it cost him much more than he had intended to pay.

David didn't mean to create so much chaos, but distracted from the vision God had for him, he was more vulnerable to sin. It's the same way for all of us. When we're without purpose, we miss out on the joy of pursuing God's vision for our lives. It's so important to have a clear vision, an overarching purpose that gives clarity and meaning to life.

According to the Bible, the follower of Christ is to have a threefold vision: to know Christ (Matthew 22:27-28); to be like Christ (Romans 8:29); and to make Christ known (Matthew 28:19-20). Pursuing God and His purpose for our life will not be without opposition. As we have seen, there is a spiritual war going on all around us. We have an enemy who wants to keep us from staying on purpose and from living a life worthy of Christ's calling.

The harvest is plentiful, but the laborers are addicted to porn.

I recently had a conversation with a leader who is a part of a large Christian ministry that recently hired over 100 new staff. He said 100% of their new male staff and more than half of their new female staff struggle with pornography. And these are full-time ministers! I asked whether there was a plan to help these new staff walk in freedom, and he said there wasn't much of one. Six months into their new jobs, some of these new staff were still watching porn *daily*. These are the future leaders of the church! This leader hated the situation but reluctantly accepted it as the new normal.

We do not have to accept this new normal. We can offer a path to freedom and purpose for those struggling in porn. And as you may have picked up as you read this book, one of the first steps in the process is de-shaming the pornography conversation. De-shaming porn allows people to be honest, repent, and get help. And de-shaming the topic doesn't mean we don't maintain high standards for spiritual leadership. Being gracious doesn't mean we don't call people to biblical standards.

I have seen a ministry that prioritizes helping their students break free from porn and, at the same time, maintains standards for leadership. If a student commits to honesty and establishes a track record of pursuing recovery, they can be in leadership. What does pursuing recovery look like? It includes repentance, regular accountability, and making progress in leaving their porn behind.

But the ministry doesn't just focus on those entering leadership. It also creates a middle ground for students who aspire to leadership but have yet to establish a track record of moving toward freedom. They were not made full leaders, but they were given more responsibility and were invited into leadership development. They had the hope of a greater purpose, that they could become leaders and, at the same time, were shown how to get there.

If a person is given a leadership position when they have little to no commitment to recovery, it encourages sin as the status quo. In fact, I have seen how denying a person a leadership or staff position has helped them get serious about addressing their addiction. A ministry or church doesn't have to choose between encouraging vulnerability on the one hand and calling their leaders to repentance and requiring progress on the other. It can and must be both.

Sadly, many ministries do not require purity in their leadership. The apostle Paul warned us of this kind of thinking. He shared an example of God dealing with His people's sexual sin:

> We must not indulge in sexual immorality as some of them did, and twenty-three thousand fell in a single day. We must not put Christ to the test... Now these things happened to them as an example, but they were written down for our instruction... Therefore let anyone who thinks that he stands take heed lest he fall. (1 Corinthians 10:8-12)

Paul was referring to a time when the nation of Israel rebelled against God through sexual immorality. God killed 23,000 in a single day. Paul said this should be a warning to us. Sexual sin is serious and uniquely destructive, and God repeatedly warns His people against it. Paul was holding up this ancient example as a reminder that grace does not suggest a lack of holiness. We are warned not to test God in this area. We are also warned not to be over-confident that we are doing well. The lukewarm response to dealing with the pornography issue suggests that many leaders in the church need to heed this warning. We all must take heed lest we fall.

In the very next verse, Paul gives a promise from God. He says, "No temptation has overtaken you that is not common to man. God is faithful, and he will not let you be tempted beyond your ability, but with the temptation he will also provide the way of escape, that you may be able to endure it" (1 Corinthians 10:13). Paul reminds us there is no new temptation. Though internet porn delivers immorality to people like never before, the temptation to lust is the same.

Immorality is any sexual activity outside the context of marriage. God created sex to be enjoyed within a marriage between a man and a woman. For those of us who adopt the Bible's standard for sexuality, we need to heed the warning against immorality.

The temptation to seek sexual fulfillment outside of God's design is nothing new. In this passage, God promises He will always provide a way out. He doesn't say the way out will be easy. The *way of escape* from temptation that comes from porn or sex addiction is anything but easy. The way out of this sin requires growth and development in key areas of life. For most people, the way out is *not* instant deliverance, but it comes through the process of outgrowing porn.

This way of escape begins with claiming the promise that the power of sin has been broken by the death and resurrection of Christ. It's a lie to believe we can't break free. The path of freedom involves taking measures to remove temptation by identifying triggers and establishing boundaries. Freedom requires renewing one's mind with God's Word and bringing sin into the light of authentic accountability.

The path to freedom teaches a person to process their emotions, not medicate them. The way of escape means a person identifies the lies of shame deposited in their life and replaces them with truth. The way to freedom involves living out of an identity in Christ. God will provide the way of escape, but it requires our growth, trust, and obedience.

Spiritual leaders must seize on the opportunity to equip those under their leadership to pursue the way of escape in light of God's higher purpose. When the higher purpose to know Christ, be like Christ, and make Christ known is clear, the motivation to outgrow porn is stronger. God will use the process to transform His people as they pursue Him and His purposes.

Be aware of the temptation to water down the definition of freedom. Let's not define it as "less porn." The best definition I have heard for freedom comes from Ted Roberts: *no acting out for a period of two years*. His definition of freedom includes that the person establishes *healthy relationships and habits*.[3]

When a person adopts this goal of genuine freedom, they realize they *cannot* do it in their own strength. They will see the need to surrender to Christ and have the help of others. This kind of freedom involves becoming a new person with a new lifestyle of habits and convictions. Don't settle for less.

Grow by Teaching

The need for more porn-free, purpose-filled Christ followers has never been greater. Jesus said, "The harvest is plentiful but the laborers are few" (Matthew 9:37). But the laborers who can effectively disciple someone out of a porn habit are even fewer. Our ministry, The Freedom Fight, is partnering with a growing number of organizations to help them build porn-free laborers through the principles taught in this book.

After strugglers go through our online program and gain a measure of freedom, we encourage them to lead others through it. An example of this is a twenty-five-year-old engineer named Trevor. He needed to go through The Freedom Fight program twice before his freedom from porn took hold in his life. He wasn't ready to apply everything the first time, but his second time through, he did. And as he walked in new freedom, he volunteered to lead a group of younger men and grew even more in that role. In this way, the truth went deeper into his life, just like I've seen it happen with so many others.

Dawson Trotman, founder of the Navigators, said, "Thoughts disentangle themselves when they pass through the lips and fingertips."[4] Teaching others helps us process the principles for ourselves in a deeper way. The truth is, every time I lead a new small group through the principles in this book, I learn something new. No one learns more than the teacher. This is the genius behind Jesus' command to make disciples. When we teach others to follow Christ, the truths go deeper into our own hearts. When the student becomes the teacher, it fills him with purpose and helps a lifestyle of recovery take root.

Helping others outgrow their porn struggle is key to making disciples. Tyler, a Cru staff member who is leading a group of college students through our program, has been surprised by the results. He said, "I believe addressing students' porn addiction could be a key to fulfilling the Great Commission. My guys have been so much more excited about their walk with God and sharing their faith after getting help with their porn struggle." Tyler discovered that he couldn't effectively disciple someone struggling with porn if he didn't address their struggle with biblical solutions.

You might feel inadequate to help others break free from porn or sex addiction. This is a normal feeling. I have felt this. I was forced to confront the issue of porn because I was helping college students follow Christ. I got equipped by learning from the people who went before me, and you can too. Commit to learn and lead, and I promise, you will make an impact.

Equipping the Saints

We are called to "equip the saints for the work of ministry" (Ephesians 4:12). This includes equipping leaders to address the current porn pandemic and preparing them for the coming tsunami. If we do it well, it will lead to an impact for Christ both inside and outside the church. Here are some key groups of people the Church must equip.

Men

A men's ministry is uniquely positioned to address the porn issue. There are typically small groups already in place, and most have dealt with the topic of porn, at least to a degree. Some pastors use a men's retreat to kick off the topic and then launch into small groups. Other pastors have used equipping groups to go through the principles in this book. After that, they transitioned into full recovery groups. Most men's ministries already have the foundation in place to help their men overcome porn, even if they need to pursue freedom with more intentionality.

Women

Shame for the Christian woman struggling with porn is extremely high. When porn is presented only as a man's issue, the shame for women who struggle multiplies. De-shaming the topic, particularly for women, is a must. When they understand that they are not alone, it encourages them to get help. The younger the woman, the more likely she struggles with porn.

Older women who get equipped in this area can help younger women find freedom. So if you're in that older generation of women, invite women to get equipped so they can help the younger generation. When the topic is de-shamed by equipping small groups (that's why this book has discussion questions in the appendix), women who are struggling can continue in a recovery group afterward.

Parents

I had a conversation with a father who had yet to have the full "sex talk" with his seven-year-old son. You can imagine the father's shock when his son asked him about anal sex. His son had questions after a friend at school showed him a video. Though they hadn't fully talked about sex, the father had already de-shamed the topic of porn by going through the book *Good Pictures, Bad Pictures* by Jansen and Poyner. It's a book that addresses the topic of pornography in an age-appropriate way. Because of this, his son felt comfortable asking him about the video.

The shame many kids feel when they see these graphic images causes them to start keeping secrets. Parents need to have both the porn talk and the sex talk in a way that de-shames it. These should be ongoing dialogues instead of just a talk. Kids need to know that sex was God's idea. God made it enjoyable. He made it for marriage. They need to know that porn undermines God's design. Parents must take initiative to fill in the blanks for their kids, or the pornified world will.

Students

Today's students must be taught that a porn habit adopted in junior high and high school will have dire consequences. If the Church doesn't warn this generation of youth about the destructive nature of porn, who will? Students need to know the truth that the younger they start this habit, the more difficult it is to break free. It will never be easier for them to break a porn addiction than it is today. With each repetition of the porn pathway, they are deepening its grip on their life. They need to know that porn sows seeds that ruin their sex life, their marriage, and their walk with God.

Addressing the issue of pornography with students brings an opportunity to teach the next generation about spiritual warfare in a practical way. Addressing the porn issue with real, biblically based solutions shows them the relevance of the Bible. They come to see that God's Word has answers for today's issues. If we do this well, we'll equip the next generation of spiritual leaders to have maximum impact in a porn-saturated world.

The Authority of God's Word

One of my prayers for this book has been that God would use it to exalt His Word and show how relevant it is. The principles in this book are powerful and effective, and not because psychologists and experts say so, though many do. The principles are effective because they are rooted in God's Word. In fact, in one passage of Scripture, Paul instructs the believers of his day to be separate from the sexualized society some of them participated in. And though he doesn't call them "roots of addiction,"

Paul mentions all six of the solutions we outlined in this book to address each of the roots in this one passage.

> Now this I say and testify in the Lord, that you must no longer walk as the Gentiles do, in the futility of their minds. They are darkened in their understanding, alienated from the life of God because of the ignorance that is in them, due to their hardness of heart. They have become callous and have given themselves up to sensuality, greedy to practice every kind of impurity. But that is not the way you learned Christ!— assuming that you have heard about him and were taught in him, as the truth is in Jesus, to put off your old self, which belongs to your former manner of life and is corrupt through deceitful desires, and to be renewed in the spirit of your minds, and to put on the new self, created after the likeness of God in true righteousness and holiness. Therefore, having put away falsehood, let each one of you speak the truth with his neighbor, for we are members one of another. Be angry and do not sin; do not let the sun go down on your anger, and give no opportunity to the devil. (Ephesians 4:17-27)

Wow! The remarkable relevance of this ancient book speaks directly to today's believers who are entangled in pornography. Apparently, many in the church at Ephesus were engaging in sexual sin like the non-believers around them: "…you must no longer walk as the Gentiles do…" (v.17). What behavior of the Gentiles did Paul point out that some in the church were following? They were controlled by their "sensuality" (meaning unbridled lust), and they were "greedy to practice every kind of impurity" (v.19). Amazingly, Paul is describing one of the disturbing elements of sex addiction. They don't just desire more sex; they desire different sex. This is why someone who starts looking at normal porn often escalates to more deviant and extreme forms. Paul exhorted the Ephesian believers, "that is not the way you learned Christ!" (v.20). He then instructed them on how to break free from the sexual sin that infected the church. The following chart shows the roots of addiction and how Paul's solutions directly address them. These roots of bondage have only been understood in the last few decades, yet the Bible has been pointing to the truth that sets us free all along.

Root of Addiction	**Solution**
The Sexualized Society	**Pursue Holiness** "... put on ... holiness." (v.24)
The Addicted Brain	**Renew the Mind** "... renewed in ... your minds ..." (v.23)
Isolation	**Develop Authentic Relationships** "... speak the truth ... we are members of one another." (v.25)
Negative Emotions	**Process Emotions** "... do not sin; do not let the sun go down on your anger ..." (v.26)
Shame	**Live out of an Identity in Christ** "... put on the new self, created after the likeness of God " (v.24)

Trauma	→	**Replace Lies with Truth** "… the truth is in Jesus … put away falsehood, let each one of you speak the truth with his neighbor …" (v.21, 25)

Make no mistake—a person doesn't simply "quit" a porn addiction; they must outgrow it. Outgrowing sexual bondage involves pursuing a new way of life. Put another way, pursuing the solutions to the roots isn't just about pursuing freedom, but it is about laying hold of the life that God has for His children.

Seizing the Opportunity

I once attended training for sex addiction professionals in Chicago. During the week, I was struck by the diversity of all the people in attendance. There were Jews, Muslims, Atheists, Christians, and many other backgrounds represented. *Every* community has been impacted by porn addiction, and they are looking for answers.

Those of us with the gospel of Jesus Christ and the Word of God have an incredible advantage. So if the Church deals with the porn issue among its members, it will be poised to bring hope and healing to *every* community. Not only is addressing the porn issue an incredible opportunity to make disciples, but it's also an opportunity to show the world that the Word of God has real answers to life's real problems.

When I first heard Josh McDowell say pornography is the greatest threat to the Church, I was skeptical. I thought, "It's bad but the *greatest threat…?*" However, the more I research and the more porn addicts I help, the more I agree with Josh. Porn is destroying more marriages, pastors, and churches and capturing the minds of more young people than anything else today.

God's Word talks about "fleshly lusts which wage war against the soul" (1 Peter 2:11 NASB), and we know this is true. As we've seen, Christians who watch porn are less likely to pray, read their Bible, and attend or serve in their church. We are at war, and porn is a powerful weapon the Church must address.

I'm convinced, if we address the six roots of addiction with the gospel-centered and holistic solutions outlined in this book, we'll experience unbelievable growth. When God's truth is applied at the deepest level of a person's life, transformation takes place. Those who experience the life change required to overcome a porn addiction will be more excited about the King and His kingdom.

In the process of bringing freedom, God is transforming His people. Indeed, the greatest threat to the Church is also the greatest opportunity for revival and growth. How do I know? Because I've seen it. And if you'll commit to the principles in this book, you'll see it too.

May it be!

Epilogue

Many Christians today point to 2 Chronicles 7:14 and the promise God gave to ancient Israel as a framework for revival. In it, God says, "If my people who are called by my name humble themselves, and pray and seek my face and turn from their wicked ways, then I will hear from heaven and will forgive their sin and heal their land." Though this was given to different people in a different time, there are timeless principles included in that passage. Specifically, the verse sets out four requirements for healing and revival. I want to highlight two of the requirements.

First, and maybe the most unpopular and least practiced, is "turning from their wicked ways." If God's people want to see healing in their own lives, they must repent from their sin. If pastors want to see revival among their people, they must turn from their wicked ways. If churches want to see a movement of God, they must confess their sin and turn from it.

There are many "wicked ways," but I'm convinced no more pervasive sin is destroying more families, churches, and young people than pornography. It is a place of compromise for many of God's people. This book shows how we can and must turn from this sin and put it to death.

The second requirement I want to highlight is prayer. Jesus taught us to ask God to "deliver us from evil" (Matthew 6:13). But prayer is meant to be embodied, and one way we can live this prayer out is by limiting the evil of porn among minors. Prayer for deliverance from evil and turning from wickedness go hand in hand. I'm praying that God will stir the hearts of His people to take this fight to the political and legal arena.

Legislative attempts to restrict porn have been unsuccessful in the past. Religious arguments have no clout in the courtroom, and the porn industry has successfully characterized any objection to pornography as a religious or moral argument. The courts have protected the porn industry from these arguments based on free speech. Yes, you read that correctly. Pornography is protected by the First Amendment as free speech.[1]

There is reason to believe that could change. There is a growing body of research showing the dangers of pornography for people and especially for adolescents. As discussed, the adolescent brain is much more susceptible to porn, and there's no denying that porn changes the brain like other addictive substances that we restrict from minors. The evidence is compelling and increasing. And we need to base legislation on this kind of scientific research.

Lawmakers in sixteen states have passed resolutions declaring pornography a public health crisis.[2] These are nonbinding resolutions, but they are an attempt to raise public awareness of the dangers of pornography so that parents and schools can be aware of the dangers. And maybe, with enough time, legislation and regulation will take hold.

When I was growing up, and still today, bookstores keep adult content out of the reach of children. This common sense must be applied to the internet. And some countries have done just that. The United Kingdom passed a Porn Block law in 2017.[3] One justification for the new law was that more than half of children and teenagers reported that they accidentally stumbled onto porn.[4] They were in the children section of the "bookstore" and found pornographic content purposefully placed there.

The common sense rule required visitors to porn sites to verify that they were eighteen. Despite good intentions, it was impossible to implement the regulation, and two years after the law passed, it was abandoned. What does this show us? Two things, actually. First, there is evidence showing the dangers of porn that governments are willing to act on. Second, it shows that more radical measures are needed.

In 2007, a bill was drafted in the US to require all porn sites to move to the .xxx domain.[5] The bill was never written, but the idea has merit. But in addition to requiring porn sites to be on .xxx domains, if a law like this is to be effective, it must require at least two things.

First, all phone and internet providers must restrict access to the .xxx domain *until* the account holder activates the .xxx domain. Right now, the burden is on parents to try to filter porn from reaching their kids. This would put the burden on the adult porn user to activate access to porn. Second, the law will only be effective if it's enforced with fines, shutting down websites that violate the standards, and even imprisoning violators.

I'm no legal expert, but many believe these kinds of regulations can withstand the free speech argument. Every adult who wants to look at porn can, while at the same time, common sense measures will protect children from getting hooked.

In light of the dangers of porn, why don't we have common sense legislation? The porn industry is very powerful and influential. It's a $100-billion industry. The porn industry conducts its own "research" on porn to contradict the truth about how destructive porn is. The goal of their research isn't necessarily to win the argument. They want to call into question legitimate research and use it as a reason to call for more research. Why? It has billions of reasons to target young minds. The porn industry has taken a page out of the tobacco industry's playbook.[6] Hooking kids on porn gives the industry a customer for life.

Any law will be challenged in the courts. With today's research showing porn's harmful impact more clearly than ever, especially among adolescents, now is the time for action.

Acknowledgements

I thank the Lord Jesus Christ for the privilege of being involved in His Kingdom work.

To my incredible wife, Amber—thank you for all your support and sacrifice that helped make this book possible. You are truly a blessing.

I want to thank each of my children—Brooke, Daniel, Kaylie, and Lindsey—for your support and encouragement on this book.

I had a lot of help with the manuscript. A huge thank you to Todd Ahrend who gave a ton of his time to help me develop the manuscript. Thanks to Selby "Teddy" Perkins and her thorough editing work throughout the process. To Seth Haines for adding his magic to the manuscript. I am grateful to Donnie and Sarah Perkins for their help in making this book possible. Thanks to all those who read sections of the book and gave feedback along the way: Heath Alexander, Stuart Hurst, and Morgan Parker. I appreciate Andrew Buck's help with all the diagrams and for being a great sounding board. A special thank you to Josh McDowell for his encouragement and support with the book. I appreciate Dave Riner and his support in writing the book and creating the Freedom Fight program in the first place.

Thank you to the awesome staff of Student Mobilization who gave feedback and insights in the building of the Freedom Fight program. Their input helped lay the foundation for this book. I want to thank Trey Smith for believing in me and investing in me all those years ago. God used those seven years to change the trajectory of my life. I am grateful to Dr. Ted Roberts for mentoring me during my training as a sex addiction professional. It was a privilege to learn from one of the best. I want to give a special thank you to all our prayer and financial supporters who have prayed for us, supported us, and encouraged us throughout this entire process. Thank you for your partnership!

Discussion Questions

Chapter 1: The Tsunami Is Coming

1. What did you find interesting about Mark's story?
2. In what ways does the author say a tsunami describes the state of the world related to pornography? Do you agree or disagree? Why?
3. In what ways did the internet change pornography consumption? What changes do you think were the most significant? Why?
4. How does the following verse apply to pornography consumption? "Do not be deceived: God is not mocked, for whatever one sows, that will he also reap. For the one who sows to his own flesh will from the flesh reap corruption" (Galatians 6:7-8).
5. What was most alarming about the examples of slow death that porn can bring? Why?
6. What ways did the four men observe the law of reaping and sowing?
7. How have you seen pornography wreak havoc in people's lives?
8. What else from the chapter stuck out to you?
9. What ways are you most tempted to sow to the flesh? How can you avoid it?

Chapter 2: How Much? So What?

1. How has access changed pornography consumption? How have you seen or experienced it?

2. Are the Barna Group statistics what you expected? Why or why not?
3. Which stats about porn consumption did you find the most interesting?
4. Why do you think porn usage among Christians and non-Christians is virtually the same?
5. Why do you think young Christians are using so much porn?
6. What caught your attention the most from the 1980s experiment showing the impact of watching pornography? Why?
7. How does viewing pornography change people?
8. Why do you think God told us to be so careful about what we let into our minds when He said, "Take every thought captive to obey Christ"?
9. How can we make this command practical?

Chapter 3: Something Is Off

1. Sexlessness, teenage erectile dysfunction, the decline of marriage, violence against women, pedophilia, and sex trafficking are all on the rise. Which of these trends is most disturbing to you? Why?
2. Do you think the increase in porn consumption is a major reason why? Why or why not?
3. Which of these trends do you see having the biggest impact on the Church? Why?
4. Why do you think so few churches address the issue of pornography?
5. According to Sociologist Dr. Mark Regnerus, what is cheap sex? How does he say it is impacting marriage rates? Do you agree or disagree? Why?
6. How does this chapter illustrate John 10:10, where Jesus says, "The thief comes only to steal and kill and destroy, but I came that they may have life and have it abundantly"?

7. In light of the research of the chapter, how does Jesus' command in Matthew 5:27-28 show God's grace and goodness? "You have heard that it was said, 'You shall not commit adultery; but I say to you that everyone who looks at a woman with lust for her has already committed adultery with her in his heart" (Matthew 5:27-28)?
8. Why is it difficult to see God's commands and boundaries as blessings? How might we change that?

Chapter 4: Hijacking the Brain

1. What caught your attention about how porn hijacks the brain?
2. How is porn like candy to the brain?
3. How does understanding the brain science of addiction help give you compassion toward the struggler who has tried to stop but can't?
4. How can the impact of porn on the brain be an example of this verse: "Flee from sexual immorality. All other sins a person commits are outside the body, but whoever sins sexually, sins against their own body" (1 Corinthians 6:18)?
5. Why is the adolescent brain more susceptible to being impacted by porn?
6. Why is just trying harder with more accountability and discipline not enough?
7. What is neuroplasticity, and why is it a reason to be hopeful?
8. How is Romans 12:2 ("Be transformed by the renewing of your mind.") an illustration of neuroplasticity? How can we renew our minds practically?

Chapter 5: War Against the Soul

1. How did porn use wage war against Alex's soul?

2. "Beloved, I urge you as aliens and strangers to abstain from fleshly lusts, which wage war against the soul" (1 Peter 2:11). What are some of the other manifestations of how pornography use wages war against the soul?
3. God repeatedly warns us against being deceived in the Bible. Which of those passages/warnings do you most need to be aware of? Why?
4. What stuck out to you about the rationalizations pastors say they hear from members of their church related to their porn use?
5. Which area of research where porn use wages war against the soul is most concerning to you? Why?
6. How do you see this spiritual attack of pornography use impacting the family and the Church?
7. Do you see people "pervert the grace of their God into a license for immorality" (Jude 4)? How so?
8. What made the difference for Alex to come back around in his faith?
9. "If you continue in My word, you are truly disciples of Mine; and you will know the truth and the truth will set you free" (John 8:31-32). How can we live this out?

Chapter 6: Till Porn Do Us Part

1. What did you learn from Sarah and Mason's story?
2. Were you surprised by the stats about how destructive porn is on marriages? Why or why not?
3. Why do you think porn is so destructive to marriages?
4. What did you learn from this chapter about the impact porn has on marriages?
5. Why doesn't marriage fix a person's porn problem?
6. How is pornography a supernormal stimulus?
7. The author said that, for many people, pornography is a gateway drug to adultery. Do you agree? Why or why not?

8. How would you explain to someone, who uses porn to spice up their sex life, that the practice will ultimately be destructive to the marriage relationship?
9. Jesus prayed that His disciples "may all be one… so that the world may believe that you have sent me" (John 17:21). How does this add to the ramifications of Christian marriages and families being destroyed? What are other ramifications of Christian marriages being destroyed?
10. How should we live in light of what we learned in this chapter?

Chapter 7: Pastors and Porn

1. What stood out to you from Antwan's story?
2. Since pornography is waging war against Christians' souls and marriages and is capturing the minds of the next generation on a massive scale, why do you think so few Christian leaders are addressing the issue?
3. Which obstacles do you think are the most significant? Would you add others?
4. Did you think the three solutions were adequate to address the obstacles? What are other solutions?
5. In your opinion, "Should a pastor be fired or asked to resign if they are found to be using porn?" Why or why not?
6. What is the punishment culture and how does the author say that it contributes to pastors and congregations staying stuck? Do you agree? Why or why not?
7. What stood out to you from the passage in James 4:4-10?
8. What do you think of the suggested restorative culture? How does a restorative culture encourage repentance?
9. Why is a restorative culture important in light of the porn use of the younger generation?
10. What did you learn from Nick's story?

11. What does getting off the beach and charging the hill look like for you?

Chapter 8: Faith and Works

1. God rebuked His leaders saying of them, "They have healed the brokenness of My people superficially, saying, 'Peace, peace,' But there is no peace" (Jeremiah 6:14). What are some of the superficial solutions being offered today for the sexual brokenness of porn addiction?
2. What's the difference between first-order change and second-order change?
3. How does 2 Peter 1:4-8 show the importance of both faith and works in living an effective and fruitful Christian life?
4. What do we learn from Austin's example? Why were both faith and works important to him?
5. Why do you think it is important to deal with the roots of porn addiction?
6. Which of the six roots are the most surprising? Why?
7. Which are you most looking forward to learning about? Why?
8. The author says those who find freedom must "outgrow porn" by developing in certain areas of their lives. Which area of growth interests you the most? Why?
9. Why do some Christians address the roots of their addiction and outgrow porn while others do not and settle for first-order change?
10. What were some of the results in Brandon's life of him addressing the roots of addiction?

Chapter 9: Sexualized Society

1. What caught your attention from Parker's story?

2. What aspects of our sexualized culture make it most challenging for you to walk in holiness and purity?
3. How do these words of Jesus capture the idea of walking in holiness in the midst of a sexualized society? "For the gate is wide and the way is easy that leads to destruction, and those who enter by it are many. For the gate is narrow and the way is hard that leads to life, and those who find it are few" (Matthew 7:13-14).
4. What stuck out to you from the holiness section?
5. Why is growing in holiness an important step to walking in freedom for the long haul?
6. Why do you think Jesus called for such a radical approach when it comes to lust (Matthew 5:27-29)? Does going ninety days without a relapse seem doable to you? Why or why not?
7. What did you learn about triggers? Why is it important to know your triggers? What are some of your biggest triggers?
8. What boundaries have you put in place to help you address triggers? What other potential boundaries do you still need?
9. What biblical attitudes should we have toward temptation (Matthew 26:41,1 Corinthians 6:18, 2 Timothy 2:22)? What temptations are you tempted to flirt with instead of flee?
10. What did you learn about the importance of accountability and anticipation?
11. Do you see the drift toward worldliness around you? In you? In what ways?
12. What action steps do you need to focus on? What are you specifically going to do?

Chapter 10: The Addicted Brain

1. What can we learn from the Navy SEALs to help with the addicted brain?

2. What did you learn about how porn hijacks the brain?
3. How does the limbic system—the emotional brain— overpower the PFC—the logical brain?
4. How do we fix our brakes (PFC)?
5. How does each aspect of BRACE help overcome the addicted brain and resist temptation?
6. What part of BRACE do you think would be most helpful? Why?
7. What did the author mean when he said, "Repetition got you into the addiction and repetition will help get you out?" How does BRACE help you build a new brain pathway?
8. What are the promises God gives about His Word in Joshua 1:8 and Isaiah 55:11? How has God's Word impacted your life?
9. How does a habit/relapse contract help a person renew their mind?
10. What did you think of the example contract given? How could this be an example of Paul "disciplining his body and keeping it under control" (1 Corinthians 9:27)?
11. What are some benefits of doing a crash report?
12. Which action steps do you need to prioritize? What's your specific plan this week?

Chapter 11: Isolation

1. What stood out to you about Rat Park?
2. What does it mean that the opposite of addiction isn't sobriety, it's connection?
3. Why do you think we tend to hide from God and others (Genesis 3:7-8)? How do you see this tendency in your own life?
4. What is Jesus claiming when He says, "If anyone thirsts, let him come to me and drink. Whoever believes in me, as the Scripture has said, out of his heart will flow rivers of living

water" (John 7:37-38)? Have you ever experienced this? How?

5. Why do you think Jesus likens the decision to trust Him to being born again — "unless one is born again he cannot see the kingdom of God" (John 3:3)?
6. What do you think about bonding to porn?
7. How do porn and isolation feed one another?
8. What can we learn from Noah and his response to temptation?
9. What does it mean to live in reality? What makes it challenging?
10. "It is more blessed to give than to receive" (Acts 20:35). How does the author say this can apply to someone in recovery?
11. What action steps do you need to prioritize? What is your specific plan?

Chapter 12: Negative Emotions

1. How is porn like a "comfort food"? What are some of your "comfort foods"?
2. What is self-awareness and emotional intelligence?
3. Proverbs 14:8 says, "The wisdom of the prudent is to give thought to their ways" (NIV). Why is it wise to give thought to your ways? How can this apply to our emotions and our response to our emotions?
4. Which of the BLASSTED emotions are most often triggers for you?
5. What can we learn from David about processing his emotions with God? "Search me, O God, and know my heart; try me and know my anxious thoughts; and see if there be any hurtful way in me, And lead me in the everlasting way" (Psalm 139:23-24, NASB).

6. What does it say about God that He commands us to "Cast your cares on the Lord and he will sustain you" (Psalm 55:22)? What does he say about us if we refuse to (1 Peter 5:6)?
7. Have you learned to anticipate your emotions? How?
8. What did you learn about the importance of lifestyle balance? What self-care practices do you need to make sure are a regular part of your schedule?
9. What are the benefits of regular check-ins?
10. Which of the action steps do you need to prioritize? What is a way to make them practical?

Chapter 13: Shame

1. What stood out to you from the Prince and Dragon story?
2. Shame researcher Brené Brown defines shame as "an intensely painful feeling or experience of believing we are flawed and therefore unworthy of acceptance and belonging." How is this different from guilt?
3. What did you learn about how shame is connected to the other roots of addiction?
4. How is a shame identity formed? What are the different factors?
5. Which factors do you feel are the most significant contributors to a shame identity? Why?
6. Have you experienced any of those? How?
7. How does a person's identity impact their behavior?
8. When you look at the prodigal son story in Luke 15 through the lens of shame, what are some fresh insights?
9. The author says God's Word must define reality for us—not our feelings, shame, or the enemy's accusations. How do you think we can do that practically?
10. What action steps do you need to prioritize? How can you make them practical this week?

Chapter 14: Identity Defeats Shame

1. What did you learn about shame from Brendan's story?
2. In the Understanding Shame section, how does shame keep a Christian porn user stuck in their sin?
3. What did you learn from the shame river illustration? Which tributaries have delivered the most shame in your life?
4. Why is a person's worth such an important part of them overcoming shame? (hint: last of shame river section).
5. What resonated with you from the Worth that Transcends Shame section?
6. How would you explain the Great Exchange to someone without a church background?
7. How is shame a spiritual attack? 2 Corinthians 10:3-5 What is a stronghold? How do you destroy them?
8. How do we take thoughts captive and make them obey Christ?
9. Which practices in putting it all together do you think would be the most helpful? Why?
10. What were some of the right moves Brendan made after his wife discovered his secret?
11. What action steps do you need to prioritize? How can you make them practical this week?

Chapter 15: Vulnerability Defeats Shame

1. What aspect of Roosevelt's speech resonates most with you?
2. What were your thoughts on the research showing the importance of vulnerability? Why do you think vulnerability is essential to defeating shame?
3. "Therefore, confess your sins to one another and pray for one another, that you may be healed" (James 5:16). How is vulnerability essential for confession? Why is going beyond

just being vulnerable and admitting sin so important to healing?

4. What were some observations that stuck out to you about the rest of Brendan's story?
5. How does this verse make the case for vulnerability? "My grace is sufficient for you, for my power is made perfect in weakness. Therefore I will boast all the more gladly of my weaknesses, so that the power of Christ may rest upon me" (2 Corinthians 12:9). Why is being vulnerable challenging to do?
6. What were some examples of the power of vulnerability that resonated with you?
7. Have you experienced the power of vulnerability in your own life or seen it in others? How?
8. Why does vulnerability take practice?
9. Which of the four practices seem the most helpful? Doable? Challenging?
10. What thoughts or observations did you have about the Restored After Shame section?
11. What action steps do you need to prioritize? How can you make them practical this week?

Chapter 16: Healing Trauma with Truth

1. What did you learn about trauma's impact on porn use from Maggie's story?
2. How is shame a manifestation of spiritual warfare? What aspect of trauma makes it so damaging? 2 Corinthians 10:3-5
3. What stuck out to you in the Exploring Trauma section?
4. Why are small groups such an important part of helping someone heal their trauma?
5. What are your thoughts about the ten worst moments exercise? How might that be helpful?

6. What makes a father so influential in a person's life?
7. What did you think about the principles to process your pain?
8. Which seems particularly helpful?
9. What stuck out to you from Eric's story? Mason's story?
10. What did you find interesting about the trauma and porn genre?
11. Why is it important to ask the tough questions when you wrestle with your trauma?
12. How does Romans 8:28,35-39 speak specifically to shame?
13. What action steps do you need to prioritize? How can you make them practical this week?

Chapter 17: May It Be

1. Based on what we've learned in this book, what is the tsunami caused by porn that is going to hit? Why don't people seem concerned about it?
2. What do we learn from David in 2 Samuel 11:1-2 about the importance of purpose related to walking in purity?
3. Do you believe the threefold vision the author mentions is for every follower of Christ? To know Christ (Matthew 22:27-28); to be like Christ (Romans 8:29); and to make Christ known (Matthew 28:19-20). Why or why not?
4. What caught your attention from the Harvest Is Plentiful section?
5. What did the author mean when he talked about Grow by Teaching?
6. What stuck out to you about the different arenas to equip within the Church?
7. Paul described the world the Ephesian Christians lived in as, "They have become callous and have given themselves up to sensuality, greedy to practice every kind of impuri-

ty?" (Ephesians 4:19). How does this describe our pornified world?

8. What do you think about how Ephesians 4:17-27 parallels the roots of addiction and their solutions?
9. How do followers of Christ have an advantage in dealing with a porn addiction over other communities?
10. Do you believe that addressing the porn issue is an opportunity for growth and revival in the Church? Why or why not?

Appendix

Chapter 6: How should a husband tell his wife about his porn struggle?

In the vast majority of marriages struggling because of porn, it is the husband's porn habit that is wreaking havoc. The Freedom Fight program, which is free, has a married men's module that walks the married man through the important steps for healing his marriage.

The husband needs to start recovery as soon as possible and develop a track record of sobriety before he tells his wife. This has proven to serve both the husband and wife and their marriage. When a husband establishes sobriety first, it keeps him from re-traumatizing his wife with regular relapses. When the husband gains a measure of sobriety, he is also in a better place to be completely honest instead of giving a staggered disclosure over time. A staggered disclosure is devastating for a wife who thinks she knows the whole story only to be hurt over and over by new revelations.

In responding to her husband's porn usage, the wife who is firm yet gracious has the best outcomes. When she shames her husband for his sinful behavior, he often shuts down and goes into hiding. She has a right to be angry and to share that anger and hurt, but she should avoid trying to shame him. Wives need to establish boundaries to protect themselves.

Wives need to connect with others who have gone through the same thing. The book *Beyond Betrayal* by Lisa Taylor is an excellent resource for wives who have experienced betrayal by their husband's porn or sex addiction. Lisa also has an online community for wives (https://beyondbetrayal.community) with encouraging resources.

Chapter 7: Equipping Class or Equipping Small Group

Men

- Read and discuss selected chapters out of *The Freedom Fight* (discussion questions in the appendix)
- Conquer Series – ten videos – (Men specific) Watch selected videos and discuss

Women

- Read and discuss selected chapters out of *The Freedom Fight*

After the equipping class/small group, those who are struggling can be invited to an FF recovery group (thefreedomfight.org). Our free program has leaders' resources to help you lead an effective recovery group.

Chapter 9: Why Masturbation Is a Relapse

A relapse is engaging in unwanted sexual behavior (porn, masturbation, hooking up, etc.). Some people argue that under the right conditions, masturbation should not be considered a relapse. Here are the reasons why I believe masturbation is a relapse and should be avoided.

1. Masturbation violates the biblical principle that teaches that sexual passion should be reserved for marriage.

   "Therefore consider the members of your earthly body as dead to immorality, impurity, passion, evil desire, and greed, which amounts to idolatry" (Colossians 3:5 NASB).

   The parts of the body are to be dead to passion. When someone masturbates, even if they could do so without lusting, the members of their body are not dead to passion. Sexual arousal is designed to lead to sexual intercourse and climax. These activities are intended for marriage. Outside of marriage, the members of our body are to be dead to passion.

2. The secular organization International Institute for Trauma and Addiction Professionals, which trains every certified sex addiction therapist, considers masturbation a relapse. Through masturbation, a person reinforces the porn pathways that teach that sex is all about them. Masturbation feeds the craving for more self-focused sex, which porn is often a part of. It strengthens the brain pathway that people need to avoid if they want freedom.

3. Masturbation has consequences in marriage. It undermines the foundation of healthy sex in marriage. Sex and sexual energy are intended for a spouse within marriage. Masturbation diverts the sexual focus toward self. When masturbation is an option, people will be tempted to get the quick fix instead of investing in their marriages.

Masturbation sets people up for disappointment when married. Urologist Harry Fisch says:

> A man who masturbates frequently can soon develop erection problems when he's with his partner. Add porn to the mix, and he can become unable to have sex. A penis that has grown accustomed to a particular kind of sensation leading to rapid ejaculation will not work the same way when it's aroused differently. Orgasm is delayed or doesn't happen at all. [2]

People who rationalize a masturbation habit are setting themselves up for problems once they get married. Many people's masturbation addiction undermines their marriage and sex life significantly. The same principle applies to women who train their bodies to respond to self-stimulation. This can undercut sex with a husband.

Masturbation and fantasy are typically the last stronghold for someone to break to walk in freedom. This stronghold destroys marriages and keeps many in bondage. Any rationalization for masturbation is against freedom, sexual health, and marital intimacy.

Locking up Devices

Go to our website: thefreedomfight.org where we give resources to show you step-by-step how to whitelist an iPhone and lock up an Android. We also give other recommendations for filtering and accountability software.

Chapter 10: Verses to meditate on when using BRACE

- Job 31:1
- Ephesians 5:3
- 1 Corinthians 6:18-20
- Matthew 5:27-28
- 1 Thessalonians 4:3-4
- Colossians 3:5
- Psalm 119:9-11
- Hebrews 13:4
- Romans 13:12-13
- Philippians 4:8
- Colossians 3:1-2
- Romans 12:2
- Galatians 5:1
- Hebrews 12:1
- Matthew 5:8
- James 5:16
- 1 Corinthians 10:13

Relapse Contract (printed in Chapter 10)

A Crash Report can be found in the resource section of our website (thefreedomfight.org).

Chapter 11: Have you made a decision to follow Christ?

When we trust in Jesus' death on the cross as payment for our sins and invite Him to live His life through us, He will indwell us. This is when our relationship with God begins. There may have been previous steps taken toward Christ along the way, but this decision to surrender your life to Him is when you commit yourself fully to Him—much like I can look back on my relationship with my wife and recount the different stages of our relationship. I can see where I took steps toward committing my life to her.

Meeting-->Friendship-->Dating-->Engagement-->Marriage

Still, it wasn't until I fully committed myself to my wife that we were married. In a similar way, we can look at our relationship with God in different stages. We can take steps to get to know *about* God. We can learn what He is like and how He has provided salvation through His one and only Son.

Just knowing about God and what He has done isn't enough. Each person must decide to turn from their sin and trust Christ to save them and lead them. This is the "marriage" decision to go all in. The Bible says of making this decision, "If you confess with your mouth that Jesus is Lord and believe in your heart that God raised him from the dead, you will be saved. For with the heart one believes and is justified, and with the mouth one confesses and is saved" (Romans 10:9-10).

This all-important decision of faith in Christ can be expressed through the words much like marriage vows. If the words of the prayer below reflect the desire of your heart, consider praying something like it yourself to receive Christ.

A Prayer to Receive Christ

> God, I admit to You that I'm a sinner and I know I'm separated from you. Thank you for sending Jesus to die on the cross for my sins. Lord, I want to receive the forgiveness and righteousness that comes through Jesus. Lord, will You come into my life and lead me and make me the person you want me to be. Thank you for eternal life.

If you make this decision to receive Christ, let someone know and begin to deepen your relationship with God and with others who are following Him. Daily Bible reading and prayer are essential to growing in your relationship with God. The YouVersion Bible App has many Bible reading plans to choose from to help you get started. Get plugged in to a church or small group Bible study with other followers of Christ.

Chapter 14: Truth Statements of Identity in Christ

- I am God's child, for I am born again of the incorruptible seed of the Word of God that lives and abides forever. (1 Peter 1:23)
- I am forgiven of all my sins and washed in the blood. (Ephesians 1:7, Hebrews 9:14; Colossians 1:14; 1 John 2:12; 1 John 1:9)
- I am a new creation. (2 Corinthians 5:17)
- I am a temple where the Holy Spirit lives. (1 Corinthians 6:19)
- I am delivered from the power of darkness: Christ brings me into God's kingdom. (Colossians 1:13)
- I am redeemed from the curse of the law. (1 Peter 1:18-19)
- I am holy and without blame before God. (Ephesians 1:4)
- I am established to the end. (1 Corinthians 1:8)
- I have been brought closer to God through the blood of Christ. (Ephesians 2:13)
- I am victorious. (Revelation 21:7)

- I am set free. (John 8:31-32)
- I am strong in the Lord. (Ephesians 6:10)
- I am dead to sin. (Romans 6:2, 11; 1 Peter 2:24)
- I am more than a conqueror. (Romans 8:37)
- I am a co-heir with Christ. (Romans 8:16-17)
- I am sealed with the Holy Spirit of promise. (Ephesians 1:13)
- I am in Christ Jesus by His doing. (1 Corinthians 1:30)
- I am accepted in Jesus Christ. (Ephesians 1:5-6)
- I am complete in Him. (Colossians 2:10)
- I am crucified with Christ. (Galatians 2:20)
- I am alive with Christ. (Ephesians 2:4-5)
- I am free from condemnation. (Romans 8:1)
- I am reconciled to God. (2 Corinthians 5:18)
- I am qualified to share in His inheritance. (Colossians 1:12)
- I am firmly rooted, established in my faith and overflowing with gratefulness and thankfulness. (Colossians 2:7)
- I am called of God. (2 Timothy 1:9)
- I am chosen. (1 Thessalonians 1:4; Ephesians 1:4; 1 Peter 2:9)
- I am an ambassador of Christ. (2 Corinthians 5:20)
- I am God's workmanship created in Christ Jesus for good works. (Ephesians 2:10)

- I am the apple of my Father's eye. (Deuteronomy 32:10; Psalm 17:8)
- I am healed by the stripes of Jesus. (1 Peter 2:24; Isaiah 53:6)
- I am being changed into his image. (2 Corinthians 3:18; Philippians 1:6)
- I am raised up with Christ and am seated in heavenly places. (Ephesians 2:6)
- I am beloved of God. (Colossians 3:12; Romans 1:7; 1 Thessalonians 1:4)
- I have obtained an inheritance. (Ephesians 1:11)
- I have access by one Spirit to the Father. (Ephesians 2:18)
- I have overcome the world. (1 John 5:4)
- I have everlasting life and will not be condemned. (John 5:24; John 6:47)
- I walk in Christ Jesus. (Colossians 2:6)
- I can do all things (everything) in and through Christ Jesus. (Philippians 4:13)
- I possess the Great One in me because greater is He who is in me than he who is in the world. (1 John 4:4)
- I always triumph in Christ. (2 Corinthians 2:14)
- My life shows forth his praise. (1 Peter 2:9)
- My life is hidden with Christ in God. (Colossians 3:3)

Notes

Chapter 1

[1] ITAP Dr. Patrick Carnes Organization Trains Certified Sex Addiction Therapist. This is the training I went through, but since I practice in a ministry context my designation is a pastoral sex addiction professional-supervisor. You have two years to complete four modules and get 30 hours of clinical supervision. I trained under Dr. Ted Roberts, founder of Pure Desire Ministries, and Dr. Kevin Skinner, author of *Treating Pornography Addiction*.

[2] Tsunami of 2004, https://en.wikipedia.org/wiki/2004_Indian_Ocean_earthquake_and_tsunami

[3] Pandemic lockdown sees spike in porn use http://www.insider.com/porn-views-have-increased-worldwide-since-onset-of-covid-19-2020-3

[4] 24% increase after giving away premium, https://www.pornhub.com/insights/coronavirus-update-may-26

[5] Supreme Court strikes down law protecting kids, https://www.mtsu.edu/first-amendment/article/1070/communications-decency-act-of-1996

[6] *Your Brain on Porn*, pg. 38, Gary Wilson, Testimony of the Impact of High-Speed Porn

[7] *Addicted to Lust*, Samuel Perry, pg. 77

[8] *Psychology Today*, https://www.psychologytoday.com/us/blog/inside-porn-addiction/201112/is-porn-really-destroying-500000-marriages-annually

[9] People who watch porn are less satisfied with their sex lives than those who don't, https://fightthenewdrug.org/huge-study-men-watch-porn-unhappier-in-relationship/

[10] *Addicted to Lust*, Samuel Perry, pg. 82

[11] Russell Brand story, https://www.lifesitenews.com/blogs/russell-brand-just-destroyed-porn-in-one-of-the-most-jaw-droppingly-awesome

[12] Terry Crews, https://www.huffpost.com/entry/terry-crews-pornography-addiction_n_56cf3a43e4b0bf0dab311588

[13] Gary Wilson, https://fightthenewdrug.org/your-brain-on-porn-gary-wilsons-porn-fighting-ba-website-working/

[14] *Playboy* magazine interview with John Mayer, February 10, 2010, He admits to preferring fantasy and masturbation to sex with a woman.

[15] John Mayer, https://www.rollingstone.com/music/music-news/the-dirty-mind-and-lonely-heart-of-john-mayer-2-100951/

[16] Melodie Shekia, *Life After Freedom from Pornography Addiction*, Chapters 1-3

Chapter 2

[1] *The Relentless Fight*, Andy Cimbala, pg. 14

[2] Freed from Pornography-Right Now Media, Hannah's story, https://www.rightnowmedia.org/Content/illustration/205985

[3] Pornhub Insights 2019, 81% are on smartphones and another 7% on mobile devices, This is for all users so it is a safe bet based on our FF survey that the 81% figure for smartphones, if just for teenagers would be over 90%, https://www.pornhub.com/insights/2019-year-in-review

[4] 95% of teens now report they have a smartphone or access to one, https://www.pewinternet.org/2018/05/31/teens-social-media-technology-2018/, Only 23% of teens owned a phone in 2011,

https://www.pewinternet.org/2013/03/13/teens-and-technology-2013/

[5] Definition of addiction or habit, https://fightthenewdrug.org/habit-vs-addiction-why-its-scientifically-possible-anyone-get-hooked/

[6] Compulsive Sexual Behavior classified as a disorder, https://www.thefix.com/world-health-organization-adds-sex-addiction-disease-list

[7] Sixteen States declare pornography a public health crisis, https://fightthenewdrug.org/here-are-the-states-that-have-passed-resolutions/

[8] 2019 Pornhub Insights, https://www.pornhub.com/insights/2019-year-in-review

[9] Daily porn consumption in US, https://www.scribd.com/presentation/87502444/Porn-Facts

[10] *Cheap Sex*, pg.114-115, Unless otherwise stated, this is the average for the whole adult population (18 and up). Notice that the frequency in the last statistic was monthly, while the 2015 Relationships in America survey of over 15,000 respondents states that 43% of men and 9% of women between ages 18 and 60 are watching porn at least *weekly*. If you drop the age to 39 and younger, the percentages rise to 46% and 16%, respectively. This follows the general pattern that the younger the age group, the more porn they watch. 66% of men and 41% of women view pornography monthly in the United States, American Psychiatric Association (2013), Diagnostic and statistical manual of mental disorders: DSM-5, Washington, D.C: American Psychiatric Association Cheap Sex, Mark Regnerus, pg.116-19% of women 18-29 view porn weekly while only 3% of women in their 50's did so.

[11] Proven Men Porn Survey (conducted by Barna Group), located at https://www.provenmen.org/2014PornSurvey/

[12] Percentage of men viewing porn several times a week, www.covenanteyes.com › 2015-porn-stats-covenant-eyes, Proven Men Porn Survey (conducted by Barna Group), located at https://www.provenmen.org/2014PornSurvey/

[13] 2019 Pornhub Insights, Women comprise 32% of visitors, https://www.pornhub.com/insights/2019-year-in-review

[14] Women viewing porn at least once a month, Proven Men Porn Survey (conducted by Barna Group), located at https://www.provenmen.org/2014PornSurvey/

[15] Survey of 560 college students in 2008 https://enough.org/stats-youth-and-porn. Chiara Sabina, Janis Wolak, and David Finkelhor, "The nature and dynamics of Internet pornography exposure for youth," CyberPsychology and Behavior 11 (2008): 691-693.

[16] Proven Men Porn Survey (conducted by Barna Group), located at https://www.provenmen.org/2014PornSurvey/

[17] The 2019 Freedom Fight national Christian student survey. Over 550 women and over 750 men from over 30 Universities across the U.S. These are Christian students involved with a ministry on their campus who indicated that their faith was important or very important (over 85% indicated that it was very important). Many of these students are in leadership positions.

[18] The 2019 Freedom Fight national Christian student survey. Over 550 women and over 750 men from over 30 Universities across the U.S. These are Christian students involved with a ministry on their campus who indicated that there faith was important or very important (over 85% indicated that it was very important). Many of these students are in leadership positions.

[19] Jessica Harris https://madeinhisimage.org/hello-my-name-is-jessica-and-im-addicted-to-porn/

[20] University of Montreal cancels porn study because they couldn't find any men in their 20's who hadn't seen it. https://www.dailymail.co.uk/news/article-2261377/Porn-study-scrapped-researchers-failed-ANY-20-males-hadn-t-watched-it.html

[21] Zillman, D. & Bryant, J. (1988) Pornography's impact on sexual satisfaction. Journal of Applied Social Psychology, 18, 438-453. doi: 10.1111/j.1559-1816.1988.tb00027.x https://profiles.nlm.nih.gov/ps/access/nnbckv.pdf Effects of Prolonged Consumption of Pornography Dolf Zillman Layden, M. A.

(2010). Pornography And Violence: A New Look At The Research. In J. Stoner & D. Hughes (Eds.) Dr. Mary Layden, Presentation at the Set Free Summit, April 2016.

[22] The Porn Phenomenon, Barna Group, https://www.barna.com/research/porn-in-the-digital-age-new-research-reveals-10-trends/

[23] The Porn Phenomenon, Barna Group, https://www.barna.com/research/porn-in-the-digital-age-new-research-reveals-10-trends/

[24] The Brain that Changes Itself, Norman Doidge, pg. 101-102

[25] The Report on Digital Sexuality 2019 https://www.yourbrainonporn.com/rebooting-porn-use-faqs/is-my-fetish-porn-induced/the-more-porn-you-watch-the-more-likely-you-are-to-be-bisexual-study-2019/

[26] Permission Giving beliefs, Dr. Mary Anne Layden in a presentation at the Set Free summit April, 2016

Chapter 3

[1] Survey shows Americans not having sex tripled in last 10 years, https://www.washingtonpost.com/business/2019/03/29/share-americans-not-having-sex-has-reached-record-high/?utm_term=.4d7d002bb327

[2] *Playboy*, Interview, John Mayer, February 10, 2010

[3] Inability to climax a result of porn, https://www.ncbi.nlm.nih.gov/pmc/articles/PMC5039517/, Behav Sci (Basel). 2016 Sep; 6(3): 17, Published online 2016 Aug 5. doi: 10.3390/bs6030017, Is Internet Pornography Causing Sexual Dysfunctions? A Review with Clinical Reports

[4] *Your Brain on Porn*, Gary Wilson, pg. 38

[5] TIME, April 2016, Why young men who grew up on internet porn are becoming advocates of turning it off

[6] Dr. Abraham Morgentaler, who's the clinical professor of urology at Harvard Medical School, says that many young men today suffer from what he calls porn-induced erectile dysfunction. These men are young, healthy men that can't maintain an erection with the person that they're with sexually. But they can get an erection watching porn, https://www.covenanteyes.com/2015/02/27/porn-cause-erectile-dysfunction/?_ga=2.193688685.1717636998.1587738322-929581036.1558531859

[7] A 2016 study on Canadian adolescents showed that 45.3% admitted to problems in erectile functioning, https://www.jahonline.org/article/S1054-139X(16)30056-8/fulltext

[8] Zillman, D. & Bryant, J. (1988), Pornography's impact on sexual satisfaction, *Journal of Applied Social Psychology*, 18, 438-453

[9] *Cheap Sex*, Mark Regnerus, pg. 95-98 (sexual hookups)

[10] Increasing extreme and deviance, https://fightthenewdrug.org/this-years-most-popular-genre-of-porn-is-pretty-messed-up/

[11] More extreme porn, https://www.yourbrainonporn.com/rebooting-porn-use-faqs/is-my-fetish-porn-induced/

[12] *Your Brain on Porn*, Gary Wilson, pg. 38

[13] The Brain That Changes Itself, Renowned psychiatrist Dr. Norman Doidge says of one of his porn-addicted patients, "His feeling that sexual intercourse was a violent act upset him greatly, yet excited him. Thoughts of sexual intercourse immediately led to thoughts of violence and thoughts of violence to sex."

[14] Anna Bridges, A study of the twenty-five most popular pornographic movies

[15] Foubert, over one hundred studies have shown pornography use increases the likelihood that a man will commit violence against a woman, Malamuth, N. M, Addison, T. & Koss, M. P. (2000), Pornography and sexual aggression: Are there reliable effects and can we understand them? *Annual Review of Sex Research*, 11, 26-91.

[16] Increase in sexual violence, https://www.nbcchicago.com/news/national-international/FBI-Report-Shows-Almost-20-Percent-Increase-in-Rape-Reports-495065881.html

[17] Robert Johnson, https://www.thestar.com/news/2015/08/31/how-robert-johnson-became-addicted-to-child-pornography-.html

[18] 2500% increase in child pornography arrests, https://www.thetrumpet.com/17188-pedophilia-is-more-common-than-you-think

[19] 85% of those arrested for Child porn admit to abusing children, https://innocentjustice.org/know-more/

[20] 100 Southern Baptist Youth Pastors, https://www.houstonchronicle.com/news/investigations/article/All-too-often-Southern-Baptist-youth-pastors-13588292.php

[21] Tommy Nelson, April 30, 2018, Student Mobilization staff training

[22] The Freedom Fight national student survey—89% of growing Christian men watch porn at least occasionally and more than 60% watch it at least weekly

[23] 300,000 Americans minors lured into sex trafficking, https://arkofhopeforchildren.org/child-trafficking/child-trafficking-statistics

[24] 49% of women who are sex trafficked are filmed while trafficked, https://fightthenewdrug.org/by-the-numbers-porn-sex-trafficking-connected/

[25] Testimony of female survivor of sex trafficking sex positive productions, https://fightthenewdrug.org/how-porn-fuels-sex-trafficking

[26] Anti-Pornhub petition gains steam, accuses adult video giant of facilitating sex trafficking, https://www.foxnews.com/faith-values/anti-pornhub-petition-sex-trafficking

[27] Sex Trafficking Increase, https://www.washingtonexaminer.com/washington-secrets/human-sex-trafficking-up-842-california-leads

[28] 13 is average age of entering sex trafficking in the US, http://fortune.com/2019/04/14/human-sex-trafficking-us-slavery/

[29] Porn and sex trafficking connected-one feeds the other, https://fightthenewdrug.org/by-the-numbers-porn-sex-trafficking-connected/

[30] Dr. Regnerus is associate professor of sociology at the University of Texas at Austin. This essay is adapted from his new book, *Cheap Sex: The Transformation of Men, Marriage and Monogamy* (Oxford University Press), https://www.wsj.com/articles/cheap-sex-and-the-decline-of-marriage-1506690454?mod=djcm_OBV1_092216&Paid&nan_pid=1864075905&ad_id=8030479

[31] *Cheap Sex*, Mark Regnerus, pg. 128

[32] *Cheap Sex* Mark Regnerus, pg. 121

[33] Steven Ruggles of the University of Minnesota predicted that a third of Americans in their twenties will never wed. Triple the historic norm, http://users.hist.umn.edu/~ruggles/Articles/Ruggles_Marriage_2014.pdf

[34] Marrieds have more and better sex, https://www.huffpost.com/entry/want-more-and-better-sex-get-married-and-stay-married_b_5967b618e4b022bb9372aff2

[35] Marrieds have more and better Sex, https://www.huffpost.com/entry/want-more-and-better-sex-get-married-and-stay-married_b_5967b618e4b022bb9372aff2

[36] Porn users report lower sexual satisfaction, https://fightthenewdrug.org/study-finds-regular-porn-use-leads-to-lower-sexual-satisfaction/

Chapter 4

[1] Joean Senatore's testimony, https://www1.cbn.com/700club/secret-life-female-porn-addict

[2] Dopamine released when you experience pleasure, https://www.news-medical.net/health/Dopamine-Functions.aspx

[3] These estimates were made by giving rats these different stimulants and observing their dopamine levels. Of course there is no rat porn so this was estimated based on interviews with men and women who have had years of porn use and years of sex with a spouse, https://www.pbs.org/wgbh/pages/frontline/meth/body/methbrainnoflash.html, The estimate on porn production of dopamine in the brain is also based on Dr. Michael Barta's research with Begin Again Institute in a webinar *Covid-19 and Pornography Addiction,* June 2, 2020, "Pornography can produce up to 10 times more dopamine in the brain than relational sex."

[4] Dopamine released when you experience pleasure and causes cravings to pursue in the future, https://www.news-medical.net/health/Dopamine-Functions.aspx

[5] Dr. Michael Barta with Begin Again Institute in a webinar *Covid-19 and Pornography Addiction,* June 2, 2020, "Pornography can produce up to 10 times more dopamine in the brain than relational sex"

[6] Sherese's, Ryan's, and Dan's story in the porn documentary, https://brainheartworld.org/watch/the-brain/

[7] Doidge N (2007), *The Brain That Changes Itself,* 108-109, New York: Penguin Books

[8] Doidge, N. (2007), *The Brain That Changes Itself,* (242-243), New York: Penguin Books

[9] PFC appears to shrink from regular porn use, https://fightthenewdrug.org/study-shows-brain-structure-changes-porn-consumers/, Dr. Simone Kuhn Research on the brains of porn users Pornography addiction: A neuroscience perspective

[10] Donald L. Hilton, Jr and Clark Watts, Published online, 2011 Feb 21, https://www.ncbi.nlm.nih.gov/pmc/articles/PMC3050060/, https://jamanetwork.com/journals/jamapsychiatry/fullarticle/1874574?utm_source=Silverchair%20Information%20Systems&utm_medium=email&utm_campaign=JAMAPsychiatry:OnlineFirst05/28/2014#Discussion

[11] *Your Brain on Porn*, testimony, pg. 25

[12] Porn users more depressed, unmotivated, and antisocial than non-users, Weir, K. (2014, April), Is Pornography Addictive? Monitor on Psychology, 45(4) 46, Retrieved From http://www.Apa.Org/Monitor/2014/04/Pornography.Aspx. Flisher, C. (2010), Getting Plugged In: An Overview of Internet Addiction, *Journal of Paediatrics and Child Health* 46: 557–559, Doi:10.1111/J.1440-1754.2010.01879.X; Layden, M. A. (2010), Pornography and Violence: A New Look at the Research. In Stoner, J, & Hughes, D. (Eds.) The Social Costs of Pornography: A Collection of Papers (Pp. 57–68). Princeton, NJ: Witherspoon Institute; Kafka, M. P. (2000). The Paraphilia-Related Disorders: Nonparaphilic Hypersexuality And Sexual Compulsivity/Addiction. In Leiblum, S. R, & Rosen, R. C. (Eds.) Principles and Practice of Sex Therapy, 3rd Ed. (Pp. 471–503). New York: Guilford Press, https://fightthenewdrug.org/watching-porn-and-feeling-lazy-and-unmotivated/

[13] *Your Brain on Porn*, testimony, pg. 22

[14] Adolescent Brain more moldable, habits formed then harder to change, https://www.verywellmind.com/what-is-brain-plasticity-2794886, By Kendra Cherry | Medically reviewed by a board-certified physician | Updated May 28, 2019

[15] Daniel R. Weinberger, Brita Elvevag, and Jay N. Giedd, "The Adolescent Brain: A Work in Progress," https://mdcune.psych.ucla.edu/ncamp/filesfmri/NCamp_fMRI_AdolescentBrain.pdf16. Wilson, G. (2014) Your Brain on Porn, 70, Common Wealth Publishing, UK

[16] Wilson, G. (2014), *Your Brain on Porn*, 70, Common Wealth Publishing, UK

[17] Wilson, G. (2014), *Your Brain on Porn*, 87, Common Wealth Publishing, UK

[18] Addiction Starts Early in American Society, Report Finds 90% of those hooked on alcohol, tobacco, drugs starting using them before age 18, research shows, HealthDay, June 29, 2011, http://health.usnews.com/health-news/family-health/childrens-

health/articles/2011/06/29/addiction-starts-early-in-american-society-report-finds

[19] Teen Brain has higher spikes in dopamine than adults or children's brains, https://www.theatlantic.com/health/archive/2014/01/dopamine-and-teenage-logic/282895/

[20] Wilson, G. (2014) *Your Brain on Porn*, 31, Common Wealth Publishing, UK

[21] First exposure stat eleven, https://www.huffpost.com/entry/parenting-in-the-digital-age-of-pornography_b_9301802

[22] Average age of first exposure is eight, http://thenovusproject.org/resource-hub/parents

[23] Children under 10 account for 22% of online porn consumption, https://www.netnanny.com/blog/the-detrimental-effects-of-pornography-on-small-children/

[24] Porn and sexual orientation, https://www.protectkids.com/effects/harms.htm#xii, Mental Health expert Steven Kavanagh, *Protecting Children in Cyberspace*, 58-59.

[25] US Department of Justice, https://aleteia.org/2014/08/03/6-ways-to-protect-your-kid-from-porn/

[26] Amaze Sex Education targets children, https://www.lawenforcementtoday.com/online-curriculum-tells-kids-that-watching-porn-is-normal-and-thats-not-all/

[27] What is Neuroplasticity? https://www.positivepsychology.com/neuroplasticity/

Chapter 5

[1] 65% of Christian men watch porn monthly Barna Group Survey 2014, https://www.provenmen.org/pornography-survey-statistics-2014/

[2] Dr. Ted Roberts, the Founder of Pure Desire ministry and Host of the Conquer Series, who has helped people for over thirty years find freedom from pornography, in a correspondence on July 5, 2019, estimated that less than 10% of Christian men who are struggling with porn are seeking recovery in a meaningful way. He believes shame is the biggest factor keeping believers in the shadows.

[3] Dr. Samuel Perry, in email correspondence July 3, 2019, His research leads him to believe that Christian women under-report their porn use because of shame.

[4] Seeing is (Not) Believing: How Viewing Pornography Shapes the Religious Lives of Young Americans, Samuel L. Perry, George M. Hayward, https://academic.oup.com/sf/article/95/4/1757/2877697

[5] *Addicted to Lust,* Samuel Perry, pg. 77-78

[6] Ibid.

[7] Ibid.

[8] *Addicted to Lust,* Samuel Perry, pg. 79

[9] *Addicted to Lust,* Samuel Perry, pg. 79-80

[10] *Addicted to Lust,* Samuel Perry, pg.80

[11] How Pornography Use Reduces Participation in Congregational Leadership: Samuel Perry, March 2019, Volume 61, Issue 1, https://link.springer.com/article/10.1007/s13644-018-0355-4

[12] *Addicted to Lust,* Samuel Perry, pg., 84

[13] *Addicted to Lust,* Samuel Perry, pg. 60

[14] Freedom Fight National Christian College Students Survey 2019, Over 1200 respondents from over 30 college campuses across the country. An anonymous Survey of Christian college students who are plugged into a campus ministry many in leadership positions. 96% of respondents say their faith is important or very important. 82% of respondents say their faith is very important. At least 40% of respondents are involved in leadership of their campus ministry.

[15] Pornography Consumption as a Threat to Religious Socialization, Samuel L. Perry, *Sociology of Religion,* Volume 76, Issue 4, WINTER

2015, Pages 436–458, https://doi.org/10.1093/socrel/srv043Published: 08 September 2015 https://academic.oup.com/socrel/article/76/4/436/2461553

Chapter 6

[1] *Psychology Today*, Kevin, Skinner, Is Porn Really Destroying 500,000 marriages annually? https://www.psychologytoday.com/us/blog/inside-porn-addiction/201112/is-porn-really-destroying-500000-marriages-annually

[2] Samuel L. Perry & Cyrus Schleifer, Till Porn Do Us Part? A Longitudinal Examination of Pornography Use and Divorce, 12 May 2017, https://www.tandfonline.com/doi/abs/10.1080/00224499.2017.1317709

[3] Teenage women much more likely to consume porn than those over 25, [2] Barna Group, "News Conference on Barna's New Study: 'The Porn Phenomenon,'" (January 15, 2016), https://www.barna.org/blog/culture-media/barna-group/porn-press-conference#.VrS9OrSJndl

[4] *USA Today*, Sixteen States declare, https://www.usatoday.com/story/news/nation/2019/05/09/pornography-public-health-crisis-states-adopt-measures-against-porn/1159001001/

[5] Dannah Gresh, The Lure of Porn is never quenched, https://www1.cbn.com/cbnnews/health/2019/april/the-lure-of-porn-is-never-quenched-how-porn-is-affecting-single-men

[6] Supernormal Stimulus, https://en.wikipedia.org/wiki/Nikolaas_Tinbergen, Film:Brain Heart World https://brainheartworld.org/?_ga=2.57723373.656888474.1562453980-581897632.1557322574&_gac=1.182069845.1561742915.CjwKCAjw9dboBRBUEi-

wA7VrrzX0yjN9AU_pWsqXowiykMb3y5WqRJjHvZmgimNOKZ73iBjIeNwp2pBoCiQMQAvD_BwE

[7] Regnerus, *Cheap Sex*, pg.109-110,

[8] Porn users 318 % more likely to cheat, https://www.theatlantic.com/magazine/archive/2008/10/is-pornography-adultery/306989/, pg. 119, Till porn do us part—less relationships, 120,125

[9] Ashley Madison stats, https://www.foxbusiness.com/lifestyle/coronavirus-ashley-madison-membership

[10] How Porn Kills Love, https://fightthenewdrug.org/how-porn-kills-love/

[11] *Addicted to Lust*, Samuel Perry, pg.124

[12] John Doyel podcast from 180recover.com, https://180recover.com/2019/09/19/the-clear-obvious-but-difficult-choice-podcast/

[13] Non-porn users happier in relationships, Maddox, A. M, Rhoades, G. K, & Markman, H. J. (2009), Viewing Sexually-Explicit Materials Alone or Together: Associations with Relationship Quality, Archives of Sexual Behavior, 40(2), 441-448. doi:10.1007/s10508-009-9585-4

[14] *Addicted to Lust*, Samuel Perry, pg. 125

[15] Open Letter on Pornography, John Gottman, https://www.gottman.com/blog/an-open-letter-on-porn/, https://www.ncbi.nlm.nih.gov/pmc/articles/PMC3490543/

[16] Porn Industry using tobacco industry tactics, https://fightthenewdrug.org/porn-industry-uses-tobacco-industry-tactics-to-hide-the-truth/, Inventing Conflicts of Interest: A History of Tobacco Industry Tactics, Allan M. Brandt, PhD

[17] *Addicted to Lust*, Samuel Perry, pg. 120

[18] Dr. Mary Anne Layden, Presentation at Set Free Summit, April 5, 2016

[19] Letter to ex-Husband, https://www.theguardian.com/lifeandstyle/2015/jun/13/a-letter-to-my-ex-husband-who-preferred-pornography-to-me

[20] *Worthy of Her Trust*, Arterburn and Martinkus, pg. 35

[21] Harry Fisch Quote. Cole, G. (2011). A Strange Invitation: On the Ordinary Problem of Pornography. Studies in Gender and Sexuality, 12, 254-267. Doi:10.1080/15240657.2011.610240 ("Porn Tells Us It Is About Sex, but the Effect of Porn Often Leads Away From Actually Having Sex With Another Person."); Paul, P. (2010). From Pornography to Porno to Porn: How Porn Became the Norm. In J. Stoner and D. Hughes (Eds.) The Social Costs of Pornography: A Collection of Papers (Pp. 3–20). Princeton, N.J.: Witherspoon Institute; Doidge, N. (2007). The Brain That Changes Itself. New York: Penguin Books. https://fightthenewdrug.org/porn-is-taking-away-mens-ability-to-have-actual-sex/

[22] Gary Wilson, *Your Brain on Porn*, pg. 44

[23] Bridges, A. J. (2010). Pornography's Effect on Interpersonal Relationships. In J. Stoner and D. Hughes (Eds.) The Social Costs of Pornography: A Collection of Papers (Pp. 89-110). Princeton, NJ: Witherspoon Institute; Paul, P. (2007). Pornified: How Pornography Is Transforming Our Lives, Our Relationships, and Our Families. New York: Henry Hold and Co, 153; Zillmann, D. (2004). Pornografie. In R. Mangold, P. Vorderer, and G. Bente (Eds.) Lehrbuch Der Medienpsychologie (Pp. 565–85). Gottingen, Germany: Hogrefe Verlag;

[24] The Freedom Fight Survey of over 700 Committed Christian College Men from over 30 college campuses across the country. 60% said that porn was their primary sex educator.

[25] Psychology Today, Kevin, Skinner, Is Porn Really Destroying 500,000 marriages annually? https://www.psychologytoday.com/us/blog/inside-porn-addiction/201112/is-porn-really-destroying-500000-marriages-annually

Both porn use and the divorce rate are basically the same for Christians versus non-Christians. Dr. Samuel Perry says that Christian wives have a greater problem with their husband's porn use; therefore, Christian porn users have more struggles in their marriage because of porn.

Chapter 7

[1] Only 7% of pastors say their church has a program to help their people with porn, Barna Survey, https://www.charismanews.com/us/73208-15-statistics-about-the-church-and-pornography-that-will-blow-your-mind

[2] A Pastors.com anonymous survey in 2002 of over 1300 pastors showed that 54% viewed porn in the last 12 months and 30% in the last month.

Addicted to Lust, Samuel L. Perry, pg. 30, An anonymous Survey by Promise Keepers showed that 54% of pastors had viewed porn in the last seven days. Dr. Perry lists two more sources showing that at least half of pastors struggle with porn.

[3] More than half of pastors say porn addiction is the most damaging issue in their congregation, https://www.charismanews.com/us/73208-15-statistics-about-the-church-and-pornography-that-will-blow-your-mind. 57% of pastors say porn addiction is the most damaging issue in their congregation. And 69% say porn has adversely impacted the church.

[4] Only 7% of pastors say their church has a program to help their people with porn, Barna Survey, https://www.charismanews.com/us/73208-15-statistics-about-the-church-and-pornography-that-will-blow-your-mind

[5] Dr. Ted Roberts in email correspondence, July 5, 2019, "I would estimate under 10% are seeking meaningful recovery"

[6] Barna-Pastors, https://www.barna.com/the-porn-phenomenon/

[7] Piper says figures are low, https://www.desiringgod.org/interviews/does-porn-use-disqualify-a-pastor

[8] John Doyel, https://www.christianitytoday.com/pastors/2017/september-web-exclusives/sexual-addiction-destroyed-my-pastorate.html

[9] Kenny Smith now mentors men to help with this. You can connect with Kenny who helps pastors and others find freedom Mended-Mentors.com.

[10] *Addicted to Lust,* Samuel L. Perry, pg. 115

[11] Pure Desire helps churches establish a restorative culture, *Restorative Policy:* As long as you haven't done anything illegal or with another person and as long as you are committed to recovery, you can get help for your porn addiction without the fear of punishment. The goal is restoration.[9.1]

[12] Dr. Ted Roberts, founder of Pure Desire Ministry, has helped 15 pastors struggling with porn find freedom and get restored to their church. The pastor has to be committed to working toward recovery.

[13] Storming the beaches of Normandy, George Taylor (1), https://www.politico.com/magazine/story/2014/06/the-man-who-took-omaha-beach-107509?o=0

[14] *Setting Us Free,* Nick Stumbo

Chapter 8

[1] Dr. Ted Roberts, email correspondence, July 25, 2019

[2] *Healing the Wounds of Sexual Addiction,* Dr. Mark Laaser, pg. 121

[3] *Addicted to Lust,* Samuel Perry, pg. 147-175

[4] Chasing the Scream, Johann Hari, 2015, https://www.youtube.com/watch?v=ao8L-0nSYzg

Chapter 9

[1] Daily porn consumption in US (2 billion pornographic emails sent daily), https://www.scribd.com/presentation/87502444/Porn-Facts

[2] Sexualizing girls, https://www.verywellmind.com/damaging-effects-of-sexualizing-girls-4778062

[3] Netflix's makes mature content more available than ever, https://endsexualexploitation.org/articles/netflix-nc17-r-rated-content/

[4] Netflix shows mostly adult content, https://www.movieguide.org/news-articles/61-of-netflix-originals-have-mature-content-few-are-family-friendly.html

[5] Netflix mature content easily assessable for kids even if you don't have Netflix, https://www.vox.com/2019/4/8/18300256/netflix-password-sharing-14-percent-survey-content-experience-moffettnathanson

[6] Half view porn as morally acceptable, In 2018, 43% of Americans said that pornography is morally acceptable. This is an increase of 12% points in the last five years. So it is a safe assumption that at the time of the writing of the book, this figure had risen to at least 45%, https://news.gallup.com/poll/235280/americans-say-pornography-morally-acceptable.aspx

[7] A.W. Tozer quote, https://worthychristianbooks.com/aw-tozer/knowledge-of-the-holy/chapter-21-the-holiness-of-god/

[8] Aaron Ralston Hiking accident, https://en.wikipedia.org/wiki/Aron_Ralston

[9] Joel Hesch, *Proven Men*, pg. 166

[10] Pavlov Conditioning, https://study.com/academy/lesson/ivan-pavlov-and-classical-conditioning-theory-experiments-contributions-to-psychology.html

[11] Dopamine surges in rats to initiate salivation, https://www.nature.com/news/brain-s-chemical-signals-seen-in-real-time-1.20458

[12] A variation of the original sex addiction cycle by Dr. Patrick Carnes. He originally came up with the Addiction cycle. He used the word ritual where I use routine.

[13] Nick Stumbo, Pure Desire Roundtable, September 25, 2019, Talking to ministry partners about an alarming trend of younger ministry leaders lowering the biblical standards for purity.

[14] For the Love of God – Volume Two, D. A. Carson, Chapter 23

Chapter 10

[1] Lone Survivor, https://www.history.com/news/the-real-life-story-behind-lone-survivor

[2] Prefrontal Cortex and Limbic system in addiction, https://www.addictionpolicy.org/the-brain-science-of-addiction

[3] Limbic system, https://www.neuroscientificallychallenged.com/blog/know-your-brain-reward-system

[4] The Prefrontal Cortex, Jan 4, 2017 | Matthew Dahlitz, Neuroscience, https://www.thescienceofpsychotherapy.com/prefrontal-cortex/

[5] Amygdala Hijack: When Emotion Takes Over, https://www.healthline.com/health/stress/amygdala-hijack

[6] How addiction hijacks our Reward System, Cynthia M. Kuhn, PhD, Wilkie A. Wilson, PhD, https://www.dana.org/article/how-addiction-hijacks-our-reward-system/

[7] Repetition and Brakes on Brain going out, https://www.mayoclinic.org/diseases-conditions/compulsive-sexual-behavior/diagnosis-treatment/drc-20360453

[8] The American Society for Addiction Medicine (ASAM), https://www.asam.org/docs/default-source/publications/asam-news-archives/vol26-3.pdf?sfvrsn=0

[9] Hypofrontality, https://www.yourbrainonporn.com/relevant-research-and-articles-about-the-studies/hypofrontality/

[10] Healing from Hypofrontality, https://www.covenanteyes.com/2014/02/28/hypofrontality/https://www.yourbrainonporn.com/relevant-research-and-articles-about-the-studies/brain-studies-on-porn-users-sex-addicts/#brain

[11] *Atomic Habits*, James Clear, pg. 145,146, how many repetitions are required to make a habit automatic?

[12] *Atomic Habits*, James Clear, pg. 144

[13] Paul Meier, *Renewing Your Mind in a Secular World*, p. 25, https://bible.org/article/biblical-meditation

[14] *Atomic Habits*, James Clear, pg. 206, Immediate negative consequences help break a bad habit

[15] Ethopian Airliner-black box, https://www.wired.com/story/boeing-737-max-8-ethiopia-crash-black-box-data-lion-air/

Chapter 11

[1] Chasing the Scream, Johann Hari, 2015, https://www.youtube.com/watch?v=ao8L-0nSYzg

[2] Ibid.

[3] Ibid.

[4] Ibid.

[5] Sex Addiction: An Intimacy Disorder, https://health.usnews.com/health-news/health-wellness/articles/2013/09/30/sex-addiction-an-intimacy-disorder

[6] Key Factors to Overcome a Sex Addiction, Patrick Carnes, https://www.iitap.com/wp-

content/uploads/2016/02/ARTICLE_18.4-Sexual- Addiction-Patrick-Carnes.pdf

[7] John Doyel podcast and blog, https://180recover.com/2019/09/17/killing-the-roots-of-sexual-brokenness-podcast/

[8] Bonding to Porn, http://healthland.time.com/2011/02/09/do-men-really-bond-with-porn-spoiling-them-for-real-life-sex/

[9] Andrea Kuszewski Oxytocin a biochemical love potion, http://healthland.time.com/2011/02/09/do-men-really-bond-with-porn-spoiling-them-for-real-life-sex/

[10] Anonymous man in recovery shares about his bonding with porn, https://www.ibelieveinlove.com/could-i-really-be-emotionally-attached-to-porn/

[11] *Life After Freedom from Pornography Addiction*, Melodie Shekia, Chapters 1-3

[12] People turn to porn when lonely, https://www.xxxchurch.com/men/people-turn-porn-theyre-lonely.html

[13] Loneliest Generation, https://eab.com/insights/daily-briefing/student-affairs/gen-z-may-be-the-loneliest-generation/

[14] Millennial Loneliness, https://www.vox.com/science-and-health/2019/8/1/20750047/millennials-poll-loneliness

[15] Naomi Wolf-Porn and loneliness, https://fightthenewdrug.org/porn-can-make-you-more-depressed-and-lonely/

[16] Freedom Fight National Survey of Christian College students over 1200 college men and women from over 30 different campuses from across the US. These are students who say their faith is important or very important. 59% said porn use hurt their closest relationships. It is suspected that the real number is even higher because most Christian porn users have a lack of self-awareness and denial that keeps them from seeing the negative consequences fully.

[17] 30 of 31 measure show that porn is negative on relationships, https://www.academia.edu/41339575/Pornography_and_Relationship_Quality_Establishing_the_Dominant_Pattern_by_Examining_Pornogra-phy_Use_and_31_Measures_of_Relationship_Quality_across_30_National_Surveys?email_work_card=view-paper

Archives of Sexual Behavior, Pornography and Relationship Quality: Establishing the Dominant Pattern by Examining Pornography Use and 31 Measures of Relationship Quality across 30 National Surveys, Samuel L. Perry, *University of Oklahoma*

[18] Samuel L. Perry & Cyrus Schleifer, Till Porn Do Us Part? A Longitudinal Examination of Pornography Use and Divorce, 12 May 2017, https://www.tandfonline.com/doi/abs/10.1080/00224499.2017.1317709

[19] Porn and loneliness, https://www1.cbn.com/cbnnews/health/2019/september/how-the-loneliness-epidemic-is-linked-to-pornography

[20] Porn makes people more depressed on lonely, https://fightthenewdrug.org/porn-can-make-you-more-depressed-and-lonely/

[21] *The Genesis Process,* Michael Dye, pg. 110-112

[22] Steve's testimony, https://www.xxxchurch.com/men/people-turn-porn-theyre-lonely.html

[23] *The Genesis Process,* Michael Dye, pg. 114

[24] *Facing the Shadow,* Dr. Patrick Carnes, pg. 396

Chapter 12

[1] Irresistible, Adam Alter, pg. 73-74

[2] Dr. Michael Barta with Begin Again Institute in a webinar, *Covid-19 and Pornography Addiction,* June 2, 2020, "Pornography can produce up to 10 times more dopamine in the brain than relational sex"

[3] Hannah, Right Now Media, https://www.rightnowmedia.org/Content/illustration/205985

[4] Pastor John Doyel testimony, https://www.christianitytoday.com/pastors/2017/september-web-exclusives/sexual-addiction-destroyed-my-pastorate.html

[5] Definition of self-awareness, https://www.dictionary.com/browse/self-awareness?s=t

[6] Dr. Gary Oliver, *Healthy Leaders, Flourishing Ministries*, pg. 30, If you bury your emotions you bury them alive and they will come back.

[7] Name it to tame it – To Name It Is to Tame It; yes, I believe we can tame the unconscious. Timothy A. Pychyl PhD, https://www.psychologytoday.com/us/blog/dont-delay/201004/name-it-is-tame-it

[8] Dictionary.com, bored

[9] Dictionary.com, loneliness

[10] Dictionary.com, anxiety

[11] Dictionary.com, stress

[12] Dictionary.com, depressed

[13] The gifts of imperfection, Brené Brown, Numb the dark you numb the light

[14] Sometimes Embracing Emotional Distress Is the Best Medicine, By Joanna Cheek on June 7, 2016, https://blogs.scientificamerican.com/mind-guest-blog/sometimes-embracing-emotional-distress-is-the-best-medicine/

[15] *The Porn Phenomenon*, Barna Group, pg. 50-55

[16] Dr. Patrick Carnes, *Facing the Shadow*, pg. 277, 2001,2015, Craziness manifests itself in lapses in routine and self-maintenance.

[17] *Insight*, Tasha Eurich, pg. 110

Chapter 13

[1] It's a Shame: The symptoms of shame and how to combat it, Lauren Carrane, blog post, https://www.yellowbrickprogram.com/blog/shame-symptoms-shame-combat

[2] The Prince and the Dragon, Melinda Reinicke, Parables for Personal Growth (San Diego, CA: Recovery Publications, Inc, 1993), pp. 5-9, permission received

[3] *Unwanted,* Jay Stringer, pg. 143

[4] *Soul of Shame,* Thompson, pg. 24

[5] *Daring Greatly,* Brené Brown, pg. 69

[6] *Soul of Shame,* Thompson, pg. 144

[7] How shame impacts the brain and triggers fear response of the emotional brain, http://themonkeytherapist.com/science-behind-guilt-shame/

[8] *Soul of Shame,* Thompson, pg. 40, 67

[9] *Soul of Shame,* Thompson, pg. 51

[10] *Soul of Shame,* Thompson, pg. 24

[11] *Soul of Shame,* Thompson, pg. 31

[12] *Soul of Shame,* Thompson, pg. 32

[13] *Soul of Shame,* Thompson, pg. 72

[14] *Soul of Shame,* Thompson, pg. 63

[15] *Soul of Shame,* Thompson, pg. 67

[16] *Your Brain on Porn,* Gary Wilson, pg.133

[17] *Atomic Habits,* James Clear, pg. 34

[18] *Atomic Habits,* James Clear, pg. 35

[19] Ibid.

[20] Recovery Roadblocks: The Addict's Art of Self-Sabotage by Matt Berry, https://www.recovery.org/recovery-roadblocks-the-addicts-art-of-self-sabotage/

[21] In 2019, the Freedom Fight conducted a survey of over 1,200 college students (700 men and 500 women) who say their faith is important to them and who are involved in a collegiate campus ministry. 87% of the men and 51% of the women said they viewed porn at least three times in the last 12 months. Of this group who watched porn, 89% said they felt self-hatred afterward.

[22] Theology Professor at Talbot Matt Williams, http://magazine.biola.edu/article/10-summer/the-prodigal-sons-father-shouldnt-have-run/

Chapter 14

[1] *Daring Greatly*, Brené Brown, pg. 72

[2] Email with Dr. Ted Roberts sharing that he estimates that less than 10% of men are seeking recovery for their porn struggle.

[3] *Soul of Shame*, Curt Thompson, pg. 48

[4] Mississippi River Facts, https://www.nps.gov/miss/riverfacts.htm

[5] Brené Brown Blog, Definition of Shame, https://Brenébrown.com/blog/2013/01/14/shame-v-guilt/

[6] *Daring Greatly*, Brené Brown, pg.66

[7] *Daring Greatly*, Brené Brown, pg. 65

[8] *Treating Pornography Addiction*, Kevin Skinner, pg. 57

Chapter 15

[1] The Man in the Arena, Selected writings of Theodore Roosevelt

[2] Being vulnerable means being susceptible to being wounded or hurt, https://www.dictionary.com/browse/vulnerable?s=t

[3] *Daring Greatly*, Brené Brown, pg. 82

[4] Ibid.

[5] *Daring Greatly*, Brené Brown, pg. 65-66

[6] Jay Stringer, Interview, https://www.youtube.com/watch?v=1wG9_FdgzJ8, In a survey of over 3,800 men and women, those who sought out others to share their shame with had 22% less porn usage than those who didn't.

[7] Brené Brown on how shame dies when shame is heard with empathy, https://www.huffpost.com/entry/Brené-brown-shame_n_3807115

[8] *Daring Greatly*, Brené Brown, pg. 67

[9] From Sermon by Pastor Mike Bickley of Journey Church at Men's Expedition 2018

Chapter 16

[1] The compulsion to repeat the trauma, Reenactment, revictimization, and masochism, van der Kolk BA, https://www.ncbi.nlm.nih.gov/pubmed/2664732

[2] Trapped in Trauma: Why Reenactment? Suzanne Titkemeyer, https://www.patheos.com/blogs/nolongerquivering/2016/03/Trapped-in-Trauma-why-Reenactment/

[3] *The Body Keeps the Score*, VanDer Kolk, pg. 18

[4] *The Body Keeps the Score*, VanDer Kolk, pg. 26-27

[5] The connection between Trauma and Addictions, https://carrierclinic.org/2019/08/06/trauma-and-addiction/

[6] *The Making of a Sex Addict*, Patrick J. Carnes, PhD, 1998 https://m.recoveryonpurpose.com/upload/ARTICLE_The%20Making%20of%20a%20Sex%20Addict_PCarnes.pdf

[7] Ibid.

[8] https://www.ncbi.nlm.nih.gov/pmc/articles/PMC2648973/, Childhood trauma, trauma in adulthood, and psychiatric diagnoses, Caron Zlotnick, Jennifer Johnson, Robert Kohn, Benjamin Vicente, Pedro Rioseco, and Sandra Saldivia

[9] *The Body Keeps the Score*, VanDer Kolk, pg. 4

[10] Dr. Ted Roberts was my supervising mentor as I received my training to be a pastoral sex addiction professional. I heard this phrase dozens of times from him during my training. It is also repeated in his excellent book on sex addiction, *Pure Desire.*

[11] *Facing the Shadow*, Patrick Carnes, pg. 160

[12] *Game Plan*, Joe Dallas, pg. 108

[13] Statistics on fatherlessness, https://fightingdads.com/fatherless-children-statistics/

[14] *The Body Keeps the Score*, Bessel Van Der Kolk, pg. 21

[15] *The Body Keeps the Score*, Bessel Van Der Kolk, pg. 237

[16] Research shows that the individuals who never connect the dots between their trauma and their addiction are more likely to continue to be tripped up by past trauma, https://www.psychologytoday.com/us/blog/compassion-matters/201803/dealing-unresolved-trauma

[17] Psychologist Dr. Lisa Firestone wrote about trauma, https://www.psychologytoday.com/us/blog/compassion-matters/201803/dealing-unresolved-trauma

[18] Jay Stringer, Interview, https://www.youtube.com/watch?v=1wG9_FdgzJ8

[19] *Unwanted*, Jay Stringer, pg. 120

[20] *Unwanted*, Jay Stringer, pg. 121

Chapter 17

[1] Tsunami article about meteorological meeting just before the tsunami hit, https://www.wsws.org/en/articles/2005/01/warn-j03.html

[2] *Unwanted,* Jay Stringer, pg. 98

[3] Definition of Freedom, email correspondence with Dr. Ted Roberts, September 18, 2019

[4] Dawson Trotman quote, https://www.azquotes.com/quote/747725

Epilogue

[1] Porn Protected as free speech, https://www.americanbar.org/groups/crsj/publications/human_rights_magazine_home/the-ongoing-challenge-to-define-free-speech/sexual-expression-and-free-speech/

[2] Sixteen states declare pornography a public health crisis, https://www.governing.com/topics/health-human-services/gov-pornography-public-health-crisis-states.html

[3] UK Porn Block Law, https://www.wired.co.uk/article/porn-block-uk-wired-explains

[4] More than half of children and teenagers accidentally find porn, https://www.wired.co.uk/article/porn-block-uk-wired-explains

[5] Interview with former US Senator Mark Pryor, June 14, 2019, He was a co-sponsor on the proposed bill to move all pornography to .xxx domain

[6] Porn industry adopts tobacco industry strategy, https://fightthenewdrug.org/porn-industry-uses-tobacco-industry-tactics-to-hide-the-truth/

Made in the USA
Middletown, DE
17 July 2024

57408918R00201